AS/400
ASSOCIATE SYSTEM OPERATOR
CERTIFICATION STUDY GUIDE

AS/400
ASSOCIATE SYSTEM OPERATOR
CERTIFICATION STUDY GUIDE

Rochester Community and Technical College
Steve Murray

MIDRANGE
COMPUTING
IIR PUBLICATIONS INC.

First Edition

First Printing—September 1999

© 1999 Midrange Computing
ISBN: 1-58347-007-7

Midrange Computing
5650 El Camino Real, Suite 225
Carlsbad, CA 92008
www.midrangecomputing.com

V4R3

ACKNOWLEDGMENTS

We would like to acknowledge and thank the following individuals:

Warren Kemplin, Director of the AS/400 University program at Rochester Community and Technical College, for his vision toward implementing AS/400 certification programs at RCTC.

Scott Sahs, Information Technology Representative at RCTC, for his enthusiasm toward helping to kick start AS/400 certification programs at RCTC.

Ellen Nelson, Dean of Continuing Education and Workforce Development at RCTC, for leadership and making it all happen.

Dennis Kronebusch and Josh Strickler, AS/400 Operations Specialists, for serving as a sounding board for the ideas in this book and for testing the lab exercises.

Bill Schmidt, AS/400 Technical Support Education at IBM Rochester, for his initial ideas toward the creation of this book and for his technical review of the subject matter.

Jason Dahl, IBM Global Services in Rochester, for his expertise in providing a technical review of this book.

Steve Myers, AS/400 Development at IBM Rochester, for helping put together instructor slides to supplement the material in this book.

Gary Brun, AS/400 Technical Support Manager at IBM Rochester, as manager of AS/400 service, support, and education strategies at IBM, as well as product technical support.

Don Heller, Project Manager, AS/400 World Wide Assessment and Certification, IBM Corporation.

Steven Bolt, Midrange Computing Book Editor.

Marianne Krcma, Editorial Services, copyeditor.

To the students of the initial class taught from the material in this book, for their feedback and suggestions.

CONTENTS

ROCHESTER COMMUNITY AND
TECHNICAL COLLEGE AND THE AS/400 UNIVERSITY xiii

FOREWORD xv

Chapter 1   EXPLORING BASIC OS/400 OPERATIONAL CONCEPTS 1

IDENTIFYING THE PURPOSE AND BENEFITS OF OS/400 2

RECOGNIZING THE MAJOR FUNCTIONS OF OS/400 3

Object Management 3

Storage Management 4

Database Management 4

User Management 5

Security Management 5

Work Management 6

Message Management 8

Print Management 8

UNDERSTANDING OS/400 DISPLAY TYPES 9

Sign-on Screen 9

Menu Displays 12

Displaying a Menu Using the GO Command 16

Entry Displays 18

List Displays 21

Information Displays 23

RECOGNIZING THE OPERATIONAL ASSISTANT 24

CHOOSING ASSISTANCE LEVELS 26
    Basic Assistance Level 27
    Intermediate Assistance Level 27
    Advanced Assistance Level 27
    Changing the Assistance Level 28
WORKING WITH AS/400 HELP FACILITIES 29
    Online Help 29
    Information Assistant 36
    InfoSeeker 37
    AS/400 Online Library on the Internet 38
    Other Resources 39
USING CL COMMANDS 40
    Structure of CL Commands 41
    Where to Enter CL Commands 42
    Finding a List of Commands on the AS/400 44
    Entering CL Commands 48
EXERCISE 1: CREATING LIBRARIES
    WITH MENUS AND COMMANDS 55

Chapter 2   **MANAGING OS/400 OBJECTS** **63**
UNDERSTANDING OBJECTS AND THEIR ATTRIBUTES 64
    Objects Are of Specific Types 64
    Objects Have Names 64
    Objects Belong to Libraries 65
    Objects Are Referenced by Name, Not by Location 65
    Objects Are Explicitly Created 66
    Objects Have a Description and Content 67
FINDING OBJECTS 67
WORKING WITH OBJECTS 71
    Copying an Object 72
    Moving an Object 72
    Authorizing an Object 72
    Deleting an Object 73
    Renaming an Object 73
    Saving and Restoring an Object 75
EXERCISE 2: WORKING WITH LIBRARIES AND OTHER OBJECTS 75

Chapter 3 CONTROLLING JOBS **97**

DEMYSTIFYING WORK MANAGEMENT 98

A Simple System. 99

A Complex System 100

A System as a Business 100

Work Management Terms Using the Business Scenario . 101

UNDERSTANDING JOBS 104

Basic Job Types 104

The Flow of a Batch Job. 105

SUBMITTING BATCH JOBS 106

WORKING WITH JOB QUEUES 108

Finding Job Queues 109

Working with Jobs in a Job Queue 110

Holding a Job Queue 112

Releasing a Job Queue 112

WORKING WITH USER JOBS 113

Holding a Job 117

Releasing a Job 118

Ending a Job. 119

Displaying Job Attributes 121

Changing a Job 122

DISPLAYING JOBS IN A SPECIFIC SUBSYSTEM 126

WORKING WITH SIGNED-ON USERS 128

Displaying Signed-on Users. 129

Finding Signed-on Users and Sorting the User List . . . 131

Finding Additional Information about Signed-on Users . 132

Sending Messages to Signed-on Users 132

Signing Users off the System 133

DISPLAYING ACTIVE JOB STATISTICS 133

EXERCISE 3: SUBMITTING JOBS
AND WORKING WITH THOSE JOBS 135

Chapter 4 MANAGING MESSAGES **149**

IDENTIFYING CHARACTERISTICS OF
MESSAGES AND MESSAGE QUEUES. 150

Message Sources 150

Message Types. 150
Message Queues. 151
SENDING MESSAGES 153
Sending Informational Messages to Users 155
Sending Informational Messages to Workstations 155
Sending Inquiry Messages. 156
Sending Break Messages to Workstations. 157
Sending Messages Using an Alternative Display 158
DISPLAYING MESSAGES 159
Replying to Inquiry Messages. 162
Displaying Messages Using
    Basic and Intermediate Assistance Levels 162
Displaying System Operator Messages 164
REMOVING MESSAGES 166
Removing Individual Messages 167
Removing All Messages in a Queue. 167
Removing All Messages Not Needing a Reply. 168
HANDLING SYSTEM AND ERROR MESSAGES. 168
Getting Help on a Message 168
Replying to System and Error Messages 172
Printing Messages. 172
DISPLAYING MESSAGE QUEUE ATTRIBUTES. 173
Delivery 174
Program 174
Severity 174
CHANGING MESSAGE QUEUES 175
EXERCISE 4: WORKING WITH USER AND SYSTEM MESSAGES . 177

Chapter 5   **CONTROLLING PRINTER OUTPUT** **191**
UNDERSTANDING AS/400 PRINTING TERMS. 192
Spooled Files 192
Output Queues. 192
Printer Writers and Printer Devices 192
Printer Device Files. 194
FINDING PRINTER OUTPUT 194
Displaying Printer Output for a User. 195

Displaying Printer Output by Job 200
Displaying Printer Output by Output Queue 201
Displaying Printer Output by Printer 204
MANAGING PRINTER OUTPUT 205
Exploring Different Views of Printer Output 205
Displaying the Contents of Printer Output 208
Holding Printer Output 209
Releasing Printer Output 210
Changing the Attributes of Printer Output 211
Changing the Same Attribute on Multiple Printer Jobs . . 213
DETERMINING WHY OUTPUT IS NOT PRINTING 215
Working with Printing Status 215
Displaying Completed Printer Output 217
Investigating Other Reasons
Why the Output Isn't Printing 218
What Determines Where Output Prints? 219
WORKING WITH LOCAL PRINTERS 221
Starting a Printer Writer 223
Ending a Printer Writer 225
Holding and Releasing a Printer Writer 227
Answering Printer Messages 229
EXERCISE 5: WORKING WITH SPOOLED FILES 231

Chapter 6   MANAGING DEVICES **251**
WORKING WITH DEVICE STATUS. 252
Displaying All Devices on Your System 252
Interpreting the Status of Devices 256
VARYING DEVICES ON AND OFF 260
When Would You Need to
Vary On or Vary Off a Device? 261
Why Can't You Vary off
a Device with an ACTIVE Status? 261
DISPLAYING DEVICE MESSAGES 264
DETERMINING THE CONTROLLERS
TO WHICH A DEVICE IS ATTACHED. 265
DISPLAYING ALL DEVICES ATTACHED TO A CONTROLLER. . . 267

VARYING CONTROLLERS ON AND OFF. 270
DISPLAYING ALL CONTROLLERS ATTACHED TO A LINE . . . 272
EXERCISE 6: WORKING WITH
    DEVICES, CONTROLLERS, AND LINES. 277

Chapter 7   **SAVING AND RESTORING** **293**
UNDERSTANDING OS/400 SAVE AND RESTORE 294
   Why You Need to Save Data on the AS/400. 295
   What You Can Save on the AS/400 297
   Is There Anything You Can't Save?. 298
   Media You Can Use to Save Data. 298
   How to Recover Saved Data. 299
PREPARING TAPES FOR A BACKUP 300
   Rotating Tapes. 300
   Cleaning Tape Units. 301
   Initializing a Tape. 302
   Displaying Tape Contents. 307
   Handling Tape Errors. 312
RUNNING A SIMPLE BACKUP. 313
   The Save Menu 314
   Save Commands. 316
   Restricting Access to the System 318
   Saving and Restoring a Library Using Tape 319
EXERCISE 7: SAVING A LIBRARY TO
    AND RESTORING IT FROM A SAVE FILE 329

RESOURCES **339**

INDEX **343**

Rochester Community and Technical College and the AS/400 University

RCTC

RCTC's Department of Continuing Education and Workforce Development provides custom training in computer software and professional certifications for computer skills. Among the computer skills and professional certifications currently provided are:

- AS/400 professional training and certifications

- A+ Certification (hardware expertise)

- MCSE certification (Microsoft networking)

- MOUS certification (Microsoft Office software expertise)

- Lotus Notes professional training and certifications

- SmartSuite software training and expertise

- Corel 8 training

- Training in Adobe graphical software such as PhotoShop and Illustrator

- Webmaster training (using FrontPage and/or Netfusion)

RCTC's Department of Continuing Education and Workforce Development is a charter member of the IBM AS/400 University, as well as a Microsoft Authorized Technical Education Center and a CISCO Networking Academy. They provide certification in these and other programs through their on-site Sylvan

Prometric Testing facilities. For more information about what RCTC can do for you, contact them at:

Rochester Community and Technical College
851 30th Avenue Southeast
Rochester, MN 55904-4999
Phone: 1-800-247-1296 or 507-280-3157
Fax: 507-280-3168

workforce.education@roch.edu

AS/400 University at RCTC

RCTC is a premier AS/400 University education partner. In partnership with IBM, which manufactures AS/400 and RS/6000 computers in Rochester, Minnesota, RCTC offers both credit and non-credit classes toward industry-recognized certifications as operators, administrators, networking specialists, and programmers. In addition, RCTC offers continuing education programs for AS/400 professionals, including such specialties as Web/Domino servers, Java programming, and new releases of RPG.

Credit classes are a continuing part of RCTC curriculum, providing a two-year Associates Degree in computer science and a one-year Advanced Certificate. The curriculum focuses on the AS/400 business computer.

The AS/400 University program for non-credit certifications is offered continuously year-round. RCTC offers two professional pathways to AS/400 credentials: an AS/400 Operator and an AS/400 Administrator, both of which can be further enhanced with programming and computer networking skills. A full certification can be completed in less than six months.

Throughout the year, AS/400 University at RCTC, in partnership with the Education Connection, also a premier AS/400 University education partner, provides corporate training sessions to educate AS/400 professionals around the globe. Detailed sessions are taught by a group of AS/400 experts who are recognized as industry leaders in their respective fields; in fact, many are award-winning speakers. Instructors such as Al Barsa, Wayne Evans, Dick Grenham, and Skip Marchesani combine seminars with hands-on labs.

FOREWORD

AS/400 customers, business partners, and professionals benefit from proof of measurable skills. Consequently, measuring the knowledge, skills, and abilities of AS/400 professionals has become a crucial task. The need to evaluate AS/400 knowledge, skills, and abilities is the key reason IBM launched a world-class AS/400 certification program in 1997. This certification program establishes standards that identify minimum levels of competency for individuals who work on the AS/400. To learn more about AS/400 certification programs, visit IBM's certification home page on the Internet (www.ibm.com/certify).

Various certification tests are offered based upon crucial roles required to run, manage, or program an AS/400. IBM's certification program provides information technology (IT) professionals with the knowledge and confidence to successfully implement the dynamic features of the AS/400. Capability will continue to be added to the AS/400 at an aggressive rate.

In March 1999, Rochester Community and Technical College accepted the challenge of developing educational interventions for these AS/400 certifications. The book you're now holding is the first in a series of certification guides—in this case, for the IBM Certified Specialist, AS/400 Associate System Operator—to be written to address the certification test objectives.

RCTC also has developed traditional classroom system operations classes to prepare IT personnel for the real world of operating an AS/400. These classes continue to enjoy wide success.

This text is an excellent source of educational material for classroom use in any AS/400 operations curriculum or as a self-study guide for the individual who might not have the time to attend a formal class. The concepts are presented at a down-to-earth, practical level. This is the first text I have seen based directly on the AS/400 system operator test objectives. While no test or course can guarantee passing a certification test, the material in this book will prepare the qualified student to master real-life AS/400 system operations. And this text provides readers with a practical, effective means with which to prepare for the certification examination.

We often talk about the shortage of skilled workers in the IT world and how businesses struggle with providing their staff with the right quality training to keep technical skills current with the rapid speed of change. This book and subsequent offerings from RCTC directly address the skill-shortage dilemma.

Don Heller
Project Manager,
AS/400 World Wide Assessment and Certification
IBM Corporation

EXPLORING BASIC OS/400 OPERATIONAL CONCEPTS

This chapter includes sections on the following topics:

- Identifying the purpose and benefits of OS/400

- Recognizing the major functions of OS/400

- Understanding OS/400 display types

- Recognizing Operational Assistant

- Choosing assistance levels.

- Working with AS/400 help facilities

- Using CL commands

IDENTIFYING THE PURPOSE AND BENEFITS OF OS/400

The AS/400 system is a powerful, tremendously versatile computer system, designed to be suitable for a wide range of commercial applications. The operating system of the AS/400, referred to simply as the *OS/400*, provides the tools you use to run the AS/400 system. It allows you to run multiple jobs regardless of any other programs running at the same time.

Like all operating systems, the main purpose of the OS/400 is to ensure that all hardware and software resources are used efficiently. When OS/400 executes any program or service, it communicates directly with the machine on your behalf. Benefits of the OS/400 include its ease of use, responsiveness, versatility, economy, and frequent updates.

Ease of use: The integrated nature and menu-driven structure of OS/400 make it one of the easiest operating systems in its class to use and operate.

Responsiveness: The AS/400 system architecture enables customers to smoothly incorporate new hardware and software. This system's architecture helps businesses respond quickly to a changing business environment, while maintaining their competitive edge.

Versatility: More business solutions are available today for the AS/400 than for any other business system. Moreover, the streamlined nature of OS/400, as well as the extensive array of existing business solutions, should lighten the programming workload for most users.

Economy: OS/400 enables the use of new, lower-cost technology with minimal or no impact to the customer. Your applications, software, and hardware are protected as you move to new applications and technologies.

Frequent Updates: OS/400 is a dynamic operating system that is continuously improved for optimum efficiency. These improvements consist of versions, releases, modifications, and Program Temporary Fixes (PTFs). IBM produces new releases of OS/400 frequently. It is always beneficial to know what version, release, or modification of the operating system you have when you need to report problems to IBM (e.g. V4R3M1). PTFs are what IBM uses to correct problems or potential problems within IBM-licensed programs. PTFs may fix problems that appear to be hardware failures, or they may provide new functions. Generally, PTFs are incorporated in a future release of the system.

RECOGNIZING THE MAJOR FUNCTIONS OF OS/400

OS/400 fully integrates a relational database, communications applications, networking capabilities, and many software components used in most business environments. The following major functions of the OS/400 program make this seamless operation possible:

- Object management
- Storage management
- Database management
- User management
- Security management
- Work management
- Message management
- Print management

Object Management

Everything on the AS/400 that can be stored or retrieved is contained in an *object*. An object combines data and the valid methods of using that data into a single entity. In one sense, an object is something you can touch or see. An object's *attributes* or *data* are things that describe the object, and the *methods* are actions you can perform on an object. Just remember that all things in the operating system are called objects. Objects include programs, files, folders, queues, job descriptions, device descriptions, user profiles, and more. Each object has different characteristics. For example, a program contains instructions, while a file contains data.

A *library* is an object used to group objects and to find objects by name. A library is similar to a directory on a personal computer. Unlike directories, however, libraries cannot contain other libraries. QSYS, the system library for the

AS/400, is the exception. It is the only library that can contain other libraries. In addition to containing other libraries, QSYS contains the programs, user profiles, and other objects that make up OS/400. (For details on how to find objects on the AS/400, see chapter 2.)

Storage Management

Single-level storage distinguishes the AS/400 from the storage systems of other hardware manufacturers. While competitors separate storage management into two distinct hardware components of memory (also known as main storage) and disk (also known as auxiliary storage or DASD), the AS/400 combines main storage and auxiliary storage into one logical unit, called *single-level storage*. Keep in mind that main and auxiliary storage must be functioning and properly integrated or users will not be able to access data on the AS/400.

With single-level storage, all objects are treated as if they dwell in a single address space. Thus, a user needs to know only an object's name, not its location. Consider a person's mailing address. If someone has a P.O. box number, you don't have to know that person's street address in order to send mail. Likewise, when you know an object's name, you don't need to know the place where it resides on the system. An object could actually be split up into different areas of the system. All you have to do is ask for the object, and OS/400 finds all the pieces for you.

Database Management

The AS/400 data management function is a full-fledged relational database called *DB2/400*, which is an integral part of the operating system. Traditional systems use a segmented structure, requiring the computer to search each file area separately for data relating to a single record. The AS/400 uses a consistent, integrated, data management function with standardized data descriptions. Individual programming statements are not needed for each task. The AS/400 operates more efficiently because it separates a program's view of the data from the way the data is physically stored on the system.

User Management

The AS/400 can support as many users as the customer needs. To be accepted by the AS/400, you must have a *user profile*. Your user profile tells the AS/400 which system resources you have been given permission to use, as well as the manner in which you need to have information displayed in order to do your job. Basically, it's a list of things the AS/400 needs to know about you.

The various pieces of information contained in the user profile regarding which resources you have been given permission to use is referred to as *user authority*. Depending on your user authority and other information in your user profile, certain options may not appear on your displays, and certain commands may not be available to you. As a system operator, you should have access to most functions on the AS/400. You are expected to accomplish such tasks as controlling jobs, handling system messages and print output, managing communications with the system, and saving and restoring objects. Your user profile indicates the special authorities you need to perform such tasks.

The AS/400 ships with several default user profiles, each representing different authority levels, so that system administrators have a basis on which to start creating unique user profiles. Examples of IBM-supplied user profiles include QSECOFR (security officer), QSYSOPR (system operator), and QUSER (AS/400 end user). The security officer can do anything on the system except service functions, which are better left to the IBM CE (customer engineer). The security officer has unlimited power to access objects on the system. Most user profiles in a business are based on the QUSER profile, since they are running the business applications on the AS/400 but not administering or operating the system.

Security Management

The ability to protect information from accidental or deliberate loss or destruction is one of the most vital features of the AS/400. Information stored on a computer system is one of the most important assets of a business. This is especially true in today's "e-business" environment, where companies use the World Wide Web to communicate and transact business with employees, business partners, and end users. There has never been a documented virus on an AS/400.

Security is built into the operating system (OS/400), not an add-on feature of an application. The security tools provided in OS/400 control who can use the system, who can use objects, and what rights of access each user has. Security of information assets does not happen by accident. A business must have a comprehensive security plan to prevent access to objects by unauthorized people.

The AS/400 is shipped at a certain security level defined by the QSECURITY system value. (System values allow the security officer or users with the proper authority to customize many characteristics of the system.) QSECURITY determines how much security is enforced on the whole machine. The major differences between the various security levels lie in whether a valid user ID and password are required to sign on to the AS/400, and whether authority is required to work with objects on the system. When your AS/400 is set up, the system administrator probably set the security level to at least require a password to log on and to require authority to individual objects.

Work Management

OS/400 comes installed with a work management environment that supports concurrent interactive, batch, spooled, and communications jobs. This environment can be tailored for individual users. All the work done on the AS/400 is submitted through work management functions. OS/400 coordinates workflow and the use of resources in a predefined operating environment called a *subsystem*. Each subsystem is specialized to perform certain types of tasks. In other words, a subsystem is a place to do work. Just like your office, everything you need is there to do your work (PC, telephone, lights, coffee mug, etc.). OS/400 includes several subsystems, all operating independently of each other but sharing system resources. Examples of IBM-supplied subsystems are QBASE, QINTER, and QBATCH. You can also create your own subsystems. A subsystem consists of resources such as these:

- Subsystem descriptions (SBSD), which describe the kind of work a subsystem does.

    If there is no description, there is no subsystem. A SBSD is analogous to a blueprint for a house. If there is no blueprint, builders don't know what style of house to build.

- Main storage to enable the system to load and run programs.

- Display stations to start and run interactive jobs.

- Job queues to start batch jobs.

- Communication devices and locations.

A subsystem creates a suitable work environment for the completion of a task. Each piece of work running in a subsystem is called a *job*. A job is the way OS/400 organizes and manages your work. OS/400 assigns a job number to each job and associates a *job description* with that job telling the system how the work is to be accomplished. Job descriptions contain pieces of information such as user IDs, job queues, and routing data. A job usually includes all necessary computer programs, files, and instructions to the operating system. You can initiate a job through control language (CL) commands or through one or more programs. OS/400 uses two types of processes to manage work: *interactive jobs* and *batch jobs*.

Interactive Jobs

Interactive jobs begin when a user signs on to the AS/400. These jobs typically have a higher priority than other tasks. With interactive jobs, the user runs programs or types commands on a display station, waits for the system to display the requested material, and repeats this sequence until the user signs off the system. As part of an interactive job, you might do a variety of tasks, such as creating a user profile or changing the authority to a library.

You guessed it: interactive jobs are run in subsystem QINTER by default.

Batch Jobs

Unlike interactive jobs, batch jobs do not usually require user interaction or immediate system feedback. They typically run at a lower priority than interactive jobs. In other words, they run in the background without any intervention from you.

A batch job begins when a user requests it. Then, the system creates the job and places it in a job queue. Since several users can simultaneously request batch jobs, but only a limited number of batch jobs can actually run at the same time, the system must temporarily place each job in a job queue. As the system finishes each batch job, it searches the job queue for the next batch job to run.

A batch job runs when the OS/400 has time available or when you determine it should run. For example, you can schedule a batch job to automatically run nightly at 11:00 P.M. You might want to schedule such a batch job for the nightly deletion of work files before a system backup. The job scheduler feature allows you to control when a job is submitted to the job queue or released from the job queue.

There's no secret here; batch jobs are run in subsystem QBATCH by default. (For details on working with jobs on the AS/400, see chapter 3.)

Message Management

A message is a communication sent to one system user or program by another. Many predefined messages are supplied with OS/400 for identifying status or error conditions, for communicating between programs within the system, or for communicating between the system and system users. A user can also communicate with other system users through messages that are created at the same time they are sent, by issuing the SNDMSG command. OS/400 Message Handler places messages in various queues. It places messages for you in your private queue, where only you can access them. Some messages are informational. Others, called *inquiry messages*, require a response from the receiver. (For details on working with messages, see chapter 4.)

Print Management

OS/400 incorporates a set of functions that are designed to provide consistent access to printing. *Print spooling* enables a user to send a document to a file that temporarily holds print jobs, arranges them in order of importance, and places them on an output queue. This frees the job producing the output to continue processing independently of the speed or availability of printers. The *virtual printer* function enables users of personal computers attached to an AS/400 to route print jobs to the system's spool queues and printers. (For details on working with printer output, see chapter 5.)

UNDERSTANDING OS/400 DISPLAY TYPES

All of the work you do with the AS/400 system centers around displays, the information shown on your workstation display. The various AS/400 display screens standardize and organize system information for you, so that you can communicate with the system easily and efficiently. There are four major types of displays:

- Menu
- Entry
- List
- Information

Although the four kinds of displays look and act differently, they have three things in common:

- They have titles.
- They list their active function keys.
- They explain their purpose.

You don't have to keep track of whether you're using a menu, entry, list, or information display. You will use them all so often you will not even think about what kind they are. This chapter is simply meant to help you become familiar with the different types of AS/400 displays.

Sign-on Screen

Before going any further with AS/400 displays, let's not overlook the most important display on the system—the AS/400 Sign-On screen. The Sign-On screen, shown in Figure 1.1, is your ticket to performing AS/400 operations. At the very least, you must have a user ID and password to get in.

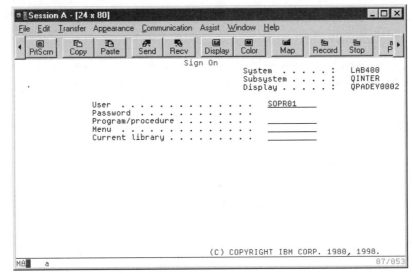

Figure 1.1: The AS/400 Sign-On screen.

The upper-right corner of the Sign-On display lists the name of the AS/400 system you are using, the subsystem the system is using, and the name of the display device you are using to access the AS/400. More discussion about these values come in later chapters.

For the User field, you must enter a user ID that matches the name of a user profile.

The Password field is displayed only if password security is active on the system. Effective with V3R7 of OS/400, the system comes straight from the factory with password security active, meaning that the system requires a password to sign on. However, before V3R7, the default security level for the system does not require a password to sign on. If your system is at a release prior to V3R7, and the password field is not available, contact your system administrator to activate password security. Without it, anyone can get access to the system, which poses a huge security risk.

Follow these steps to sign on now:

1. Type your user ID.

2. Press Tab.

3. Type your password.

4. Press Enter.

The AS/400 Main Menu should appear, as shown in Figure 1.2.

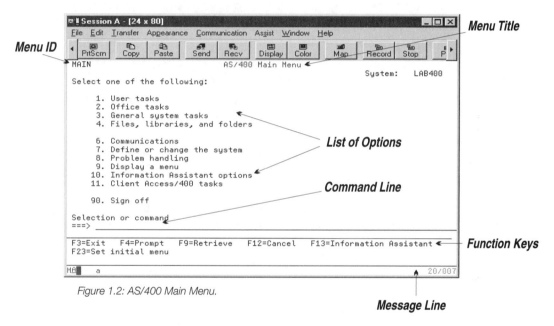

Figure 1.2: AS/400 Main Menu.

Once a user has signed on, a menu is typically displayed. The AS/400 Main Menu is the most powerful menu provided by OS/400. From this menu, just by typing the number of a menu option, you can get to any operation to which you are authorized. Except for option 90, all options on this menu cause some other menu to be displayed.

Notice option 5 is not displayed, which means the user does not have authority to this option. If the user had authority, option *5 for Programming* would be shown. Because a system operator has a great deal of authority, most options are available.

Menu Displays

The AS/400 Main Menu is an example of a menu display, which offer you a list of items from which to choose. Menus provide an easy and efficient way to select work items. Using the AS/400 Main Menu, let's examine the six main parts of a menu:

1. The *title* is in the middle of the top line.

2. The *menu ID* is in the upper-left corner. You can use the menu ID to get to a particular menu quickly. Menus are the only type of display that have IDs.

3. The list of *options* includes the number and option description of each function you can perform from this menu. To perform a function, enter the option number on the command line.

4. The *command line* is an input area for entering the number of a menu option or a CL command.

5. A list of *function keys* is provided below the command line. Function keys differ from display to display. If there are more function keys than can be shown on a single display, "F24 = More keys" appears and allows you to display these additional keys.

6. The *message line*, located at the bottom of the display, is blank or contains copyright information. When the AS/400 communicates with you, a message appears here.

Notes: If your menus have missing option numbers, don't panic; nothing is wrong. The system administrator might have eliminated some options to simplify your job.

On keyboards where there is only one row of function keys (F1 through F12), F13 through F24 are accessed by using the F1 through F12 keys with the Shift key. For example, to use F24, press Shift and F12; to use F17, press Shift and F5, and so forth.

There are a couple of ways that you can display a menu. You can enter menu options to "walk" through many menus, or you can use the GO command to take a shortcut to a menu. To use the GO command, you must know the menu ID.

Displaying a Menu Using a Menu Path

You can use a series of menus known as a *menu path* to get to the menu of choice. You select an item from one menu, and a second menu is displayed, offering additional items. You select an item from the second menu, and a third menu offers even more items. This menu path continues until you reach your destination menu.

With the menu-path method of running tasks, the system prompts you through each step of your task selection. This method eliminates the use of lengthy command strings. However, as you become a more advanced user of the AS/400, you might find that using the CL commands are a more efficient way to accomplish tasks. (See the subheading Using CL Commands for more details.)

As an example, consider the menu path method to work with printers:

On the AS/400 Main Menu (MAIN), type 3 for General system tasks, and press Enter. The General System Tasks menu appears, as shown in Figure 1.3. Take a few moments to explore the different options on the General System Tasks menu. You will become, or maybe you already are, very intimate with these types of tasks in your daily work as a system operator.

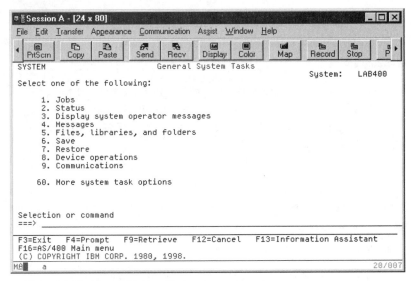

Figure 1.3: The General System Tasks menu.

On the General System Tasks (SYSTEM) menu, type 8 for Device operations, and press Enter. The Device Operations menu appears, as shown in Figure 1.4.

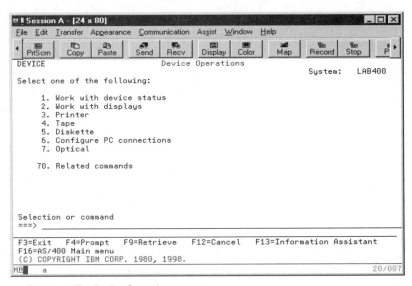

Figure 1.4: The Device Operations menu.

On the Device Operations (DEVICE) menu, type 3 for Printer, and press Enter.
The Printer menu appears, as shown in Figure 1.5. From the Printer (PRINTER)
menu, option 2 allows you to work with printers—your destination.

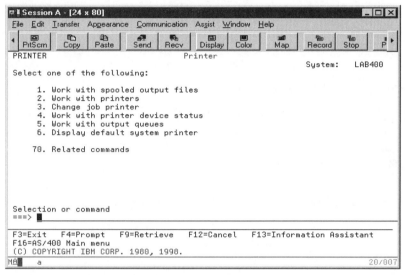

Figure 1.5: The Printer menu.

In this example, you "walked" through four different menus to get to your destination. Knowing that the menu ID of the Printer menu is PRINTER, you could
have taken a fast path to this menu. (The fast path method, or GO command, is
discussed under the following subheading, Displaying a Menu Using the GO
Command.)

Function keys 3 and 12 (F3 and F12) allow you to step back through previous
menus. F12 always displays the previous menu in the path, while F3 may skip
one or more menus. In this example, pressing F12 on the Printer menu returns us
to the Device Operations menu. However, pressing F3 from the Printer menu returns you all the way back to the menu from which you started—in this case, the
AS/400 Main Menu.

> ***Tip:*** If you want a particular menu to display after you sign on, display that menu and press F23 (Set Initial menu), which is Shift and F11. For example, to display the Printer menu after you sign on, access that menu and press F23. F23 might not be listed on every menu, but it can be used on any menu. Pressing F23 resets your user profile. To see how your profile was changed, type the CL command CHGPRF and press F4. The Change Profile (CHGPRF) display appears, as shown in Figure 1.6. Note the Initial menu field.

Displaying a Menu Using the GO Command

You can get to any menu on the AS/400 quickly by entering GO and the menu ID on any command line. For example, if you want to work with printers, you can get to the Printer menu by entering GO PRINTER on any command line. The menu ID is shown in the top left corner of the display.

To find a list of all menus on the system, type either one of the following commands and press Enter:

```
WRKMNU *ALL
GO *ALL
```

> ***Tip:*** If you need to display a menu, but can only remember the first character or two of its menu ID, use the GO *x** form of this command. Replace the *x* with the beginning characters of the menu ID that you remember. For example, if you enter GO DEV*, OS/400 displays a list of all menus whose names begin with those characters and allows you to select the one you want to display.

The following is a list of menus that are useful in controlling and operating the system. You can get to any of these menus directly from any display having a command line. Just type GO and a menu ID from the following list:

ASSIST: The Operational Assistant menu simplifies some of the common operator and user tasks, such as working with printer output, jobs, messages, and changing your password. In addition, users with the proper authority can select options to manage or customize the system, check the system status, clean up objects, power the system on and off, enroll users, change some system options, and collect disk space information.

CLEANUP: The Cleanup menu allows you to start, end, or change automatic cleanup. The cleanup function deletes old job logs, history logs, messages, office calendar items, and journal receivers that take up storage space.

DEVICESTS: The Device Status menu allows you to choose options for working with system devices, such as display stations, printers, tape drives, and diskette drives.

DISKTASKS: The Disk Space Tasks menu provides the option for collecting disk space information to help show how storage is being used on your system. After collecting the information, you can specify what information to include in a report, and then print the report.

FILE: The Files menu allows you to work with files on the system.

INFO: The Information Assistant Options menu allows you to find out where to look for information about your AS/400 system and how to comment on that information. You can also use this menu to find out what is new in this release of the AS/400 system and what new enhancements and functions are to be available in the next release.

LIBRARY: The Libraries menu allows you to work with the libraries.

MANAGESYS: The Manage Your System, Users, and Devices menu allows you to display what activity is going on in the system, run a backup, and work with the devices on the system.

POWER: The Power On and Off Tasks menu allows you to display the power-on and -off schedule. If you have the correct authority, you can also change the schedule or power off the system and then power it on again.

PRINTER: The Printer menu allows you to work with spooled files, output queues, and the status of printer devices.

PROBLEM: The Problem Handling menu allows you to work with problems, ask questions, and receive answers using the question and answer database, display system operator messages, display the history log, and start system service tools (SST).

RESTORE: The Restore menu allows you to restore saved information from tape, or a save file on the system.

SAVE: The Save menu allows you to select a menu option to specify the type of backup you want to run.

SETUP: The Customize Your System, Users, and Devices menu lets you customize automatic cleanup, schedule when your system is to power on and off, and enroll users.

STATUS: The Status menu allows you to display the status of jobs, devices, and system activities.

SYSTEM: The General System Tasks menu allows you to control system operations, devices, and all jobs on the system.

TAPE: The Tape menu allows you to use and control tape devices, as well as initialize the tapes that are used during backup.

TECHHELP: The Technical Support Tasks menu provides options to help resolve problems on the system.

USERHELP: The Information and Problem Handling menu provides additional information about the system and is useful in attempting to resolve problems.

Entry Displays

An entry display prompts or asks you to type information. Because the form and quantity of this information varies depending on what the display is trying to do, entry displays can appear in many ways. All entry displays have one purpose: they request the user to enter information that is appropriate to the type of display and the desired action.

The Change Profile (CHGPRF) display, shown in Figure 1.6, is an example of an entry display.

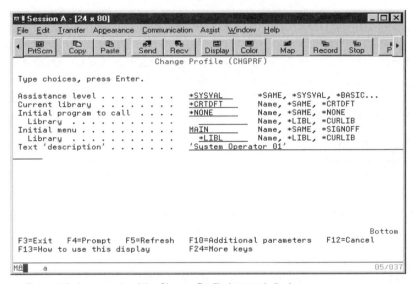

Figure 1.6: An example of the Change Profile (CHGPRF) display.

To get to this display using a menu path, complete the following steps:

1. On the AS/400 Main Menu, type 1 for User tasks and press Enter.

2. On the User Tasks menu, type 9 for Change your user profile and press Enter.

Notice that, like menus, entry displays contain a centered title, function keys appropriate to the display, and a blank area below the function keys for system messages. The title typically includes the name of the command that is executed. For example, Figure 1.6 shows that the command CHGPRF is running to change your profile. You can also enter a command directly, versus choosing a menu option associated with the command.

The first time you use any entry display, the system provides most field values for you. These are referred to as *default values*. Default values are used until you decide to change them.

Blank fields, on the other hand, may require user-assigned values. Examples of entry fields that require user-assigned values include user name, password, and message fields. Some blank fields can be skipped because the system doesn't really need the information to perform the function. Don't worry about leaving out anything vital. If you press the Enter key before filling in a required field, the system prompts you to enter the required information.

> **Tip:** To change an existing entry, just type the new value over the current value (being careful to get rid of any extra characters). After you've finished typing the new values, press the Enter key to make them the new values. If you accidentally type a value for a field, just clear the field completely. OS/400 puts the default value back in when the Enter key is pressed.

Choices for each field are listed to the right of the entry field. If there is an ellipsis (…) after the last choice, more values are available to choose from. You can ask, or prompt, the system for all possible choices for an entry field by placing the cursor somewhere within the field and pressing F4 (Prompt). This works whether a field has a current value or is blank.

On some entry displays, such as Change Profile, certain fields (also known as *parameters*) are not shown on the display, because these fields or parameters are not commonly used. You can request that they be shown, in which case F10 (Additional parameters) becomes available. Pressing F10 shows more parameters available on that display. Figure 1.7 shows an example of the Change Profile (CHGPRF) display with additional parameters.

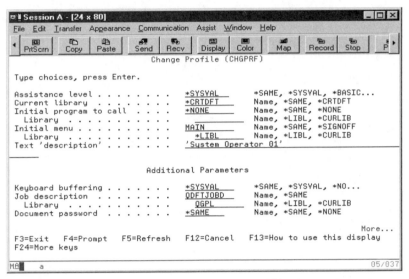

Figure 1.7: The Change Profile (CHGPRF) display with additional parameters.

List Displays

A *list display* is a list of objects or data, such as jobs, output queues, spooled files, libraries, and so forth. List displays are usually shown in response to a request for system information. List displays are also called *Work with* displays because you can do several types of work with the items on the list by typing one or more of the option numbers. The Work with All Spooled Files display shown in Figure 1.8 is an example of a list display.

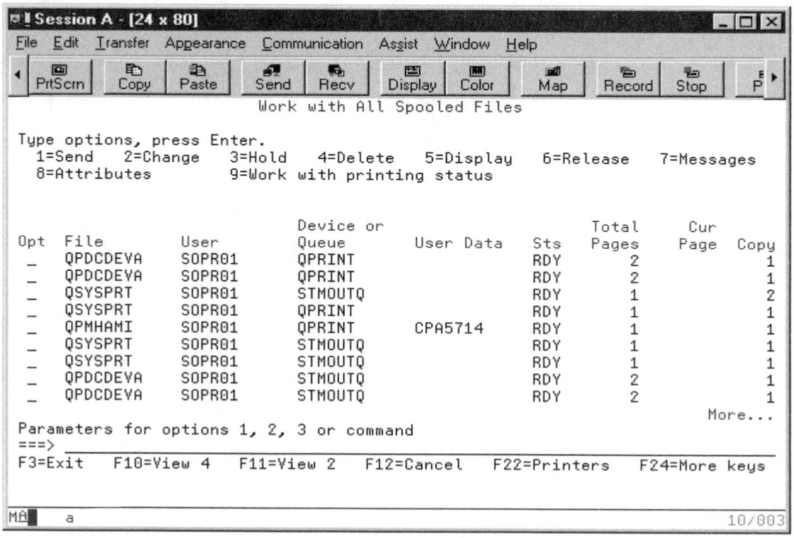

Figure 1.8: A Work with display screen, called Work with All Spooled Files.

Notice that the information is arranged in columns, each with a short title. The Opt column, to the left of each item, is an input field. In this column, an option number may be typed. Use the arrow keys, or the Tab key, to move up and down in the Opt column. The options available are shown in the upper part of the display. These options vary depending on the purpose of the display and your user authority. Sometimes all of the options are not shown. If additional options are available, "F23 = More options" is shown and may be selected.

A CL command is run for each option you select. For example, option 2 (Change) invokes the command CHGSPLFA (Change Spooled File Attributes). The command line allows you to enter a parameter for the command associated with an option listed, or to enter an entire CL command. On the Work with All Spooled Files display, you can enter parameters for options 1, 2, or 3. For example, you could type 2 (Change) next to a file or multiple files, tab to the command line, and type COPIES(<number>) to change the number of copies to be printed for the specified spooled files.

A list may contain more items than can be displayed on a single list display. In that case, *More...* appears in the lower-right corner of all but the last list display.

The word *Bottom* appears in the lower-right corner of the last list display. Use the scrolling keys (for example, Page Up and Page Down) to move from one display to another. Always check for the *More...* on your screen to make sure you're not missing anything.

The Work with All Spooled Files display is also an example of an *extended list*. The information on this type of list display does not fit within the width of the screen. On this particular display, F10 and F11 allow you to toggle between different columns of information. On other list displays, these function keys may not be shown, but may still be available. If additional function keys are available, "F24 = More keys" is shown on the display.

Information Displays

An *information display* contains information only. You cannot enter any data or make any changes. Press the Help or F1 key on an AS/400 display to see a typical information display, as shown in Figure 1.9.

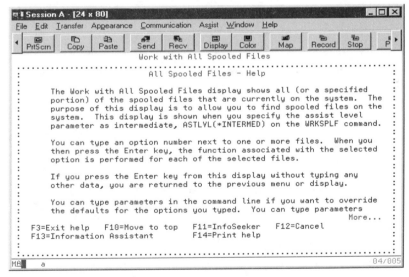

Figure 1.9: An information display for online help.

Another example of an information display is shown in Figure 1.10. The Display Work Station User screen provides information about your sign-on. Throughout this book, you are sure to get plenty of experience using the various types of OS/400 displays.

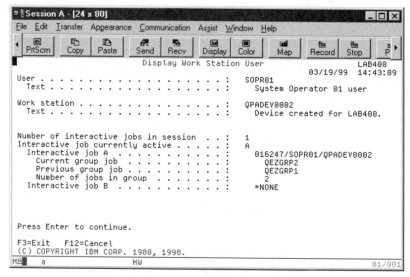

Figure 1.10: An information display for a signed-on user.

Tip: One way to get to the Display Work Station User display is to enter the command DSPWSUSR on any AS/400 command line. Information about the user profile you're signed on as is shown. This is handy information in case you need to quickly find out the name of the workstation device where you're signed on.

RECOGNIZING THE OPERATIONAL ASSISTANT

When you want to perform basic AS/400 tasks, the Operational Assistant is the place to start. It's designed to simplify common tasks such as managing printer output and controlling jobs by using more friendly terminology. In addition, users with proper authority can select options to manage or customize the system, check the system status, clean up objects, power the system on and off, enroll users, change some system options, and collect disk space information.

However, as you move toward more advanced AS/400 tasks, depending on Operational Assistant does not help you. Some options that have more complex displays are not accessible through the Operational Assistant. As a system operator, you are frequently the initial contact point for resolving user problems. You are expected to accomplish such tasks as controlling jobs, handling system messages and print output, managing communications with the system, and saving and restoring objects. You need to become very familiar with AS/400 operations and commands that Operational Assistant displays do not provide. This section introduces you to the Operational Assistant so that you know it's available, but the Operational Assistant is rarely referenced in any other chapter.

You can access Operational Assistant in one of the following ways:

Exploring Basic OS/400 Operational Concepts

- Press the Attention (Attn) key on non-programmable terminals, or the Escape (Esc) key on a personal computer. For this to work, the system value QATNPGM must be set to *ASSIST, which is the default value, and the user profile parameter, Attention program, must be set to *SYSVAL, which is the default value.

- Type GO ASSIST on a command line.

Tip: To display a system value, enter the command DSPSYSVAL <name of system value>.

Select the option for Operational Assistant from an application menu where it is available. Figure 1.11 shows the AS/400 Operational Assistant Menu. You must have at least a user class of *SYSOPR to see all the options on this menu. The user class is specified in your user profile.

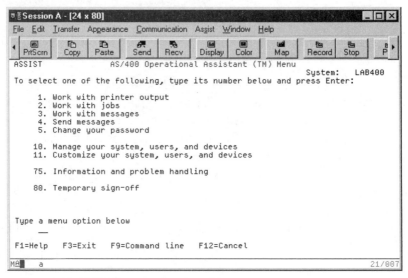

Figure 1.11: AS/400 Operational Assistant Menu.

Notice that there isn't a command line on the Operational Assistant Menu. Pressing F9 (Command line) displays a command line. Some AS/400 users may not have access to a command line because restricting access to the command line is a rudimentary form of security. However, system operators typically have access to command lines because there are many CL commands an operator uses that don't have an associated menu option.

CHOOSING ASSISTANCE LEVELS

You can choose the amount of help you want to receive as you interact with the AS/400. The various degrees of help offered are referred to as *assistance levels*. Assistance levels differ from one another in the terminology used, types of tasks that can be performed, and the number of functions and options supported that are actually shown on the display.

The AS/400 provides three assistance levels from which to choose:

- Basic
- Intermediate
- Advanced

Basic Assistance Level

The basic assistance level uses the type of display that provides the most assistance. It supports the more common user and operator tasks without the use of computer terminology. For example, the term "printer output" is used instead of "spooled file." When working with device status (a device can be a printer, tape drive, display station, and so forth), the terms "make available" and "make unavailable" are used instead of "vary on" and "vary off."

When you select a basic assistance level, the system simplifies your work by reducing the number of choices you need to make in performing your tasks. When you select the intermediate or advanced assistance level, you accept more of the responsibility involved for performing your tasks. You might be wondering why anyone would want less assistance from the system. Well, having the ability to choose from a variety of options and functions can offer greater flexibility when performing more complex tasks.

Intermediate Assistance Level

The intermediate assistance level uses displays that support all of the tasks that can be done on the AS/400 system. It uses computer terminology to describe the options and functions available from each display, as well as the tasks that can be done. This assistance level allows very complex tasks to be performed with greater flexibility. This book is designed around the intermediate assistance level.

Advanced Assistance Level

The advanced assistance level provides displays that offer the same functions and options as the intermediate assistance level. However, to increase the amount of workspace on the display, options and function keys are not shown. Therefore, you really need to know these options well in order to effectively use this level. The advanced assistance level is only available on a few displays.

Changing the Assistance Level

The following displays are common examples of where you can change the assistance level:

- Display Messages (DSPMSG)

- Display System Status (DSPSYSSTS)

- Work with Configuration Status (WRKCFGSTS)

- Work with Messages (WRKMSG)

- Work with Spooled Files (WRKSPLF)

- Work with System Status (WRKSYSSTS)

- Work with User Jobs (WRKUSRJOB)

- Work with User Profiles (WRKUSRPRF)

- Work with Writers (WRKWTR)

To change assistance levels on any of the applicable displays, just press F21 (SE-LECT ASSISTANCE LEVEL) and choose the assistance level you want to use. The display you see corresponds to the assistance level you've selected. You can also change the assistance level when you run one of the above-listed CL commands. Type the command you want to run, followed by the ASTLVL parameter. For example, to work with your spooled files at the basic level, enter WRKSPLF ASTLVL(*BASIC), and the Work with Printer Output display appears.

The assistance level is set for each command, so that you can use the basic assistance level for some displays and the intermediate assistance level for other displays. Your current assistance level for each command is stored. Therefore, when you sign on again, your assistance level remains the same.

To use the same assistance level on all displays, change the Assistance level parameter in your user profile. Type CHGPRF on a command line and press F4. An example of the Change Profile (CHGPRF) display is shown in Figure 1.6, earlier in this chapter. *SYSVAL uses the system default for the assistance level, as determined by the QASTLVL system value.

> ***Tip:*** To display the QASTLVL system value, enter the command DSPSYSVAL QASTLVL. If you have the authority, the assistance level may be changed for the entire system (thus affecting all users) via the command CHGSYSVAL QASTLVL; or, as mentioned above, you can change it in your user profile (thus affecting only how you see the displays).

WORKING WITH AS/400 HELP FACILITIES

The AS/400 has a wealth of information available to help you do your job as a system operator. This section introduces you to several help functions that are used to find the information you need when you need it. The Help resources are as follows:

- Online help

- Information Assistant

- InfoSeeker

- AS/400 Online Library on the Internet

Online Help

Online help is built into OS/400 and is therefore available to all system users. The Help or F1 key is your link to online help on the AS/400. The following on-line help information is available for all types of displays:

- What the display is used for.

- How to use the display.

- How to use the command line.

- How to use input fields.

- Which function keys are available and what they do.

Help is available for options on menus, fields on entry displays, and columns on list displays. To get help on a menu option, type the option and press the F1 key, or put the cursor on the menu option and press F1. To get help for a particular field, put the cursor on the field and press F1. To get help on a column of information, put the cursor anywhere on that column and press F1. You can also get help on a particular command. Just type the command on a command line and press F1.

The information that is shown depends on how online help is accessed. Two categories of online help are available: context-sensitive help and extended help.

Context-Sensitive Help

What you see when you press F1 generally depends on where the cursor is positioned when the key is pressed. This kind of help is referred to as context-sensitive help. You can use context-sensitive help on any OS/400 display: menu, entry, list, or information.

Menu Displays

Let's look at the help information that gets displayed when the cursor is positioned in three different areas on the AS/400 Main Menu. Start by pressing F1 while the cursor is positioned on the command line or in the menu title area to get help for the entire menu. All help available for that display (including the purpose of the display, options, and function keys) is shown in a help window, as depicted in Figure 1.12.

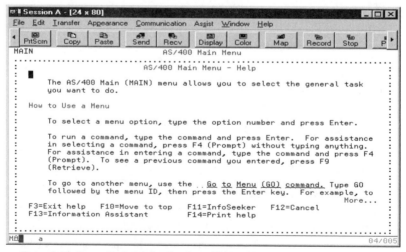

Figure 1.12: General help information from AS/400 Main Menu.

More... indicates that additional help information is available. Use the scrolling keys (Page Up and Down) to view all of the information.

Now, press F1 while the cursor is positioned on the function keys to get help for only the function keys. A help window describing the function keys appears, as shown in Figure 1.13.

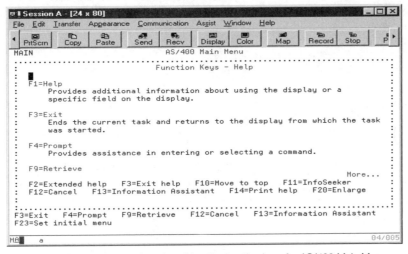

Figure 1.13: The Help window describing the function keys for AS/400 Main Menu.

Finally, press F1 while the cursor is positioned on the line of a menu option to get help for only that option. Maybe you want to go directly to help for option 8 (Problem handling) on the AS/400 Main Menu. Put your cursor anywhere on line 8 (Problem handling), and press F1. A help window describing that option appears, as shown in Figure 1.14.

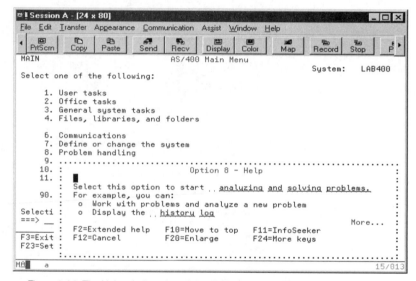

Figure 1.14: The Help window describing Option 8 from AS/400 Main Menu.

In this last example, notice the words and phrases that are underlined. Underlining indicates that a *hypertext link* to more information is available. Hypertext is a series of AS/400 help displays that are linked together by keywords or phrases. To move through hypertext links, put the cursor on the underlined term and press Enter. For example, by pressing Enter on the "analyzing and solving problems phrase," a help window with more information is displayed. This help window is shown in Figure 1.15.

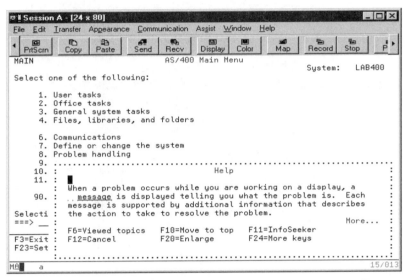

Figure 1.15: The Help window with more information regarding problem handling.

Likewise, if you pressed Enter on the hypertext term "message" in this example, you would get a description of what a message is and the different types of AS/400 messages.

Notice F6 (Viewed topics). This means that you can press F6 to list all of the hypertext displays in the order in which you viewed them, and then select a topic to jump to. Alternately, you can use F12 to back track through the topics one-by-one.

Entry Displays

Context-sensitive help is most common on entry, or prompt, displays where you enter values for command parameters. The parameter the cursor is positioned on when F1 is pressed determines the information that is provided.

You use this type of help most often when you don't understand a parameter or the values available to choose from. Just move the cursor to the field and press F1. A help window describing only that field appears.

Figure 1.16 shows help for the Configuration description parameter on the Work with Configuration Status (WRKCFGSTS) entry display.

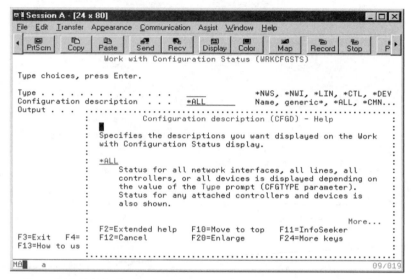

Figure 1.16: Help for the Configuration description parameter on the WRKCFGSTS entry display.

More… indicates that additional help information is available. Use the scrolling keys (Page Up and Down) to view a description of all possible values for this parameter. Alternately, press F20 (Enlarge) to enlarge the window, so that you can read more information at once without having to page down.

List Displays

Context-sensitive help for columns on list displays provides information about the meaning of data in a column. Put the cursor anywhere on the column, and press F1 to get help specific to that column.

Figure 1.17 is an example of help for the Status (Sts) column on the Work with All Spooled Files display.

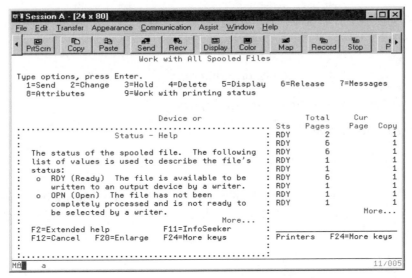

Figure 1.17: The Help display for the Status (Sts) column on the Work with All Spooled Files display.

Information Displays

You can also display context-sensitive help for any field on an information display, except for help displays. If you press F1 anywhere on a help display, another level of help information appears with a title of How to Use Help.

Extended Help

You can get extended help information on any AS/400 display. (Figure 1.12 shows an example of extended help.) Extended help provides different types of information about the entire display:

- An explanation of what the display does.

- An explanation of how to use the display.

- A description of the available options and function keys.

To get extended help, press F1 when your cursor is on one of the following:

- Any part of the display's title line.

- A blank menu option line or command line.

- A completely blank line on the display.

- Any instruction.

- A blank selection line.

To get extended help on certain help windows, such as those shown in Figures 1.13, 1.14, 1.16, and 1.17, press F2 (Extended help). Help for the entire display is shown.

Information Assistant

You can get additional information about the AS/400 by using Information Assistant, which is available to all users. You can access Information Assistant in one of the following ways:

- Select option 10 on the AS/400 Main Menu.

- Select option 2 on the Information and Problem Handling (USERHELP) menu.

- Type GO INFO on a command line.

- Press F13 on a help window.

Figure 1.18 shows the Information Assistant Options menu.

From the Information Assistant Options menu, you can find out how to look for online AS/400 manuals, search the system help index, start an online education module, or analyze and report problems. To get more information about a particular item, just press F1.

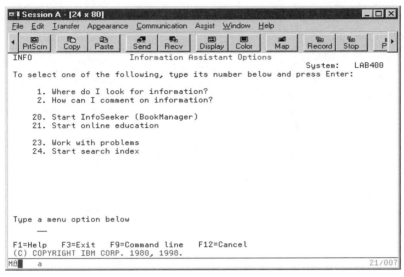

Figure 1.18: The Information Assistant Options menu.

InfoSeeker

You might have noticed that you received very few manuals with your AS/400. Instead, you received a Softcopy Library on a CD-ROM. The Softcopy Library can be installed on the AS/400 to be accessible to every user on the system, or it can be installed on a standalone PC to be viewed from that PC. Also, you can choose to just read the library (without installing it) directly from the AS/400 CD-ROM drive or from a PC's CD-ROM drive. (Note: The Softcopy Library is also available on tape, if your AS/400 does not have a CD-ROM drive.)

The books in the Softcopy Library are organized in "bookshelves," which group a set of related books together for easy access. You have some of the following bookshelves available:

- OS/400 Commonly Used Books

- Day-to-Day Operations

- Release and Information Overview

- Planning and Installation

You can also create your own bookshelf by grouping together the books that you most often reference.

InfoSeeker is the tool that allows you to view the Softcopy Library on the AS/400. InfoSeeker's search function finds information within an IBM book-shelf, a user-defined bookshelf, a set of online books, or a single online book. To help you read online books, InfoSeeker provides the following capabilities:

- Displays IBM-defined bookshelves.

- Searches across a set of books.

- Searches within a single book or topic within the book.

- Uses hypertext linking from one topic to another.

- Prints or copies a topic or sequence of topics.

- Organizes books into a custom bookshelf for a user.

You can start InfoSeeker in one of the following ways:

- Press F11 on any help display.

- Press F13 on most menus.

- Select option 20 on the Information Assistant (Info) menu.

- Enter STRINFSKR on a command line.

When you request the InfoSeeker function, the bookshelves that pertain to the version and release of your OS/400 are listed. (For more information on other functions of InfoSeeker, see the book *OS/400 InfoSeeker—Getting Started*. For detailed information on using InfoSeeker, see the book *OS/400 InfoSeeker Use*.)

AS/400 Online Library on the Internet

If you have Internet access, you can search for the AS/400 manuals on the Internet. Manuals are organized by the version and release of OS/400. You can search for an individual book available with the release of your OS/400, or you can search by a bookshelf, like you do if you use InfoSeeker on the AS/400. You can also order manuals from IBM via the AS/400 Online Library.

To find AS/400 manuals on the Internet, follow these steps:

1. Enter the following URL in your browser to display the AS/400 On-line Library:

    ```
    http://publib.boulder.ibm.com/pubs/html/as400/onlinelib.htm
    ```

    Bookmark this URL; you are sure to access it frequently.

2. Choose your language, and click the GO button.

3. On the Library Contents page, select the version and release of your OS/400. For example, to find manuals available with V4R3, click V4R3.

4. On the V4R3 Publications page, click Category bookshelves for V4R3. A list of V4R3 publications by category is shown.

5. Click Day-to-Day Operations. The suggested books for System Operators are listed.

6. Click the HTML version of one of these books. The Table of Contents for the selected book appears. You can now search for anything in that book.

You also have the option of downloading a PDF version of the book. This offers a printable version of the book, as though you bought it from IBM. You can save it for reprint. A printer with two-sided printing capabilities offers the best print results, as some IBM manuals can be quite long. (Downloading the PDF version takes time and bandwidth. Use this option only if you need to print the book. Searching for information in the PDF version is much slower than the HTML version.)

Other Resources

If you are new to the AS/400, a good reference book is the *System Operation for New Users: SC41-3200*. Use it as review of basic system operator functions, such as signing on and off an AS/400, using the keyboard and function keys, using on-line help, using CL commands, and sending and receiving messages. This manual also shows the various types of keyboards that can be used with terminals and PCs. The kind of keyboard you have and the program you are running determine the way you use your function keys.

System Operation SC41-4203 is another handy reference book for system opera-tors. This manual contains helpful information on job and print control, message handling, and device management.

Basic System Operation, Administration, and Problem Handling: SC41-5206 contains fast-path instructions for common system operator tasks, but it also in-cludes tasks that are typically performed by system administrators.

Another source of help is the online course "AS/400: Getting to Know Your Sys-tem." This course is shipped free on a CD-ROM with every AS/400 system. You can install it on the AS/400 so that it is available to all users of the system from option 21 on the Information Assistant Options menu (see Figure 1.18) . You can also load the course on a standalone PC, since the course uses AS/400 display simulation. In other words, you don't need to be connected to an AS/400 to run this course. It is an invaluable tool to use for a "refresher study" as needed.

USING CL COMMANDS

As a system operator, you have the ability to directly control the AS/400 by typ-ing control language commands. In addition to using menus, you can also type commands along with specific parameters to instruct the AS/400 to do some-thing. Entering commands is often faster and more efficient than using menu paths to perform an operation. Sometimes you need to travel through several menu layers to get to a certain display, whereas a single command may take you directly to that display.

Control language (CL) is simply the language that you use to communicate with the operating system, OS/400. CL consists of commands. A CL command can be run by a user or included in a program. It can be processed interactively (where there is two-way communication between a user and the AS/400), or it can be processed in batch. (A batch process means that after a user enters a command, the AS/400 uses the command with no further interaction with the user).

The following pages explain specific elements of using CL:

- The structure of CL commands.
- The place to enter CL commands.
- The place to find a list of commands on the AS/400.
- The way to enter CL commands.

Structure of CL Commands

Every Control Language command is made up of two parts: the command name and parameters.

Command Name

The naming structure of CL commands is English-like, which makes the commands easy to understand. CL commands can consist of a verb and a noun, or a verb, an adjective, and a noun. For example, the command WRKSPLF (Work with Spooled Files) consists of a verb, an adjective, and a noun.

You can easily tell the action each command performs and on what item the action is performed. Table 1.1 shows some command abbreviations along with examples.

Table 1.1: Command Abbreviations.				
Action	**Item (example)**	**Command Prefix**	**Command Suffix**	**Command**
Change	Message queue	CHG	MSGQ	CHGMSGQ
Create	Library	CRT	LIB	CRTLIB
Copy	File	CPY	F	CPYF
Delete	Library	DLT	LIB	DLTLIB
Display	Message	DSP	MSG	DSPMSG
Start	Printer writer	STR	PRTWTR	STRPRTWTR
Work with	Spooled files	WRK	SPLF	WRKSPLF

There are over 1,800 commands available on the AS/400. Even the most experienced users are seldom familiar with more than a few hundred of them.

Parameters

Every CL command consists of a command name, sometimes followed by one or more parameters. Usually only a few parameters are specified. A parameter has two parts: a keyword followed by a value in parentheses. For some parameters, you can specify multiple values.

The following is the general format for a command:

```
COMMAND NAME    KEYWORD(VALUE)    KEYWORD(VALUE)...
                     |                 |
                 Parameter 1       Parameter 2
```

Any CL command that has parameters is structured this way. For example, to create a library named PAYROLL, you could enter the following command:

```
CRTLIB LIB(PAYROLL)
```

where CRTLIB is the command name and LIB(PAYROLL) is a parameter, of which LIB is the keyword and PAYROLL is the value for that keyword.

Where to Enter CL Commands

You can enter a command either on a menu or list display command line or on the Command Entry display. Most menus and list displays have a line reserved for entering commands. This command line is especially useful when entering only one or two commands, because it is easy to use and readily accessible. On system menus (such as the AS/400 Main Menu) and list displays, the command line is located near the bottom of the display. On Operational Assistant menus, press F9 (Command line), and a command line appears near the bottom of the display.

The Command Entry display is specifically designed for entering commands. It allows you to enter efficiently commands, view previously entered commands, duplicate commands for reuse, and receive additional error message assistance. Use this display when you want to list or keep track of several commands at one time.

To access the Command Entry display, type CALL QCMD on any display command line. Figure 1.19 shows a Command Entry display.

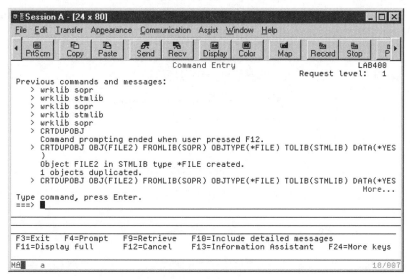

Figure 1.19: A Command Entry display.

In this example, previously entered commands are listed in the history area of the display. To list all previously entered commands since signing on, press F10 (Include detailed messages). One advantage of the Command Entry display over a menu command line is that you can go back and review which commands you have been using.

You can also re-use one of the commands by positioning the cursor on the command and pressing F9 (Retrieve). This brings back that command to the command line, which is faster than entering the command again. Or better yet, move your cursor to a line in the history area and press F4 (Prompt). The prompt screen for the command appears. You can see other choices for the parameters and optionally specify different values without entering the entire command again.

The F9 key can also be used on any menu or list display command line. Each time you press F9, the system backs up an additional command so that you can browse though previous commands until you find the one you want to repeat. If there are a lot of commands, however, it is more efficient to use the Command Entry display to look for the command you want to repeat, put your cursor on it, and then press F9 to rerun that command as is or F4 to prompt it. Pressing F9 repeatedly on a menu command line, when there are several commands, might be frustrating if you press the key too fast and miss the one you want. Your command does not come around again until F9 cycles through the whole list!

Finding a List of Commands on the AS/400

You can search for a list of all commands on the system using the Major Commands Group menu. To access this menu, do one of the following:

- Press F4 on a blank command line.

- Type a question mark (?) on a blank command line and press Enter.

- Enter the command GO MAJOR.

Figure 1.20 shows the Major Command Groups menu.

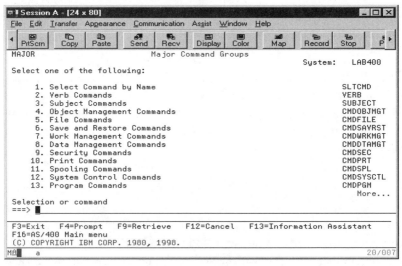

Figure 1.20: The Major Command Groups menu.

From this menu, you can select the options that lead to the proper command grouping menus. Options on the secondary grouping menus allow you to continually narrow your search until you find the command you need. Once you find the desired command, you can use the entry display help information to assist you in selecting the proper parameters.

Operators are frequently interested in spooling commands because controlling printer output is a huge part of their day-to-day work. To find a list of commands that enable you to work with printer output, your first inclination might be to select 10 for Print Commands. However, a spooled file is an intermediate-level term for printer output. Knowing this, complete the following steps, using the Major Command Groups menu:

1. Type 11 (Spooling Commands) and press Enter. The Spooling Commands (CMDSPL) menu appears, as shown in Figure 1.21. (From this menu, your first inclination might be to select 8 for User Print Info Commands. Remember, however, that a spooled file is the terminology used at the intermediate-assistance level for printer output.)

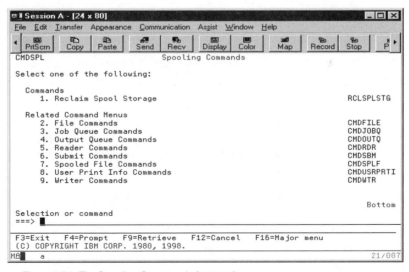

Figure 1.21: The Spooling Commands (CMDSPL) menu.

2. Type 7 (Spooled File Commands) and press Enter. The Spooled File Commands (CMDSPLF) menu appears, as shown in Figure 1.22.

Tip: To get directly to this menu, you could have entered GO CMDSPLF on a command line, thus bypassing the MAJOR and CMDSPL menus shown in Figures 1.20 and 1.21. As with any menu, you can use the GO command followed by the menu ID (always located in the upper-left corner of the display) to quickly go to a menu.

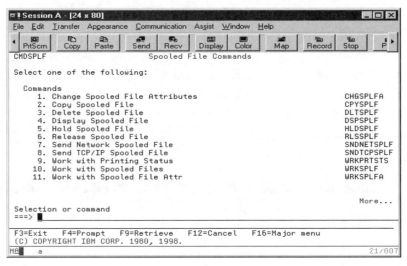

Figure 1.22: The Spooled File Commands (CMDSPLF) menu.

3. The best choice from here is option 10. Type 10 (Work with Spooled Files) and press Enter. The Work with Spooled Files (WRKSPLF) entry display appears, as shown in Figure 1.23.

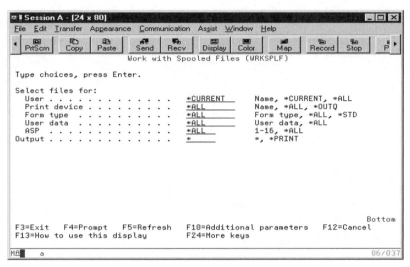

Figure 1.23: The Work with Spooled Files (WRKSPLF) entry display.

4. You can select the values you want for the parameters. When you press Enter, you're on your way to working with printer output.

Now that you know what the command is to work with printer output, in the future you don't need to traverse through these menus. The command WRKSPLF takes you directly to where you want to go. (This command and its functions are described in detail in chapter 5.)

If you know a part of a command name, but have forgotten how to spell it, you can type the characters of the command that you know followed by an asterisk (*). For example, if you know that the first four characters of the Work with Spooled Files command are WRKS, but can't remember the entire command name, type WRKS* on a command line and press Enter. The Select Command display appears, with all commands beginning with WRKS. Figure 1.24 shows an example of the Select Command display.

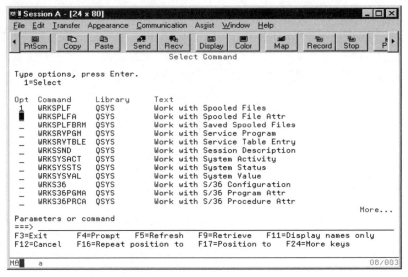

Figure 1.24: The Select Command display.

If you don't see the command you're looking for on the first display, page down until you find it. In the case of Work with Spooled Files, you must page down. On the option line next to the command, type 1 to select it and press Enter. The Work with Spooled Files (WRKSPLF) entry display appears, as shown in Figure 1.23.

If you want a more general category listing of commands, such as a list of all "Work with" commands, just enter WRK* on a command line. In this case, the Select Command display lists all commands that begin with the letters WRK. Now, you can select the desired command.

Tip: To get help on any command, just type the command name on a command line, and press F1. Online help is displayed describing the purpose of and parameters for that command.

Entering CL Commands

There are two methods for entering a CL command:

- Prompt the command to complete parameters.

- Enter the command in free form.

Command Prompting

You don't have to remember all the CL command keywords and values to complete a command. Each command has an entry display to prompt you for the command parameters. This is called *command prompting*. You can request command prompting in one of the following ways:

- Press F4 after typing the command name on a command line (e.g., DSPOBJD and F4).

- Type a question mark (?) immediately preceding the command name on a command line and press Enter (e.g., ?DSPOBJD).

In either case, the entry display shown in Figure 1.25 appears.

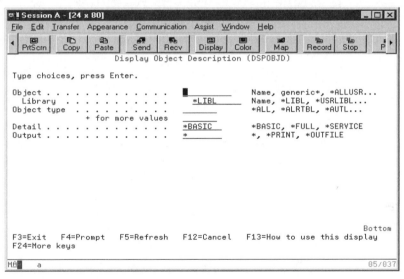

Figure 1.25: Prompted version of DSPOBJD command with parameter choices.

Each command entry display has certain characteristics. In this example, make sure to note the following characteristics:

- The descriptive name and command name at the top-center of the display.

- Choices for each parameter, as shown on the right side of the display. If an ellipsis (...) follows the last choice, more choices are available. Just put the cursor on that parameter and press F4 to list all permissible values, or press F1 to list all values along with a description of each.

Tip: To get help for the entire command, move your cursor to the title line or to any blank area of the display and press F1.

- The required versus optional parameters. Some parameters require a value, while others are optional. In Figure 1.25, Object and Object type are required parameters. If you try to enter a command without specifying any required parameters, those parameters are highlighted to let you know you need to choose a value. Optional parameters contain a default value, or what is considered to be the most common value. You can type a different value over the default value. Note that most values begin with an asterisk (*); this is IBM's way of helping you distinguish between system-provided values and user-created values, such as the name of a library.

- A plus sign (+) for more values, as shown under the Object type parameter on this display. This means that you can enter more than one value for this parameter. To specify multiple values, type the first value, type a plus sign on the next line, and press Enter. A display is shown containing multiple value lines. After entering all values, press Enter to return to the command entry display. Once this list has been entered, it can be changed.

- Function keys. Not all of the function keys may be shown on each command entry display. You may have to press F24 (More keys) multiple times to view all of the function keys. Even if the keys are not visible, they are still active. The following function keys are the most commonly used:

  ➤ F3 and F12 both cause you to exit the command entry display without running the command.

  ➤ F4 displays all of the values for a given parameter.

  ➤ F5 resets all parameters to their system default values. Any parameter values you have keyed will be lost. To reset only one parameter to its default value, just blank out its value and press Enter.

➤ F9 displays all of the parameters for a command, whether additional or conditional ones.

➤ F10 displays additional parameters that are not commonly used. The design of a command entry display is to show you only those parameters that you are most likely to need to run the command, without overwhelming you with every possible parameter available for a command. This is why F9 and F10 are available, so that you can view other parameters when needed.

➤ F11 toggles between showing either keywords or choices. You can switch from one format to the other by pressing the same function key. Figure 1.26 is an example of a display showing keywords. Compare this figure with Figure 1.25, which shows the parameter choices.

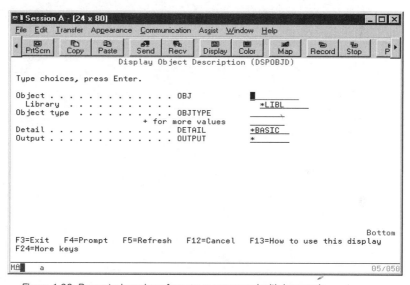

Figure 1.26: Prompted version of DSPOBJD command with keywords.

The keywords are a helpful guide if you want to use the free-format method of entering commands. Press F11 to toggle back and forth between keywords and choices. Whether keywords or parameter choices are shown each time you prompt a command depends on how your user profile is set up. Use the command CHGPRF and look for the User options (USROPT) parameter.

Some parameters have conditional parameters, which only display based on entries for previous parameters. For example, if you specify a value of *OUTFILE for the Output parameter in Figure 1.25 and press Enter, the File to receive output, Member to receive output, and Replace or add records parameters are displayed, as shown in Figure 1.27.

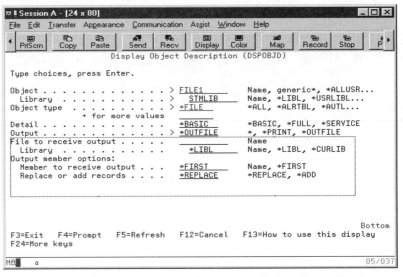

Figure 1.27: The Display Object Description (DSPOBJD) display with conditional parameters for OUTPUT(*OUTFILE).

As you can see in this example, there are several parameters. The advantage of prompting a command and using the entry display is that you do not have to know all of the parameters. You will probably use the command prompting method most of the time, especially on commands that you use infrequently. It is the easiest approach. A greater than (>) symbol next to an input field indicates that the parameter was either specified or changed from the default value.

> *Tip:* If you specify values, then decide to cancel your changes by pressing F3 or F12, you can easily retrieve those values. Just press F9 on a command line to bring back that command, and the parameters you specified are shown in the command string.

Free-Format Method

Another way to enter commands is to use the free-format method. With this method, you enter the command and its parameters on a command line as a string of characters. You use this method when you are familiar with the commands and their parameters.

> *Tip:* You can type as many parameters on the command line as you can remember, and then press F4 to prompt for more. The values you entered on the command line are filled in on the entry display.

There are two ways that you can enter a command using the free-format method: keyword form and positional form.

Keyword Form

With keyword form, you enter the command name followed by the keyword and value of each parameter you want to use. There must be a space between parameters and parentheses around values. The following is an example of the DSPOBJD command in keyword form:

```
DSPOBJD OBJ(STMLIB/FILE1) OBJTYPE(*FILE) OUTPUT(*PRINT)
```

Based on Figure 1.27, notice that you don't have to enter all of the parameters available for this command, just the required ones and any other ones you want to change (such as the OUTPUT keyword). The system uses default values for optional parameters.

Notice the parameter OBJ(STMLIB/FILE1). The value consists of two parts: the library name and the object name. When you are using the keyword form, the order of the values in a qualified name (library/object) is the reverse of the order for the same qualified name on the prompt display. That is, you cannot position the object name before the library name, for example OBJ(FILE1/STMLIB).

However, when you are using keyword form, the parameters themselves can be entered in any order, regardless of the order of the parameters on the prompt display. Therefore, the DSPOBJD command in the example could also be entered as

```
DSPOBJD OUTPUT(*PRINT) OBJ(STMLIB/FILE1) OBJTYPE(*FILE)
```

where OUTPUT(*PRINT) is now listed as the first parameter, and the command still runs successfully.

Positional Form

If you do not enter keywords, the parameters must be in the exact order as shown on the (F4) prompt display for the command. (See Figure 1.27). This is called *positional form*. Most commands limit the number of parameters that you can enter using positional notation. As an example of using positional notation, the DSPOBJD command could be typed as follows:

```
DSPOBJD STMLIB/FILE1 *FILE
```

You would get an error if you tried to enter the command like this:

```
DSPOBJD STMLIB/FILE1 *FILE *PRINT
```

In this example, the AS/400 thinks you are trying to use an invalid value (*PRINT) for the Detail parameter, which follows the Object type parameter on the Display Object Description (DSPOBJD) prompt display.

You can use a combination of keyword and positional forms. In this case, you must make sure that the positional parameters occur first. Once keywords are used, positional notation is no longer valid, and any additional parameters must be specified in keyword form. For example, the DSPOBJD command could be typed as follows:

```
DSPOBJD STMLIB/FILE1 *FILE OUTPUT(*PRINT)
```

Typing the keyword OUTPUT validates the command shown in the previous example. You're now telling the AS/400 to skip the Detail parameter and use the *PRINT value for the correct parameter (Output).

As you can see, using the positional form can be tricky. It saves typing, but entries must be accurate. Reserve this method for commands with brief parameter lists until you are more experienced using CL commands.

The easiest approach is to use command prompting, and then enter or change the parameter values you need on the command prompt display. With experience, you are sure to find it more convenient to type familiar commands directly on a command line without prompting—especially those commands that only require you to enter a parameter or two.

In the chapter exercises, you get plenty of experience entering CL commands via each of the methods described in this chapter.

EXERCISE 1: CREATING LIBRARIES WITH MENUS AND COMMANDS

Scenario: You are to create two libraries. The first library is a control library that will be used in the exercise at the end of chapter 2 for creating, copying, and moving objects. The other library is to be used as your library throughout the rest of this book. This is the library to which you copy and move the objects from the control library.

> **Important:** You must complete Exercise 1 before doing any exercises in subsequent chapters. Future exercises are contingent upon creation of the libraries in this exercise.

Procedures

1. Create a library using a menu path.

2. Create another library using the CRTLIB command.

3. Delete the second library and recreate it using commands.

Create a Library Using a Menu Path

1. Sign on with a user ID that has system operator authorities. Unless system defaults have been changed, the AS/400 Main Menu appears. If another menu or display appears immediately after sign on, type GO MAIN on a command line and press Enter. The AS/400 Main Menu (MAIN) appears.

2. On the AS/400 Main Menu, select the option for Files, libraries, and folders:

   ➤ Type 4 and press Enter.

3. On the Files, Libraries, and Folders (DATA) menu, select the option for Libraries:

   ➤ Type 2 and press Enter.

4. On the Libraries (LIBRARY) menu, select the option for Create a library:

   ➤ Type 2 and press Enter.

The Create Library (CRTLIB) entry display appears, as shown in Figure 1.28.

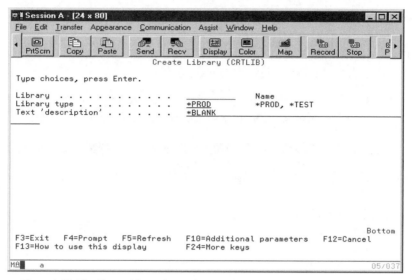

Figure 1.28: The Create Library (CRTLIB) entry display.

5. Now you can specify values for the parameters of the CRTLIB command. On the Create Library (CRTLIB) display, do the following:

    a) For *Library*, type the name of your user profile (user ID).

    b) Tab to the *Library type* field.

    c) Get help about the values *PROD and *TEST:

    ✓ Place your cursor anywhere on the Library type field and press F1. Help specific to this field appears. Read the online help for these values. After reading help, you determine that *TEST is the best choice, since this is not a library that is to be used for production. In fact, you will delete this library, once you're done with it in the exercise in chapter 2.

    ✓ In the help window, press F2 (Extended help) to view help for this entire display.

✓ Press F3 to exit help.

d) For *Library type*, type *TEST over the default value of *PROD.

e) Tab to the *Text 'description'* field.

f) For *Text 'description'*, type a short description of this library. Be creative. Figure 1.29 shows example values for this display.

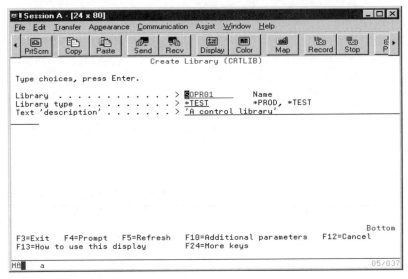

Figure 1.29: Example values for the Create Library (CRTLIB) display.

g) Press Enter to create the library.

You are returned to the Libraries (LIBRARY) menu, and a message appears at the bottom of the menu confirming that the library was created.

Tip: You can get help on a system message. Just put your cursor on the message, and press F1.

Create Another Library Using the CRTLIB Command

1. Prompt the CRTLIB command. On the command line:

    ➤ Type CRTLIB and press F4.

    The Create Library (CRTLIB) entry display appears. As you can see, using the CRTLIB CL command gets you to this display in virtually one step, whereas the menu method in the previous task required three steps.

    Tip: Although commands are shown in uppercase, you can enter them using either lowercase, uppercase, or a combination of each. In other words, it doesn't matter in what case you enter commands.

    ---

2. On the Create Library (CRTLIB) display, do the following:

    a) For *Library*, *type xxx*STUFF. (For *xxx*, use the initials of your first, middle, and last name.)

    b) Tab to the *Library-type* field.

    c) For *Library type*, type *TEST over the default value of *PROD.

    d) Tab to the *Text 'description'* field.

    e) For *Text 'description'*, type LIBRARY FOR *<your name>*. (For *<your name>*, use your first and last name.) Figure 1.30 shows example values for this display.

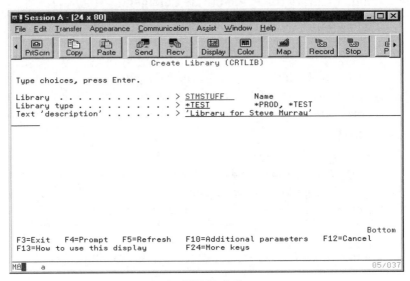

Figure 1.30: Example values for the CRTLIB display.

f) Press Enter to create the library.

You are returned to the display (probably the Libraries menu) from which you entered the command. Again, a message should appear at the bottom of the menu confirming that the library was created.

3. Retrieve the CRTLIB command:

a) Press F9. The command string (with the parameters you specified) is returned on the command line, as shown in Figure 1.31.

b) Congratulations! Take a second or two to admire what you just did. Now when you see a long command string like this in a manual or on someone else's display station, you know it's not rocket science after all!

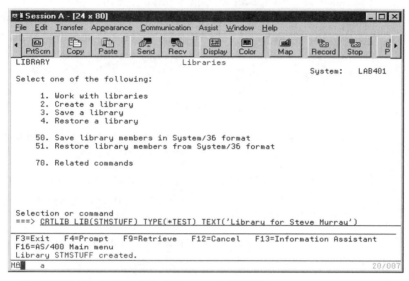

Figure 1.31: The command line from prompted CRTLIB.

You could create another library by entering a new name for the LIB parameter and optionally changing the TYPE and TEXT parameters and then pressing Enter. You can do all this right from within the command string!

Delete the Second Library and Recreate It Using Commands

> **Important:** Make sure you re-create this library. It is the library you will use as the basis of subsequent exercises in this course.

1. Clear the command line of any characters:

   ➢ Press the End key or space over the characters with the space bar.

2. Delete the library you just created. On the blank command line:

   ➢ Type DLTLIB *xxx*STUFF (where *xxx* is your initials) and press Enter.

A message should appear at the bottom of the menu confirming that the library has been deleted. This is an example of positional form for entering a CL command—the keyword LIB is not specified. You could have also entered the command using keyword notation as DLTLIB LIB(*xxx*STUFF).

3. Recreate the library you just deleted:

    a) Press F9. The DLTLIB *xxx*STUFF command string is retrieved. F9 always retrieves the most recently entered command first.

    b) Press F9 again. This time, the CRTLIB LIB(*xxx*STUFF) TYPE(*TEST) TEXT('Library for *<your name>*') command string should be returned. If it isn't, press F9 repeatedly until it is.

        Use F9 to return each command one by one until you get the one you want to repeat.

    c) Press Enter. A message should appear at the bottom of the menu confirming that the library was created.

See how easy it is to use the AS/400 to do what you need to do!

2

MANAGING OS/400 OBJECTS

This chapter includes sections on the following topics:

- Understanding objects and their attributes

- Finding objects

- Working with objects

UNDERSTANDING OBJECTS AND THEIR ATTRIBUTES

It is important to understand objects for two reasons. First, objects are the basic units of information storage on the AS/400. Second, learning about objects helps you to understand how the system functions.

Almost all information stored on the AS/400 is considered an object. AS/400 manuals and technical publications frequently refer to objects. In general, discussions about the AS/400 are centered on objects. Each type of object has a unique function. Here are some common objects:

- Programs (*PGM), which tell the system what to do (like a recipe).

- Files (*FILE), which contain records of user data (the ingredients in a recipe).

- User profiles (*USRPRF), which contain information about users on the system.

- Libraries (*LIB), which are used to group related objects, and which allow users to find objects by name.

Other objects include print (or output) queues, job queues, message queues, job descriptions, device descriptions, and yes, even menus.

The AS/400 maintains descriptive information about each object. This information is called the object's *attributes*.

Objects Are of Specific Types

Each object can be only one type, and each object has specific operations that can be performed on it. For example, you can store data in a file, but you can't run a file. Likewise, you can run a program, but you can't store data in it.

Objects Have Names

An object's name must be 10 characters or less, using a combination of the following alphanumeric characters:

- The letters A through Z.

- The numerals 0 through 9.

- The special characters $, #, @, . (period), and _ (underscore).

The first character must be alphabetic or one of the symbols $, #, or @. Since objects provided by IBM start with *Q*, to avoid any confusion between IBM-supplied objects and those you create, don't name your own objects starting with *Q*.

Objects Belong to Libraries

Libraries are not limited by size. You can have as many objects in a library as you want, as long as no two objects of the same name and type exist in the same library. You can copy an object with the same name, type, and content to a different library, in which case you have a duplicate of the original object.

> **Note:** Libraries cannot contain other libraries, with the exception of QSYS, the system master library that contains all other libraries.

Objects Are Referenced by Name, Not by Location

Recall the discussion of single-level storage in chapter 1. You don't need to know the location of the object to find it (unlike on personal computers, where you need to know the directory path in which a file resides). You just need to know its name. You can request an object by its simple name or its qualified name.

Simple Name

For example, let's say you want to work with a program called STARTJOB. On a command line, you enter the following command:

```
WRKOBJ STARTJOB
```

The system searches the job's current library list to locate an object matching the name with a type appropriate for the request.

Qualified Name

For example, let's say you want to work with the program STARTJOB, in the library SOPR. You would enter this command on the command line:

```
WRKOBJ SOPR/STARTJOB
```

The system searches only the library SOPR for the program STARTJOB.

As you can see, the name of a specific object that is located in a library can be specified as a simple name or as a qualified name. A *simple object name* is the name of the object only. A *qualified object name* is the name of the library where the object is stored followed by the name of the object. In a qualified object name, the library name is connected to the object name by a slash (/).

Objects Are Explicitly Created

When you create a new object, you describe the object type, such as *LIB, *FILE, *OUTQ, *JOBQ, and so forth. After you determine the appropriate library and place the object in it, the system can use the object. You already know how to create objects, since you created two libraries in chapter 1. You will create more objects in the exercise at the end of this chapter. An example of a CL command for creating an object is CRTLIB LIB(SOPR) TYPE(*TEST) TEXT('System Operations Library').

The user ID you use to sign on to the system typically determines ownership of objects you create. When you create an object, you automatically become its owner, unless your group profile (if you belong to one) is set up to own all objects that you create.

When an object is created, the owner is given all the object and data authorities to that object. If the ownership of the object is transferred to another user (or group of users), the original owner has the option to keep all object and data authorities the same, or to remove all authority to that object.

If the group profile is the owner of the object, then all members of the group profile have authority to the object. When a group profile owns an object, any user in that group can add, change, or delete records in the object, assuming all data authorities are provided to the users.

Group ownership of objects is especially helpful when data sharing is necessary. Consider a credit card company, where each customer representative would need to access all customer records. Each representative must be a member of a group profile that includes authority to all objects containing customer records.

Objects Have a Description and Content

Every object contains descriptive information such as name, type, creation date, size, owner, and so forth. To display an object's description, use one of the following command sequences:

- Type DSPOBJD and press F4 to prompt for the object name and type; then select option 5 (Display full attributes).

- Enter WRKOBJ *<library name>/<object name>* and select option 8 (Display description).

An object's content varies depending on its type. For example, files may contain other items, called *members*, depending on the characteristics of the main file.

FINDING OBJECTS

You can find an object using one of these several ways:

- If you know the object's name, enter the command WRKOBJ followed by its simple name (object name) or a qualified name (library name/object name). You must have some authority to the object to display it. On the Work with Objects list display (see Figure 2.3), you can choose what you want to do with that object, as long as you have the appropriate authority to perform the operation. An object can be shown on a display station or printed on a printer. Some of the information that can be shown includes the information used to create the object (object description), the attributes of the object, and the content of the object.

- If you don't know the object's name, or the library in which it resides, enter the command WRKOBJ and press F4. On the Work with Objects entry display, change each parameter to *ALL and press Enter. All objects to which you have some authority are shown. Be aware that depending on the number of objects on the system, this request could take a lot of time and adversely affect system performance. Therefore, at the very least, run this command during non-peak usage times.

Tip: If you ever find that a request seems to be taking a lot of time, you can easily end that request. This just might save you from other users complaining that your job request is slowing down their response times. Likewise, as a system operator, if you notice that response times are slowed, you can determine who or what the culprit is, and then resolve the problem. (For a more detailed discussion on this, see chapter 3.)

To end a request, complete these steps:

1. If you're using a non-programmable terminal, press and hold the Shift or Alt key (depending on the keyboard), and then press the System Request (Sys Req or Sys Rq) key. An entry line appears at the bottom of the display. If you're using a PC with 5250 display session emulation, such as found in Client Access/400, you may need to use an alternative method to access the system request line. In Client Access/400, for example, right-click the mouse to display a keypad, and click the SysRq button.

2. Type 2 on the system request line, and press Enter to end the previous request. Alternatively, you can press Enter on the system request line to display the System Request menu, as shown in Figure 2.1. This menu offers several other options.

The system request function essentially starts an alternative interactive session at your display station. Then, you can use the System Request key to switch back and forth between the primary and alternate job. An alternate job can be particularly useful for doing another task or viewing information without having to end your work.

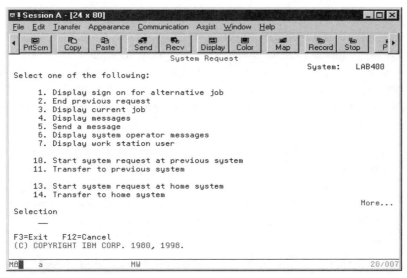

Figure 2.1: The System Request menu.

- If you just want to see all objects that you own, enter the command WRKOBJOWN. By default, only the objects that your user profile owns are listed.

- If you want to know which objects a user or group profile owns, enter the command WRKOBJOWN *<profile name>* to provide a list of all objects owned by that profile. You must have read authority to the user or group profile. On the Work with Objects by Owner display, you can use option 8 (Display description) to find out when an object was created and when it was last changed.

- If you want to see the contents of a particular library, enter the command DSPLIB *<library name>* to list all the objects in that library. You must have read authority to that library to display its contents. On the Display Libraries list display, you can use the display option to find out when a particular object was created and when it was last changed. This command is useful for monitoring user libraries.

- If you want to work with all libraries to which you have authority, enter the command WRKLIB *ALL. You are presented with those libraries to which you have some authority. On the Work with Libraries list display, you can choose what you want to do with that library, as long as you have the appropriate authority to perform the operation. You can create a library (option 1) from this display as well as work with objects (option 12) in a library. Figure 2.2 shows the Library Commands menu. Press the Page Down key to view more library commands. Note that you can quickly access this command list by entering GO CMDLIB on any command line.

Tip: You can use a menu path to access library displays and functions. On any command line, enter GO MAIN to display the AS/400 Main Menu. Choose option 4 (Files, libraries, and folders), then option 2 (Libraries). On the Libraries (LIBRARY) menu, choose option 70 (Related commands) to view all possible library commands.

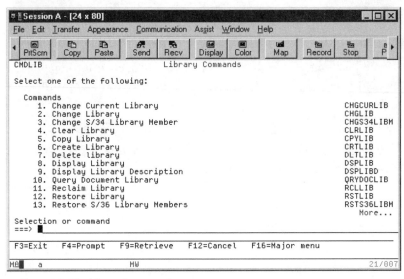

Figure 2.2: The Library Commands menu.

WORKING WITH OBJECTS

For an object to exist, it first must be created. Once the object is created, anyone who is not excluded from the object can display it on the system. Moreover, anyone who has the correct authority to the object can work with it—that is, do tasks on it. Here is a short list of operations you can perform on objects:

- Copy
- Move
- Authorize
- Delete
- Rename
- Save
- Restore

> *Tip:* To get a list of object-related commands, enter GO CMDOBJ on a command line. You can only work with the commands to which you are authorized.

An example CL command for working with an object is WRKOBJ OBJ (SOPR/STARTJOB). This example permits you to work with all objects for which you have authority that are named STARTJOB and are located in library SOPR. Figure 2.3 shows an example of the Work with Objects display.

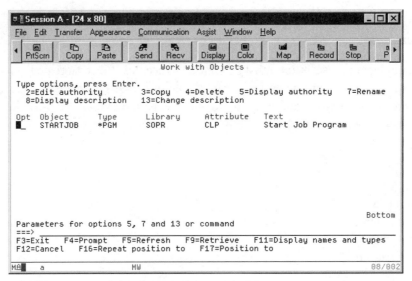

Figure 2.3: The Work with Objects display.

Copying an Object

You can copy an object to another library, and even to the same library as long as you rename the object. Then, you have two identical objects. You can copy an object in one of two ways:

- Select option 3 (Copy) on the Work with Objects display.

- Enter the CRTDUPOBJ (Create Duplicate Object) command.

Moving an Object

If you move an object, you have only one object, which is now located in a different place on the system. You can move an object by issuing the MOVOBJ (Move Object) command.

Authorizing an Object

You can control who can retrieve an object. For example, a public authority of *ALL allows all system users to use the object unless they are specifically prohibited. A public authority of *EXCLUDE means no system users can use an object unless specifically authorized to do so. There are three ways to authorize an object:

- Select option 2 (Edit authority) on the Work with Objects display.

- Enter the GRTOBJAUT (Grant Object Authority) command.

- Enter the EDTOBJAUT (Edit Object Authority) command.

A system administrator or security officer typically manages security on your AS/400. However, a system operator can display an object's authorities. There are two ways to display an object's authority:

- Select option 5 (Display authority) on the Work with Objects display.

- Enter the DSPOBJAUT (Display Object Authority) command.

Deleting an Object

When you delete an object, it is removed from its library. The reference to the object is removed, and the disk space it occupied becomes available. When you choose to delete an object, the system always offers a confirmation display so that you don't delete anything unintentionally. You can delete an object by typing 4 (Delete) next to the object on the Work with Objects display.

Renaming an Object

- You can specify a new name for an object, but this should be done only if absolutely necessary. Certain objects cannot be renamed. The following are two ways to rename an object:

  ➤ Select option 7 (Rename) on the Work with Objects display.

  ➤ Enter the RNMOBJ (Rename Object) command.

Read the online help for renaming an object, shown in Figure 2.4, to better understand the consequences of renaming. To get to this online help, complete the following steps:

1. Type WRKOBJ <*your control library name*> on a command line.

   > **Note:** See the exercise in chapter 1, if you don't remember
   > the name of the control library you created.

2. Type 7 on the option line next to the library object, but do not press Enter.

3. Press F1 and page down the help display until you see 7 = Rename.

4. Place your cursor anywhere on the hypertext phrase "Rename Object (RNMOBJ) command" and press Enter.

5. Carefully read the help, noting the Restrictions and Notes for object renaming.

   > **Tip:** It might help to enlarge the display for easier reading.
   > Just press F20 (Enlarge).

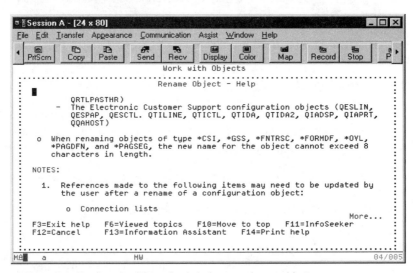

Figure 2.4: An example of the online help for renaming an object.

Saving and Restoring an Object

You can save an object to offline media, such as tape, so that you have a backup copy of the object. If you need to recover an object due to a loss of data on your system, you can easily restore it from offline media. (Chapter 7 is devoted to save and restore operations.)

EXERCISE 2: WORKING WITH LIBRARIES AND OTHER OBJECTS

Scenario: You will create some objects and put them in the control library (the one with the same name as your user profile) you created in chapter 1. Then, you will practice copying and moving the objects from the control library to the second library (the one named *xxx*STUFF, where *xxx* is your initials) that you created in chapter 1.

Note: You must complete this exercise before doing any exercises in subsequent chapters. Future exercises are contingent upon certain objects created and tasks performed in this exercise.

Procedures

1. Access the Command Entry display.

2. Create some objects in the control library you created in chapter 1.

3. Find the objects you just created.

4. Display your authority to objects you created.

5. Find library *xxx*STUFF you created in chapter 1, and display its description.

6. Rename library *xxx*STUFF to *xxx*LIB.

7. Determine if records show that your library has been changed.

8. See if library *xxx*LIB contains any objects.

9. Copy an object from the control library to your *xxx*LIB library.

10. Move objects from the control library to your *xxx*LIB library.

11. List the objects in library *xxx*LIB.

12. Delete the control library.

Access the Command Entry Display

1. Sign on with a user ID that has system operator authorities.

2. On the command line:

   ➤ Enter CALL QCMD.

   Note: Unless otherwise indicated, you must press the Enter key after typing a command string to execute the command.

   ---

3. On the Command Entry display, there should be no commands or messages listed. Display detailed messages including previously entered commands:

   ➤ Press F10.

   The first message shows that an interactive job was started. This is your sign-on. The interactive job does not end until you sign off. (To learn more about interactive jobs, see chapter 3.) The other listing should be the command CALL QCMD you just entered.

Create Some Objects in the Control Library You Created in Chapter 1

1. Create an output queue. On the Command Entry display:

   ➤ Type CRTOUTQ and press F4.

2. On the Create Output Queue (CRTOUTQ) display, do the following:

   a) In the *Output queue* field, type *xxx*OUTQ (where *xxx* is your initials).

   b) In the output queue *Library* field, type the name of your control library (the library with the same name as your user profile).

   c) Press F10 to display additional parameters.

   d) Press the Page Down key.

   e) In the *Text 'description'* field, type 'Output queue for *<your name>*'.

   Note: Advanced users and even AS/400 manuals often reference fields (parameters) by their keywords. Press F11 to toggle between showing parameter keywords and parameter choices.

   ---

   f) Press Enter.

   The Command Entry display presents a message to remind you what object you created and into which library. Make sure *xxx*OUTQ was created in your control library (the one with the same name as your user profile), as indicated by the message. (You are to move this object later in the exercise and use it in the exercise for chapter 5.) Figure 2.5 shows an example of the Command Entry display after you entered the CRTOUTQ command. Notice the command string for CRTOUTQ and the system message below it. The command string contains only those parameters that you specified. All other parameters use the default values provided by the system.

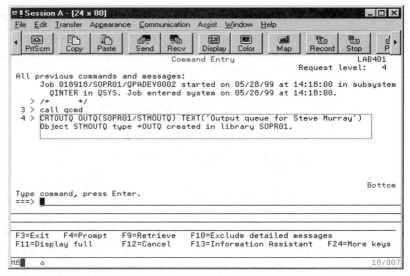

Figure 2.5: An example of the Command Entry display after the CRTOUTQ command has been entered.

3. Create a job queue. On the Command Entry display, do the following:

    a) Press F9 to bring the CRTOUTQ command string to the command line. The command line should look like this:

```
CRTOUTQ OUTQ(<control library name>/xxxOUTQ) TEXT('Output queue for <your name>')
```

    b) Change the command string to this:

```
CRTJOBQ JOBQ(<control library name>/xxxJOBQ) TEXT('Job queue for <your name>')
```

    where *xxx* is your initials. (Now you know what they mean when they say the AS/400 is flexible!)

    c) Press Enter.

    The Command Entry display presents a message to remind you what object you created and into which library. Make sure *xxx*JOBQ was created in your control library (the one with the same name as your user profile), as indicated by the message.

(You move this object later in the exercise and use it in the exercise for chapter 3.) Figure 2.6 shows an example of the Command Entry display after you entered the CRTJOBQ command. Notice the command string for CRTJOBQ and the system message below it. The command string contains only those parameters that you specified. All other parameters use the default values provided by the system.

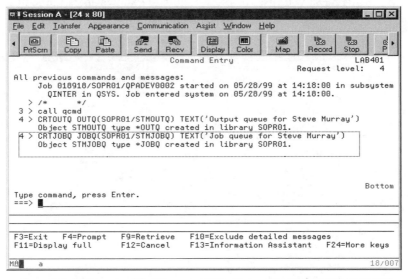

Figure 2.6: An example of the Command Entry display after the CRTJOBQ command has been entered.

4. Create a display file. On the Command Entry display:

➤ Type CRTDSPF <control library name>/FILE1.

Notice you're using positional notation here (no keywords). In keyword notation, the command would look like this:

```
CRTDSPF FILE(<control library name>/FILE1).
```

Positional notation works here because, if you had prompted (F4) this command, you would have seen that *File* is the first parameter on the prompt display.

5. Press Enter. The Command Entry display again reminds you what object you created and in which library it resides. The object should have been created in your control library (the one with the same name as your user profile). Figure 2.7 shows an example of the Command Entry display after you entered the CRTDSPF command.

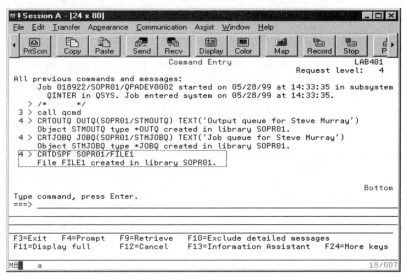

Figure 2.7: An example of the Command Entry display after the CRTDSPF command has been entered.

Note that FILE1 is a *qualified name* (library name/object name). You dictated that this file be created in a particular library. Likewise, you specified the library into which the output queue and job queue objects should be created. Thus, you also used a qualified name when creating those objects.

If you had not specified a library for any of these objects, the object would have been created in the current library, which is QGPL by default. (QGPL stands for General Purpose Library, and it is an IBM-supplied library.) For example, if you enter the command CRTDSPF FILE1, the file FILE1 would be created in library QGPL if there were no other current library specified.

Find the Objects You Just Created

1. Start with the library in which you created the objects:

   ➤ Enter WRKLIB <control library name>.

   The Work with Libraries display appears, as shown in Figure 2.8.

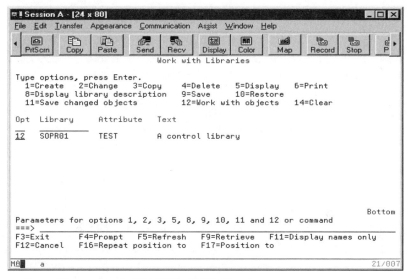

Figure 2.8: An example of the Work with Libraries display.

2. Display the objects in the library. As shown in Figure 2.8, on the option line next to the library:

   ➤ Type 12 and press Enter.

   You should now see the three objects you just created. Looking at the Work with Objects display, as shown in Figure 2.9, you realize that you would like to enter a description for the display file, FILE1.

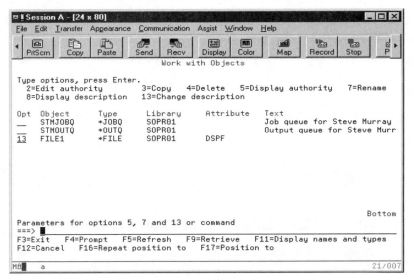

```
⊟ I Session A - [24 x 80]                                      _ □ ×
 File  Edit  Transfer  Appearance  Communication  Assist  Window  Help
 ◄  ⬚       ⬚      ⬚      ⬚      ⬚      ⬚      ⬚      ⬚      ⬚      ⬚     ⬚ ►
   PrtScrn   Copy   Paste   Send   Recv   Display  Color   Map   Record  Stop   P
                            Work with Objects
   Type options, press Enter.
     2=Edit authority       3=Copy    4=Delete    5=Display authority   7=Rename
     8=Display description  13=Change description

   Opt  Object     Type      Library     Attribute   Text
   __   STMJOBQ    *JOBQ     SOPR01                   Job queue for Steve Murray
   __   STMOUTQ    *OUTQ     SOPR01                   Output queue for Steve Murr
   13   FILE1      *FILE     SOPR01      DSPF



                                                                   Bottom
   Parameters for options 5, 7 and 13 or command
   ===> █
   F3=Exit    F4=Prompt    F5=Refresh   F9=Retrieve   F11=Display names and types
   F12=Cancel    F16=Repeat position to   F17=Position to

 MA█    a                                                        21/007
```

Figure 2.9: An example of the Work with Objects display.

3. Specify a description for your display file. As shown in Figure 2.9, on the option line next to FILE1:

➤ Type 13 and press Enter.

4. On the Change Object Description (CHGOBJD) display, for the Text *'description'* parameter, type the text *A display file* and press Enter. You should see a message at the bottom of the Work with Objects display confirming the action that you took. The description of your display file is reflected in the *Text* column.

   When you were changing the text description on the Change Object Description display, did you notice the name of the command in parentheses in the title? You also could have prompted that command to access this display. In this case, you would type CHGOBJD on the command line and press F4.

5. Do not exit the Work with Objects display.

Display Your Authority to Objects You Created

1. On the Work with Objects display, on the option line next to each object:

    ➤ Type a 5.

    The display should look similar to that in Figure 2.10.

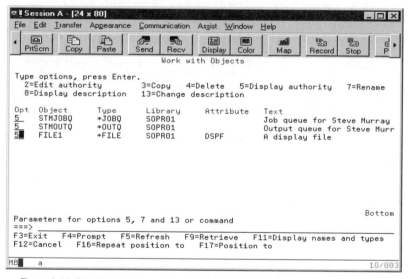

Figure 2.10: Display authority on the Work with Objects display.

2. Display the first object:

    ➤ Press Enter.

    The first object in the list appears.

3. Find your user profile (in this example, it's SOPR01). You should have *ALL authority to that object, which means you can do just about anything to the object, except operations, which only the object's owner can perform. But notice that you are the owner—you created the object! If you create an object, you can delete that object, copy it, and move it as well.

Note: The object's owner is shown in the upper-right corner of the display. Figure 2.11 shows an example of the Display Object Authority display. If a profile has *USE authority to the object, such as *PUBLIC (all users known to the AS/400), it means the profile can read (see) the object, but cannot do things like copy, move, or delete the object.

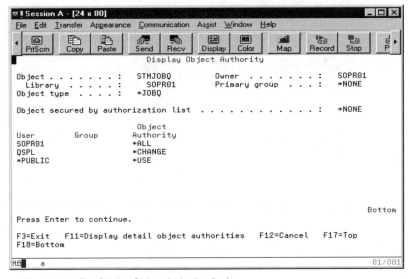

Figure 2.11: The Display Object Authority display.

4. Display the second object:

   ➤ Press Enter.

   The second object in the list appears. The object name changes in the upper-left of the display each time Enter is pressed.

5. Display remaining objects and return to the Work with Objects display:

   ➤ Continue pressing Enter.

When you type an option number next to multiple items on a list display, pressing Enter when you're finished with each item lets you continue through the remaining items.

6. Return to the Command Entry display:

> Press F3 repeatedly.

Find the Library *xxx*STUFF You
Created in Chapter 1 and Display its Description

1. On the Command Entry display:

> Enter WRKOBJ *xxx*STUFF (where *xxx* is your initials).

The Work with Objects display appears, as shown in Figure 2.12.

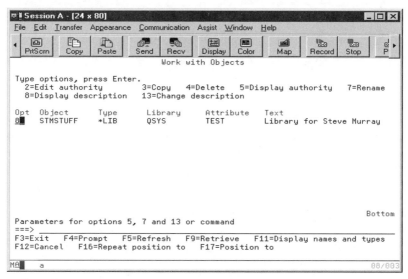

Figure 2.12: An example of the Work with Objects display.

2. Display your library's description. As shown in Figure 2.12, on the option line next to your library:

> Type 8 and press Enter.

The Display Object Description—Full display appears. You can also get to this display by using the DSPOBJD command. Notice that the first page of this display shows such information as when the object was created, the user who created it, and on what system it was created.

3. View different attributes of your library's description:

   a) On the first page of the object description, write down the creation date and time and the owner of the object:

   _____

   b) Press the PageDown key to view the next page of the object description. The second page of the object description shows when your library was last changed.

   c) Write down the change date and time:

   _____

   d) Press the PageDown key to view the next page of the object description. The third page of the object description shows storage and save/restore information. Note the size of your library. Be aware of this important display for when you need to find out how much space an object consumes. The AS/400 records size in bytes. An example of this display is shown in Figure 2.13.

4. Return to the Work with Objects display:

   ➤ Press F12.

5. Do not exit the Work with Objects display. (You will save and restore your library in the exercise at the end of chapter 7.)

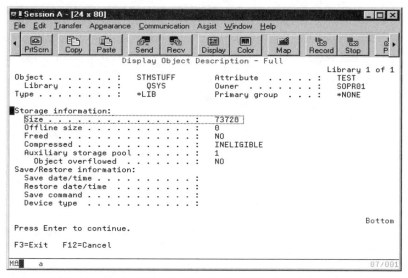

Figure 2.13: An example of page 3 of the Display Object Description (DSPOBJD) display.

Rename Library *xxx*STUFF to *xxx*LIB

1. On the Work with Objects display, on the option line next to your library:

    ➢ Type 7 and press Enter.

2. Specify a new name for your library. On the Rename Object (RNMOBJ) display, in the *New Object* field:

    ➢ Type *xxx*LIB and press Enter (where *xxx* is your initials).

    You should see a message at the bottom of the Work with Objects display confirming the rename action. The new name of your library is reflected in the Object column.

3. Do not exit the Work with Objects display.

Determine if Records Show That Your Library Has Been Changed

1. On the Work with Objects display, on the option line next to your library:

   ➤ Type 8 and press Enter.

   The first page of the Display Object Description—Full display appears.

2. Go to the second page:

   ➤ Press the PageDown key.

   The change date and time should correspond with the date/time you re-named your library.

> **Note:** This is a simple auditing measure you can take to check when an object was last updated, or to check if it has ever been updated since its creation. In the latter case, the creation date/time and change date/time would be the same. Be aware that the system audits changes if the *Object auditing value* field (listed on the second page of the object description) is set to *USRPRF, *CHANGE, or *ALL.

---

3. To get help on any field, just put your cursor on the desired field, and press F1.

4. Return to the Command Entry display:

   ➤ Press F3 repeatedly.

See if Library *xxx*LIB Contains Any Objects

1. On the Command Entry display:

   ➤ Enter WRKLIB *xxx*LIB (where *xxx* is your initials).

   The Work with Libraries display appears.

2. Work with the objects in your library. On the option line next to your library:

> Type 12 and press Enter.

There shouldn't be any objects listed. So, you are directed to move and copy objects from your control library (the one with the same name as your user profile) to your newly renamed *xxx*LIB library.

3. Return to the Command Entry display:

> Press F3 twice.

Copy an Object from
Your Control Library to Your *xxx*LIB Library

1. Retrieve the WRKLIB *<control library name>* command. On the Command Entry display:

> Put the cursor on the line of this command, press F9 to bring it down to the command line, and press Enter.

2. Display the objects in the library. On the option line next to the library:

> Type 12 and press Enter.

3. You should see three objects: *xxx*JOBQ, *xxx*OUTQ, and FILE1, as depicted in Figure 2.14.

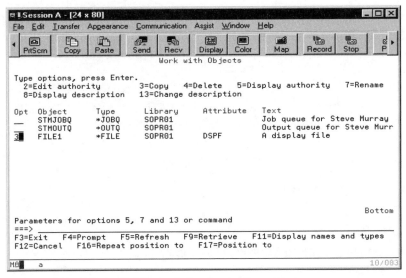

Figure 2.14: A Work with Objects display showing three objects.

4. Copy the display file. As shown in Figure 2.14, on the option line
    next to FILE1:

    ➤ Type 3 and press Enter.

5. On the Create Duplicate Object (CRTDUPOBJ) display, do the
    following:

    a) For the *To library* parameter, type *xxx*LIB (where *xxx* is your
        initials).

    b) Keep the default values for the other parameters. Figure 2.15
        shows example values for the Create Duplicate Object
        (CRTDUPOBJ) display.

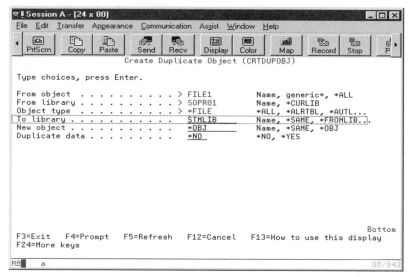

Figure 2.15: Example values for the Create Duplicate Object (CRTDUPOBJ) display.

c) Press Enter. It's business as usual again. You should see a message at the bottom of the Work with Objects display confirming the copy action. Now, FILE1 exists in two places—your *xxx*LIB in addition to your control library (the one with the same name as your user profile).

6. Do not exit the Work with Objects display.

Move Objects *xxx*JOBQ and *xxx*OUTQ from Your Control Library to Your *xxx*LIB Library

1. On the Work with Objects display:

   a) Press the Tab key to go to the command line.

   b) Type the command MOVOBJ and press F4.

2. On the Move Object (MOVOBJ) entry display, do the following:

a) Press F11 to see the keywords.

b) For OBJ, type *xxx*JOBQ (where *xxx* is your initials) for the object and the name of your control library (the one with the same name as your user profile) for the library.

c) For OBJTYPE, type *JOBQ.

d) For TOLIB, type *xxx*LIB (where *xxx* is your initials). Figure 2.16 shows example values for the Move Object (MOVOBJ) display.

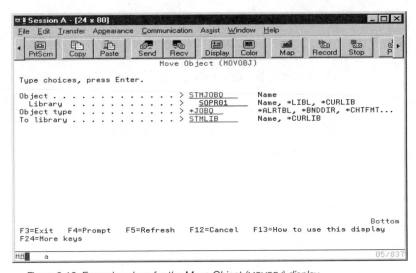

Figure 2.16: Example values for the Move Object (MOVOBJ) display.

e) Press Enter. You should see a message at the bottom of the Work with Objects display confirming the move action.

3. Refresh the Work with Objects display:

➢ Press F5.

The object *xxx*JOBQ should have disappeared. It is no longer in your control library (the one with the same name as your user profile). Now only two objects remain in the control library: *xxx*OUTQ and FILE1.

4. Retrieve the MOVOBJ command string. On the Work with Objects display:

    ➤ Press F9.

    The command line should look like this:

    ```
    MOVOBJ OBJ(<control library name>/xxxJOBQ) OBJTYPE(*JOBQ)TOLIB(xxxLIB)
    ```

5. Change the command string to this:

    ```
    MOVOBJ OBJ(<control library name>/xxxOUTQ) OBJTYPE(*OUTQ) TOLIB(xxxLIB)
    ```

    Again, *xxx* is your initials. Figure 2.17 shows an example, with the changes in lowercase.

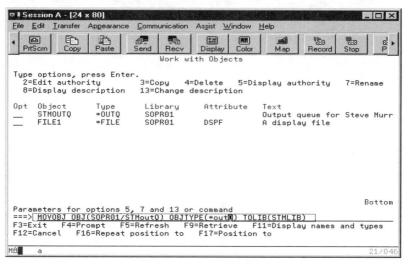

Figure 2.17: The MOVOBJ command string with changes in lowercase.

6. Press Enter.

7. Voilà! Object *xxx*OUTQ is out of your control library (the one with the same name as your user profile) and into your *xxx*LIB library. Refresh the display, and you should now only see one object left in the control library—FILE1.

8. Return to the Command Entry display:

   ➤ Press F3 repeatedly.

List the Objects in Library *xxx*LIB

1. On the Command Entry display:

   ➤ Enter DSPLIB *xxx*LIB (where *xxx* is your initials).

   The Display Library display appears, and there should be three objects: *xxx*JOBQ, *xxx*OUTQ, and FILE1. An example of this display is shown in Figure 2.18.

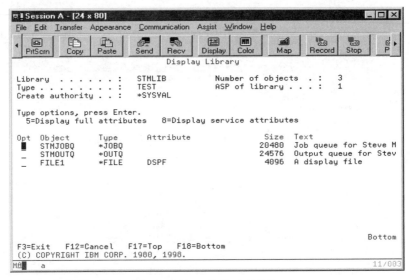

Figure 2.18: The Display Library display with three objects.

> ***Important:*** Make sure these objects exist in library *xxx*LIB. You will be using objects *xxx*OUTQ and *xxx*JOBQ in subsequent exercises in this book.

2. Optionally, display the attributes for any of these objects.

3. Return to the Command Entry display:

    ➢ Press F3.

Delete Your Control Library

1. On the Command Entry display:

    ➢ Enter DLTLIB *<control library name>*.

    Notice the two-line message that is triggered:

    ```
    Object FILE1 in <control library name> type *FILE deleted.
    Library <control library name> deleted.
    ```

    Deleting a library also deletes the objects in that library. If you are not the owner of the library, nor the owner of the objects in that library, you must have enough object authority to delete an object. Since the library you deleted is one which you created, and since you created the objects in the library, you are the owner and were able to delete the library.

2. For extra measure, try to display your control library (the one with the same name as your user profile):

    ➢ Enter DSPLIB *<control library name>*.

    You should get a message saying that the library isn't found.

CONTROLLING JOBS

This chapter includes sections on the following topics:

- Demystifying work management

- Understanding jobs

- Submitting batch jobs

- Working with job queues

- Working with user jobs

- Displaying jobs in a specific subsystem

- Working with signed-on users

- Displaying active job statistics

DEMYSTIFYING WORK MANAGEMENT

One of the most versatile aspects of the AS/400 is its ability to help you to manage your work. Many people can use the AS/400 at the same time, and the AS/400 can use many printers at the same time. Combinations of these variables could potentially result in confusion. The AS/400 is designed to prevent this from happening.

How the system manages work varies according to how much it relies on you to get the work done. For this reason, the work that the system does is one of two types:

- Interactive processing
- Batch processing

Interactive processing requires continual two-way communication between a display-station user and the system. Throughout the duration of the task being performed, the computer occasionally requires information from you.

An example of interactive processing is your current AS/400 session. This session begins when you sign on the system; the system requests sign-on information, you reply by providing the necessary information, and the computer responds by displaying a menu of options from which you may choose. This pattern of system request, user reply, and system response is repeated until you end the interactive session by signing off the system.

In contrast, *batch processing* requires only that you send the information for processing. After processing is initiated, the system needs no further information from the user to complete the task, leaving both the user and the display station free to do other things.

The AS/400 contains many system objects, and the way they interrelate helps determine the efficiency of your system. Work management functions control the work done on the system. When the Operating System/400 (OS/400) is installed, it includes a work management environment that supports all interactive and batch work. Work management supports the commands and internal functions necessary to control the system operation and the daily workload on the system.

In addition, work management contains the functions you need to distribute resources for your applications, so that your system can handle your applications.

Because IBM ships all AS/400 systems with everything necessary to run typical operations, you are not required to learn about work management to use your system. However, to change the way your system manages work to better meet your needs, affect the order your jobs are run, solve a problem, improve the system's performance, or simply look at jobs on the system, you need an understanding of work management. In other words, if you understand work management, you know what affects the various pieces of the system, and how to change them so they operate most efficiently.

Because of the system's complexity, learning about work management in stages is helpful. You could begin by deciding what work you need the system to do and how you want that work to be done. By keeping it simple from the start, you can avoid becoming frustrated by the flexibility in the system. As you become comfortable with the concept of work management, and begin to understand how each of the pieces interrelate, you are on your way to getting the most from your AS/400.

A Simple System

The purpose of the system is to perform work. Work enters, work is processed, and work leaves the system. If you think of work management in these three terms, work management is easier to understand. Work management describes where work enters the system, where and with what resources work is processed, and where output from work goes. Figure 3.1 shows the concept of a simple system.

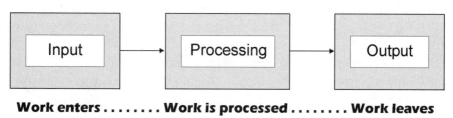

Work enters . . . . Work is processed . . . . Work leaves

Figure 3.1: The work flow in a simple system.

A Complex System

A complex system is many simple systems operating together. Using this definition, the simple systems within the AS/400 are the *subsystems*. Table 3.1 lists examples of IBM-supplied subsystems.

Table 3.1: Examples of IBM-Supplied Subsystems.	
OS/400 Subsystems	**Description**
QBASE	Base subsystem. Supports all interactive, batch, and communication jobs. Acts as the default controlling subsystem. When the AS/400 is first installed, all work (including interactive and batch jobs) is performed by QBASE.
QCTL	Controlling subsystem. Separates work load into multiple subsystems, which provides for better system performance. QCTL starts all of the following subsystems. Note: Only QBASE or QCTL should be specified as the controlling subsystem.
QINTER	Interactive subsystem. Supports interactive jobs.
QBATCH	Batch subsystem. Supports batch jobs.
QSPL	Spooling subsystem. Supports print spooling jobs.
QCMN	Communications subsystem. Supports communications jobs.
QSYSWRK	System subsystem. Starts system jobs.
Q....	And many others. Use the WRKSBSD command to work with a list of subsystems that you have authority to use.

A System as a Business

An example of a simple system is a small business. Assume there is a small store in the business of building hand-crafted wood furniture. Work enters—the business receives an order for small tables, chairs, and bookshelves. Work is processed—the carpenter calls the customer to confirm the order, and to discuss design aspects including style, size, and color. The carpenter designs each piece of furniture, gathers the necessary materials, and then builds the furniture. After the furniture is completed, it is delivered—work leaves.

Since a complex system is a combination of many simple systems, a comparable example of a complex system is a shopping mall, which has many small and large businesses in one area. Maybe the carpenter has a business in the northwest corner of the mall, and a baker has a business along the east side. The baker and the carpenter have different input and different output; that is, their orders and their products are very different. In addition, the time it takes each business to process its work is quite different, and its users know and understand that.

Work Management Terms Using the Business Scenario

But how is this related to the AS/400? A complex system (the shopping mall) is a compilation of many simple systems (the stores). Remember on the AS/400, these simple systems (the stores) are called subsystems.

Keeping in mind the mall scenario, you need to know what the business looks like. Every store has blueprints or store plans. These plans are really just descriptions, in varying detail, of the physical makeup of the business. Maybe the business has a store with two floors, five doors, three mailboxes, and two phones. On the AS/400, a *subsystem description* contains all the information about the subsystem

A subsystem creates a suitable environment in which a job can do its work. The system can contain one or many subsystems, which can be created or deleted by a user (if that user has the proper authority). As the number of different types of jobs increases in the system, more subsystems can be defined to manage those jobs. All interactive processing can occur in one subsystem. All batch processing can occur in another, while system operator jobs happen in a third, and so on. This makes it easier to control the different jobs in the system, because subsystems can be started and ended individually.

Any piece of work within the business is considered a job. An example of a piece of work might be a customer letter, a phone call, an order, or the nightly cleanup. The same is true about the AS/400—any piece of work is called a *job*. Also, each job has a unique name. A *job description* describes the work coming into the subsystem. Job descriptions contain pieces of information such as user IDs, job queues, and routing data. On the AS/400, information in the job description might compare to descriptions of jobs in a small business. In the following list, some of these job description comparisons are made:

AS/400 System Objects	Small Business
User ID	Who is the customer?
Job queue	In which mailbox did that arrive?
Job queue priority	Is that letter important?
Hold on job queue	Can that letter be handled later?
Output queue	How will the product be packaged?
Routing data	What product will suit this customer's needs?
Accounting code	Does the customer have a credit card?

Whether on the AS/400 or in the mall, the same issues have to be addressed when setting up work management.

Where does the work come from?   For the carpenter, the work comes from customer calls, from references, and from people who visit the store. On the AS/400, the work can come from many places, such as job queues, workstations, communications, autostart jobs, and prestart jobs.

Where do they find the space?   Within the mall, each business (subsystem) has a certain amount of floor space. On the AS/400, *pools* allow you to control the main storage (or floor space), in which each subsystem (business) gets to do its work. The more floor space a business (subsystem) has, the more customers, or jobs, it can fit.

How does the work come in?   Customers who cannot find the store they need find an information booth to help send them in the right direction. The same is true on the AS/400. *Routing entries* are similar to store directories or an information booth. After the routing entry is found, it guides the job to its proper place. The routing entry needs to be found first, however. That is done through *routing data*. Routing data is what the job uses to find the right routing entry.

How is the work treated?   Obviously, the carpenter needs to place a priority on each job. The chair due at the end of the week should be done before the bookshelf due at the end of the month. On the AS/400, *class* provides information about how the job is handled while in the subsystem. This information includes the following:

- Priority while running
- Maximum storage
- Maximum CPU time
- Time slice
- Purge

Each of these attributes contribute to how and when a job is processed.

Just as there are rules that affect all the stores in the mall, there are rules that affect all the subsystems on the AS/400. An example of these rules is a *system value*. System values are pieces of information that apply to the whole system. Possible system values include the following:

- Date and time
- Configuration information
- Sign-on information
- System security
- Storage handling

Each customer in a mall has information specific to him or her. The carpenter might decide to call each customer to discuss the design specifications for each piece of furniture. On the AS/400 system, the *user profile* holds information specific to a particular user. Similar to a customer's credit card, a user profile gives that user specific authorities and assigns the user attributes for his or her jobs. These *job attributes* answer such questions as:

- What job description?
- What output queue or printer device?
- What message queue?
- What accounting code?
- What scheduling priority?

This book does not describe each of these concepts in detail, but this information is provided to give you an overview of the various pieces of OS/400 work management and how they all relate to each other.

UNDERSTANDING JOBS

The key element used by the AS/400 to organize and manage work is the *job*. A job can be started by typing a command or running a program. A job usually includes all necessary programs, files, connections, and instructions to the Operating System/400 (OS/400) licensed program. A job can be one very short and simple task such as printing a report, or it can be a series of tasks. The following are types of jobs:

- Calculating total sales by product
- Calculating total sales by area
- Calculating total sales by salesperson
- Printing sales reports

Basic Job Types

As with processing, there are two basic types of jobs: interactive jobs and batch jobs.

An *interactive job* begins when you sign on to a display station and ends when you sign off. During the session, your interaction with the system is similar to a conversation. The AS/400 links together all of the tasks you do from the time you sign on until you sign off. This makes it easier for you to manage your work environment, find your output, and keep track of what you have done.

A *batch job* is any job that doesn't require continuous interaction between the system and the user after it has been submitted to be processed (run). A user submits the job (for example, printing a sales report), and it is sent to a *job queue*, where it remains until it can be run. The AS/400 needs no further information from the user once the job has been submitted because all the information for the job is stored in data files on the system.

Frequently, users submit batch jobs at about the same time. In such cases, jobs are temporarily placed in a job queue in the order in which they were submitted (which could involve a difference of only a fraction of a second). As the system finishes one batch job, it searches the job queue for more work. Batch jobs, therefore, actually start from a job queue.

The Flow of a Batch Job

It is important to know the flow of a batch job so that you can track it through the system and display or change its status. This allows you to do these tasks:

- End or hold a job
- Answer messages sent by the system
- Control printer output

The flow of a job can have up to five steps, although not all jobs need to include steps 4 and 5:

1. A user or program submits a job to be run.

2. The system places the job on a job queue.

3. The system takes the job from the job queue and runs it.

4. If this job creates some information (output) that needs to be printed, the printer output is placed on an output queue.

5. The system takes printer output from the output queue and sends it to the associated printer to be printed. Figure 3.2 shows how a batch job with printer output flows through the system.

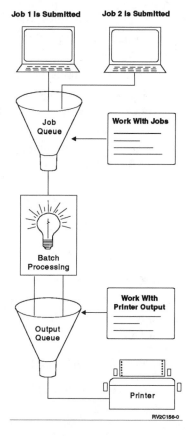

Figure 3.2: The system flow of a batch job with printer output.

Let's say that User A and User B have submitted their monthly reports at about the same time. They both want their report printed, but there is only one printer available. OS/400 simply places their jobs in a job queue in the order in which they were received. A job queue can be considered a line of jobs that are waiting to be run; generally, jobs run in the order in which they entered the job queue.

The AS/400 takes jobs from the job queue and runs them. As each job is run, the system sends any printer output to the *output queue*. The output queue is similar to the job queue, in that it can be considered a line where the printer output of each job must wait its turn to be printed. Again, printer output generally prints in the order in which it enters the output queue. Printer output remains in the output queue until it is either printed or deleted.

Finally, the printer takes the printer output from the output queue and produces the printed copy. As it happens, User B's job is printed first. However, just because one job is submitted before another doesn't mean it is printed first. A variety of factors can affect the length of time it takes for a job to run. These factors include such things as job length, the type of processing involved, and job priority. (For further details about output queues and controlling printer output, see chapter 5.)

SUBMITTING BATCH JOBS

There are two ways you can submit a batch job. You can submit it immediately, or schedule it to run later. In this chapter, only the process of submitting a batch job immediately is discussed. To submit a job that runs immediately, do one of the following:

- Follow a menu path:

   1. On the AS/400 Main Menu (MAIN), type 3, General system tasks, and press Enter.

   2. On the General System Tasks (SYSTEM) menu, type 1, Jobs, and press Enter.

   3. On the Jobs (JOB) menu, type 7, Submit a job, and press Enter.

> **Hint:** Take a fast path to the JOB menu: Enter the command GO JOB.

- Type the command SBMJOB and press F4.

The Submit Job (SBMJOB) display is shown in Figure 3.3.

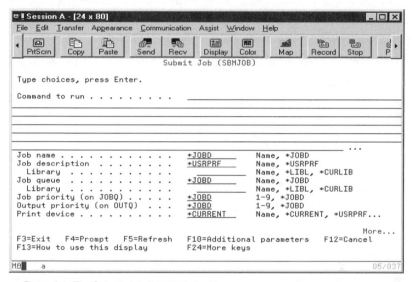

Figure 3.3: The Submit Job (SBMJOB) display.

The *Command to run* field is used to enter the command you want to run in a batch job. This field is essentially the same as the command line you see at the bottom of a display. You can call a program or specify a CL command:

- If the job you want to submit is a program, type CALL and the name of the program; for example, CALL PAYROLL. If the job you want to run is a REXX procedure, use the Start REXX Procedure (STRREXPRC) command.

- If the job you want to run is a CL command, type the name of the command. You can use prompting to assist you with the parameters for the command.

Type the name of the command, and then press F4 (Prompt), while your cursor is positioned in the Command to run field.

You can change the default values for any of the other entry fields on the Submit Job (SBMJOB) display. You get the chance to do this in the exercise at the end of this chapter.

Once you press Enter, the job is submitted. A message appears at the bottom of your display showing the *qualified job name* and the name of the job queue to which the job has been submitted. The qualified job name is used by the system and by system users to locate jobs. It consists of three parts:

- Job number—Assigned by the system to make sure every qualified job name is unique. This number helps to differentiate between two or more jobs that have been submitted by the same user and given the same user-defined name.

- User ID—The user profile under which the job is running, usually the profile of the person submitting the job.

- Job name—A short descriptive title of the job, such as PRTINV for print invoices. A programmer may define this name ahead of time. If a job name is not specified, the default name is QDFTJOBD, as specified in the *job description* parameter of your user profile.

WORKING WITH JOB QUEUES

Before a batch job is run, it waits in line on the job queue of the subsystem that runs it. The job can be waiting because other jobs are in front of it on the queue, the job is held, the job queue is held, or the job queue is not allocated to an active subsystem. A waiting job also has a priority (its place in the queue). Figure 3.4 shows an overview of a subsystem processing jobs from a job queue.

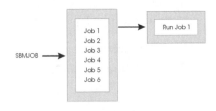

Figure 3.4: An overview of a subsystem processing jobs from a job queue.

Finding Job Queues

If you have submitted batch jobs, the Work with User Jobs display (as described in the topic "Working with User Jobs" later in this chapter) tells you the status of those jobs, including where they are on the job queue if they are waiting to run. However, you might want to know which jobs are scheduled to run ahead of your job. Or, as the system operator, you might need to monitor all user activity on the job queues. You can view this information on the Work with All Job Queues display. To find the Work with All Job Queues display, shown in Figure 3.5, do one of the following:

- On the Jobs (JOB) menu, select option 5, Work with job queues. On the Work with Job Queue (WRKJOBQ) display, press Enter to take the default (*ALL) to work with all job queues in the libraries to which you are authorized.

- On any command line, enter WRKJOBQ and by default, all job queues in the libraries to which you are authorized are listed.

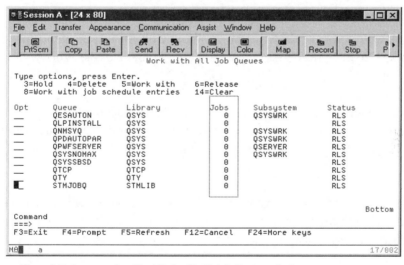

Figure 3.5: An example of the Work with All Job Queues display.

Find the name of the job queue you created in the exercise for chapter 2. Are there currently any jobs in your queue? In the exercise at the end of this chapter, you actually submit some jobs to this job queue.

The Jobs column shows the number of jobs currently in the job queue. This number increases as jobs are submitted and decreases as jobs are run. The numbers on the screen indicate the number of jobs that are in the queue only at the instant the display is requested. Press F5 (Refresh) to determine in real-time how many jobs are coming in and going out of a queue.

Notice the Subsystem column. Each job queue can be assigned to a subsystem. The subsystem specified in this column selects and runs all the jobs in its assigned job queue. If the Subsystem column is blank, the job queue is not assigned to any subsystem. You can still place jobs in this job queue, but the jobs cannot run until the job queue is assigned to a subsystem.

> **Tip:** To find priorities of any jobs that may be on a job queue, use option 5 (Work with). On the Work with Job Queue display, the Priority column contains the priority of each job in the job queue you've selected.

Working with Jobs in a Job Queue

To work with jobs in a job queue, on the Work with All Job Queues display, type 5 (Work with) and press Enter. Figure 3.6 is an example of the Work with Job Queue display.

The Work with Job Queue display shows the jobs in the job queue you've selected. The heading portion of this display, the line of information just below the screen title, identifies the name of the job queue you've selected, its library, and its status.

A status code of RLS indicates that the job queue is released, which means jobs can be processed from that queue. When the Status shows RLS/SBS, it means that this queue is also assigned to a subsystem, in which case the jobs can be run.

In the middle of the Work with Job Queue display, you can see all the jobs that are currently on the job queue, in the order in which they are to be selected for processing. In addition to the job name, this display shows the name of the user who submitted the job and a unique number for the job. In other words, the first three columns from the left comprise the fully qualified job name.

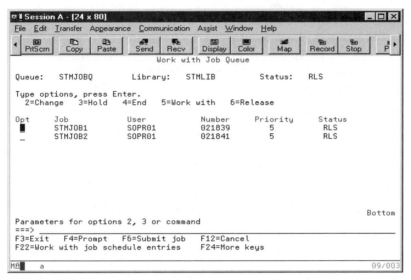

Figure 3.6: An example of the Work with Job Queue display.

Notice the Number column. It contains the sequence number assigned by the system on a first-in, first-out (often referred to by the acronym *FIFO*) basis. The same user can submit multiple jobs with the same job name because the sequence number ensures that every job has a unique identifier.

Notice the Priority column. Priority controls the sequence in which the subsystem selects jobs from the job queue. A priority of zero indicates the highest priority at which a job can run, whereas a nine indicates the lowest priority at which a job can run. For example, if job A was submitted before job B, but job A's priority is 5 and job B's priority is 1, then job B runs before job A because of the higher priority.

Note: Users may be limited as to the highest priority jobs they are allowed to run, as determined by the Highest schedule priority parameter in the user profile.

When you submit a job to the job queue, you assign it a specific priority, or you accept the default priority associated with the environment in which it runs. When multiple jobs have the same priority, the subsystem selects them on a FIFO basis. The system assigns job numbers in the same way.

For the Status column, access online help (by pressing F1 or the Help key) to find out what the different job status codes mean. (Details about changing, holding, releasing, and ending jobs are discussed in the topic "Working with User Jobs.")

Holding a Job Queue

When you put a hold on a job queue, you prevent it from doing anything until you release it. A held queue cannot provide jobs for a subsystem. However, you can still put new jobs in a held job queue. You hold a job queue when you want to do:

- Make changes to a job in that queue.
- Prevent specific jobs from running until the system is less busy.

You can hold a job queue in one of two ways:

- Select option 3 (Hold) on the Work with All Job Queues display for the job queue or queues you want to hold. Once you hold a job queue from this display, the status of the queue is changed to *HLD. The asterisk indicates that a change has just been made to that queue. Press F5 (Refresh), and the status of the queue is changed to HLD.

- Use the command HLDJOBQ JOBQ(*<library name>/<job queue name>*).

Releasing a Job Queue

When you release a held job queue, a subsystem can again select jobs from that queue for processing. You can release a job queue in one of two ways:

- Select option 6 (Release) on the Work with All Job Queues display, for the job queue or queues you want to release. Once you release a job queue from this display, the status of the queue is changed to *RLS. The asterisk indicates that a change was just made to that queue. Press F5 (Refresh), and the status of the queue is changed to RLS.

- Use the command RLSJOBQ JOBQ(*<library name>/<job queue name>*).

As shown in the list of options on the Work with All Job Queues display, you can also delete and clear job queues. When you delete a job queue, the job queue object and all jobs in that queue are deleted. When you clear a job queue, you just remove all jobs in that queue.

WORKING WITH USER JOBS

In the previous pages, you learned how to display all the jobs currently running in a particular job queue. However, that method only categorizes jobs by their job queue. You also need to know how to search for jobs by user, job status, and job type. As a system operator, you often need to determine the status of users' jobs in order to control their jobs and print output. To do this, you must access and use the Work with User Jobs display.

With the Work with User Jobs display, you can determine different things about a user's job. The following are some of the things you can determine about the job:

- Is it waiting in a job queue for processing?
- Is it running in a subsystem?
- Is it waiting in an output queue for printing?
- Is it waiting for the response to a message?

To find this display, on the Jobs (JOB) menu, select option 1, Work with jobs, and press Enter. Alternatively, you can type WRKUSRJOB and press F4 on any command line. The Work with User Jobs (WRKUSRJOB) entry display appears, as shown in Figure 3.7.

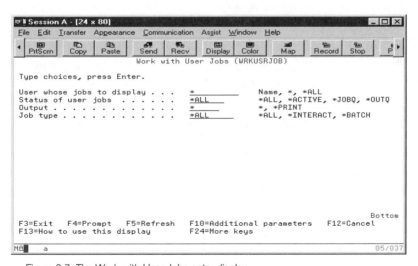

Figure 3.7: The Work with User Jobs entry display.

Notice the first, second, and fourth parameters.

The *User whose jobs to display* parameter defaults to an * (asterisk), meaning you see only your own jobs. You can specify a particular user's name as it appears in the user profile. In this case, you see only the jobs for that user. Or you can specify *ALL to see the jobs for every user in the system.

> **Note:** To view and manage the jobs of other users, you must have job control (*JOBCTL) special authority in your user profile. System operators typically have this authority.

The *Status of user jobs* parameter gives you the following choices:

- *ALL, the default value, shows you the status of every user job anywhere in the system.
- *ACTIVE limits you to the user jobs that are currently running in a subsystem.
- *JOBQ limits you to the jobs in job queues that are waiting to be started.
- *OUTQ limits you to the jobs that have completed running and have output waiting to print in output queues.

> **Tip:** To quickly find all active jobs on the system, enter WRKUSRJOB USER(*ALL) STATUS(*ACTIVE) on a command line. Or, using positional notation, just enter WRKUSRJOB *ALL *ACTIVE. (For additional information about active jobs and active job statistics, see the topics "Working with Signed-On Users" and "Displaying Active Job Statistics" later in this chapter.)

The *Job type* parameter specifies the type of user jobs to display. Here are the available choices:

- *ALL, the default value, shows every type of job, including interactive and batch. Other types of jobs you may see include autostart, prestart, and batch immediate.

- *INTERACT shows only interactive user jobs.

- *BATCH shows only batch user jobs.

Tip: To display your own jobs, just type the command WRKUSRJOB and press Enter.

To list all jobs running in the system, type *ALL for the *User whose jobs to display* parameter and press Enter. This may take some time to complete.

Caution: Displaying all user jobs may adversely affect the performance of other jobs. If there are many jobs on the system, or during peak usage times, select a user ID instead of typing *ALL for this parameter.

Figure 3.8 is an example of the Work with User Jobs display. In the heading information in the upper-right corner of the display, the name of your AS/400 is shown. This is important if your system is part of a network. The body of this display contains an entry for each job in the system. The columns on this display are described next.

```
Session A - [24 x 80]
 File  Edit  Transfer  Appearance  Communication  Assist  Window  Help

   PrtScrn   Copy   Paste   Send   Recv   Display   Color   Map   Record   Stop   P
                         Work with User Jobs                        LAB400
                                                         06/01/99  13:47:08
 Type options, press Enter.
   2=Change   3=Hold   4=End   5=Work with   6=Release   7=Display message
   8=Work with spooled files   13=Disconnect


 Opt  Job         User      Type     -----Status-----  Function
  __   QPADEV0005  JHARRIS   INTER    OUTQ
  __   QPADEV0005  SOPR01    INTER    OUTQ
  __   QPADEV0005  TEAM04    INTER    OUTQ
  __   QPADEV0007  DKRONOPR  INTER    OUTQ
  __   QPADEV0008  TEAM09    INTER    OUTQ
  __   QPASVRP     QSYS      BATCH    OUTQ
  __   QPASVRP     QSYS      AUTO     OUTQ
  __   QPASVRP     QSYS      BATCH    ACTIVE            PGM-QPASVRP
  __   QPASVRS     QSYS      BATCH    OUTQ
  __   QPASVRS     QSYS      BATCH    OUTQ
                                                            More...
 Parameters or command
 ===>
 F3=Exit      F4=Prompt    F5=Refresh    F9=Retrieve   F11=Display schedule data
 F12=Cancel   F21=Select assistance level
 MA    a                                                          09/002
```

Figure 3.8: An example of the Work with User Jobs display.

Job Column

Use the Job column, along with the User column, to identify the jobs. For an interactive job, the job name identifies the workstation where the job originated. (In Figure 3.8, QPADEV0005 would be an example of a job name identifying a workstation.)

For a batch job, the job name describes the work done by the job. For example, the name for a job that prints year-to-date sales information could be YTDSALES. A job that prints a test report for the RPG programming language could be called RPGTEST.

User Column

The User column indicates the user profile under which the job is running. For interactive jobs, it shows the user who signed (or is currently signed) on to the system. For batch jobs, it shows the user specified in the user profile assigned to the job.

Because different users can run the same batch job and use the same job name, the combination of the job name and user is often necessary to positively identify a job. Also, a user might have several jobs listed on this display. For example, an interactive job, one or more batch jobs, and some jobs on output queues could all have the same job name and user. When multiple jobs with the same job name and user exist, you can use option 5 (Work with) to access another display that includes a sequence number to further identify the job.

Status Column

The Status column indicates the state or condition of the job. Common status codes on this display include JOBQ, OUTQ, ACTIVE, MSGW, and END. Table 3.2 includes a description of the more common status codes. (See online help for details on other status codes.)

Table 3.2: Common Status Codes for User Jobs.

Status Code	Reason
JOBQ	Job is on a job queue, waiting to run.
OUTQ	Job has completed running, and its output is on an output queue, printing or waiting to be printed.
ACTIVE	Job is started in a subsystem and is trying to do its work. While a job is active, it can already have output on an output queue. However, its status doesn't change to OUTQ until it finishes running.
MSGW	Job is running; it has paused and is waiting for the response to a message.
END	When all the output of a job has been printed, its entry is either removed from this display or its status is shown as END.

Type and Function Columns

The Type column indicates the job class, such as INTER (interactive) or BATCH. The Function column indicates the operation currently being performed by an active job. For a batch job, it identifies the program being run by the job. For an interactive job, it identifies a program, menu, or command. For example, if you are signed on and looking at the Work with User Jobs display, the Function column would read CMD WRKUSRJOB.

Holding a Job

Holding a job enables you to suspend a job. When you put a hold on a job, you prevent it from doing anything until you release it. You hold a job when you want to make changes to that job. You can hold a job one of two ways:

- Select option 3 (Hold) on the Work with User Jobs display for the job or jobs you want to hold. Once you hold a job from this display, HLD appears in the Status column. Press F5 (Refresh), and the status is changed to HELD.

- Use the command HLDJOB and press F4 to specify the qualified job name and any additional parameters.

If you hold a job with a status of JOBQ or ACTIVE, the job is held on the job queue until you release it. Once a job has a status of OUTQ, it has finished running. Any reports (spooled files) that it has created are waiting to print or are printing. If you do not want these spooled files to print immediately, specify this before you hold the job. To do this, find the option line next to the job, type 3, and press F4. On the Hold Job (HLDJOB) display, type *YES for the *Hold spooled files* parameter. Figure 3.9 shows an example of the Hold Job (HLDJOB) display.

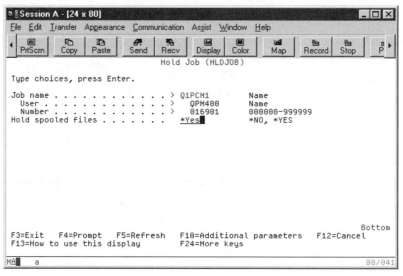

Figure 3.9: An example of the Hold Job (HLDJOB) display.

Releasing a Job

Releasing a job enables you to free a held job. A released job resumes from the point at which it was held. You can release a job one of two ways:

- Select option 6 (Release) on the Work with User Jobs display for the job or jobs you want to release. Once you release a job from this display, RLS appears in the Status column. Press F5 (Refresh), and the RLS code disappears. Everything is business as usual once again.

- Use the command RLSJOB and press F4 to specify the qualified job name and any additional parameters.

Ending a Job

Ending a job enables you to cancel a job. You can end a job one of two ways:

- Select option 4 (End) on the Work with User Jobs display for the job or jobs you want to end. Once you end a job from this display, End appears in the Status column. Press F5 (Refresh), and the End code disappears.

- Use the command ENDJOB and press F4 to specify the qualified job name and any additional parameters. For example, on the End Job (ENDJOB) display, you can specify how to end the job, whether in a controlled manner or immediately.

When you end a job and the status changes to OUTQ, it means the job has finished running. Any reports (spooled files) that the job created are either printing or waiting to print on an output queue. If you want to prevent these reports from printing, specify this before you end the job. To do this: find the option line next to the job, type 4, and press F4. On the End Job (ENDJOB) display, type *YES for the *Delete spooled files* parameter. Figure 3.10 shows an example of the End Job (ENDJOB) display.

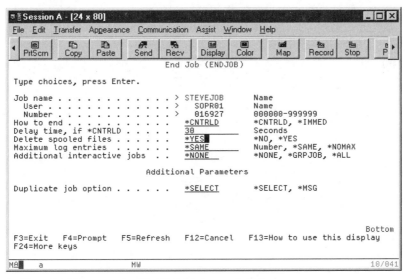

Figure 3.10: An example of the End Job (ENDJOB) display.

Before you end any job, always consider the possible consequences. For example, ending a batch job might cause problems with subsequent batch jobs that are dependent upon that job's successful completion. Ending an interactive job could result in a recovery situation. For example, if you end an order entry program while the user is entering an order, the program does not perform end-of-order processing. This might damage the database files used by the program.

When and When Not to End a Job

You can end a job if the job is waiting for a message response, or if the job is on a job queue or active in a subsystem. When you end a job with a status of JOBQ, its entry is removed from the job queue. If the job's status is ACTIVE, the job is ended.

You cannot end a job if the job is complete, and its output is in an output queue, where the job status is OUTQ. It has already ended. However, you can display the spooled files for the job (option 8, Work with spooled files, on the Work with User Jobs display), and then optionally delete the files.

> **Note:** Whenever you end a job, the system writes a job log to the output queue, regardless of whether you specify to delete the spooled files on the End Job (ENDJOB) display. To view the job log on the output queue, select option 8, Work with spooled files, for that job on the Work with User Jobs display.

You typically end a user's job when one or more of the following occurs:

- The workstation is locked up.

- The wrong job is submitted.

- The user prematurely submits a job (for example, a monthly report in which files have not been properly updated).

- The user needs to start over.

Whenever possible, you should get a user's job running again. However, sometimes the best approach is to end the job and let the user start over.

Displaying Job Attributes

The system keeps a comprehensive record of all aspects of every job. This information is available to you through the Work with Job menu. To access this menu, select option 5 (Work with) on the Work with User Jobs display for the job you want more information about, or use the command WRKJOB. Figure 3.11 shows the Work with Job menu.

Tip: To find job information for your own interactive job, just type WRKJOB and press Enter.

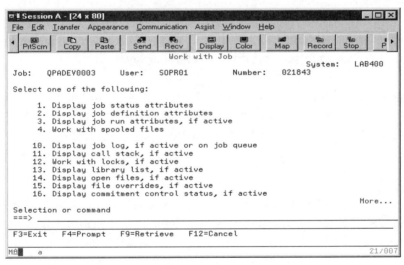

Figure 3.11: The Work with Job menu.

To help you monitor jobs and find out why problems with jobs occur, you can use the following tasks on the Work with Job menu:

- Display job status attributes
- Display job definition attributes
- Display job run attributes
- Display call stack
- Display open files

Displaying job status attributes: Select option 1 on the Work with Job menu. Now, you can see when the job entered the system and when it started running. For a batch job, this information can help you determine whether or not the job has been running too long and might be in a loop.

Displaying job definition attributes: Select option 2 on the Work with Job menu. This displays information such as job queue assignment and priority, output queue assignment and priority, message queue assignment, and logging level. Many of these definition attributes can be changed using the Change Job (CHGJOB) command or F9 (Change job) key on the Display Job Definition Attributes display. (See the next section in this chapter, for information on how to change a job.)

Displaying job run attribute: Select option 3 on the Work with Job menu. You can find out what a job's run priority is on this display.

Displaying the call stack: Select option 11 on the Work with Job menu. If an active job has stopped or seems to be in a loop, the call stack can help to determine where the problem is. It shows what program line numbers the job is currently trying to run.

Displaying open files: Select option 14 on the Work with Job menu. You can see information about all of the files that the job is currently using. The Display Open Files display is useful in detecting a program loop. Press F5 (Refresh) continually and look at the data in the Relative Record column to see if the job is repeating the same relative record number. Press F11 (Display I/O details) to access this information. You can also use this option to monitor the progress of a long-running batch job. For example, if you know that the job updates 15,000 records in a file, you can check the I/O Count column for the input/output count in that file to find out how the job is progressing. Press F5 to keep refreshing this column.

Changing a Job

Once you have used the options on the Work with Job menu (as shown in Figure 3.11) to do research, you might want to change some of the attributes of a job that is running or waiting to run. You can change attributes of a job by using one of the following methods:

- Select option 40 (Change job) on the Work with Job menu for the job referenced toward the top of the menu.

- Select option 2 (Change) on the Work with User Jobs display for the job you want to change.

- Prompt (F4) the CHGJOB command and specify a qualified job name for the job you want to change.

Any of these methods delivers the Change Job (CHGJOB) prompt display to you. An example of this display is shown in Figure 3.12.

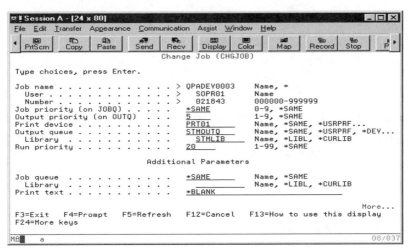

Figure 3.12: An example of the Change Job (CHGJOB) prompt display.

Tip: To display additional parameters, press F10.

You can change a number of job attributes. For example, you can do any of the following:

- Change the job priority on a job queue.
- Change the print priority.
- Assign a job to a different output queue.
- Change how an active job is run.
- Move a job to a different job queue.

Changing the Job Priority on a Job Queue

Each job on a job queue has an assigned priority (position on the queue). To change a job's position on the queue, type a number (0 to 9) in the *Job priority* field (on JOBQ) on the Change Job (CHGJOB) display. Raising a job's priority (changing the priority to a number closer to zero) can move it closer to the top of the queue. The highest priority is zero; the lowest priority is nine. Jobs with a higher priority are run before jobs with a lower priority. There may be a limit on how high you can set the priority, depending on the number specified in the Priority limit parameter (PTYLMT) of your user profile.

> **Note:** When you submit a job, the highest priority allowed is one. Priority zero is reserved for changing a job to move it to the very top of the queue.

This change only affects the job once. If the same job is submitted to the job queue again, it has its original priority. To make a permanent change to the job's priority on the job queue, change either the job description it uses or the procedure for submitting the job.

Changing the Print Priority

Printer output on an output queue has an assigned priority. (The position on the queue that it has obtained from the job's print priority.) To change this priority, type a number from 1 to 9 in the *Output priority* field (on OUTQ). Raising a job's priority (changing the priority to a number closer to one) can move the job's printer output closer to the top of the output queue. Then, it begins printing sooner than printer output with a lower priority on that output queue. Output queue priorities work in the same way as job queue priorities.

This change only affects the job once. If the same job runs again, it returns to the original output priority. To make a permanent change to the job's output priority, change either the job description it uses or change the procedure for submitting the job.

Assigning a Job to a Different Output Queue

When a batch job that creates printed output is waiting to run, you can change the output queue to which it is assigned by changing the *Output queue* field. Once the batch job starts to run, it begins creating its spooled file in its assigned output queue. At that point, you would need to move the spooled file to a different output queue. (See chapter 5 for details about moving spooled files to different output queues.)

For an interactive job, you may want to change the assigned output queue before you use the Print key to print a report or before you run a program that creates a report. This change only affects the job once. If the same job runs again, it is assigned to the original output queue. To make a permanent change to a batch job's output queue, change either the job description it uses or change the procedure for submitting the job. To make a permanent change to an interactive job's output queue, change the job description it uses, the user profile, or the workstation device description.

Changing How an Active Job Is Run

To change how a job is run, change either the *Run priority* or *Time slice* fields. The control program decides which jobs to run in what order and for how long. Here's how it happens in the control program:

- Every job has a time slice and a run priority. The time slice sets a limit on how long the processor works on one job before switching to another job. Time slices are measured in milliseconds. The run priority determines which job the processor selects next.

- Once the processor has started processing the instructions for a job, it continues with that job until one of the following events happens:

  ➢ The job reaches time slice end.

  ➢ The job needs to wait for something. For example, an interactive job might send a new display to your screen. Then, the system has to wait for you to type another request and press the Enter key.

When one of the previous events occurs, the system has to decide which job to run next. The system looks at a list of jobs that are ready to be run and chooses the highest priority job.

You can see that both run priority and time slice can affect how a job is run. You should use great care in changing either of these. If you give any job too high a priority or too long a time slice, it can negatively affect everything else running on the system.

This change only affects the job once. If the same job runs again, it returns to the original priority and time slice. To make a permanent change to how the job runs, change either the characteristics of the class it uses or have it run using a different class.

Moving a Job to a Different Job Queue

Sometimes certain job queues are set aside for work that does not require immediate running. These job queues can be released and held depending on how busy your system is, or your system may have a job queue assigned to a subsystem that has less system resources than the interactive subsystem.

To move a job from one queue to another, type the name of the new job queue in the *Job queue* field. This change only affects the job once. If the same job is submitted again in the same way, it goes to the original job queue. To make a permanent change to the queue this job uses, change either the job description it uses or the procedure for submitting the job.

DISPLAYING JOBS IN A SPECIFIC SUBSYSTEM

In the previous topics, you learned how to find jobs by the job queue in which they are running, by the user profile that initiated the job, and by their status (such as *ACTIVE) and type (such as *BATCH). It is also helpful to know how to search for jobs by the subsystem in which they are active. This is a convenient way to verify if, and how many, jobs are running in a subsystem. To do this, you must use the Work with Subsystems display, as shown in Figure 3.13.

To find this display, do one of the following:

- On the Jobs (JOB) menu, select option 6, Work with active subsystems, and press Enter.

- On any command line, enter WRKSBS.

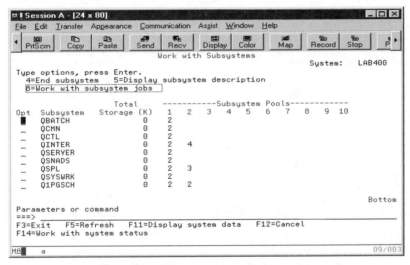

Figure 3.13: An example of the Work with Subsystems display.

Option 8 (Work with subsystem jobs) allows you to display and work with active jobs in a particular subsystem. For example, to only see interactive jobs currently running in subsystem QINTER, follow these directions:

1. In the option column next to QINTER, type 8.

2. Press Enter. The Work with Subsystem Jobs display appears, similar to the example shown in Figure 3.14.

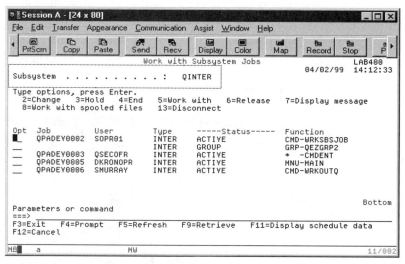

Figure 3.14: An example of the Work with Subsystem Jobs display.

Notice that the same options and columns of data are available to you on the Work with Subsystem Jobs display as on the Work with User Jobs display. (See Figure 3.8.) The difference between the two displays is that you are sorting jobs by subsystem names versus sorting jobs by user profile name. Also, the status of jobs on the Work with Subsystem Jobs display is always active, whereas with the Work with User Jobs display, you can specify any job status to work with.

Tip: To use a CL command to work with the jobs in a subsystem, enter WRKSBSJOB <subsystem name> on any command line. For example, enter WRKSBSJOB QBATCH to work with all active batch jobs in subsystem QBATCH.

WORKING WITH SIGNED-ON USERS

You can easily find out who is currently signed on to the system and what those users are currently doing. Essentially, you do this to determine the kinds of interactive jobs users are currently running. In fact, signed-on users are referred to as *interactive jobs*.

To review, an interactive job is everything a user does on the system (for example, running commands and programs) from the time the user signs on to when the user signs off. An interactive job begins when the user signs on to a workstation, and ends when the user signs off.

Interactive users may not use the largest share of AS/400 resources, but these users frequently have the highest priority for system use. Therefore, smooth functioning of interactive users' jobs is paramount.

You can perform the following tasks with signed-on users:

- Display signed-on users.

- Find signed-on users and sort the user list.

- Find additional information about signed-on users.

- Send messages to signed-on users.

- Sign users off the system.

Displaying Signed-on Users

To display all users signed on to the system, do one of the following:

- Enter GO MANAGESYS on a command line to access the Manage Your System, Users, and Devices menu. Then, select option 12, Work with Signed-On Users.

  Note: If the Work with User Jobs display appears, it means the assistance level for that display is set to intermediate. To use the Work with Signed-On Users display, press F21 to change the assistance level to basic. Once you change the assistance level for a display, the display remains at that level until you change it again. (See chapter 1 for details about OS/400 assistance levels.)

- Enter the Work with User Jobs command as follows:

```
WRKUSRJOB USER(*ALL) STATUS(*ACTIVE) JOBTYPE(*INTERACT) ASTLVL(*BASIC)
```

> **Note:** If you specify *INTERMED for ASTLVL, you see the intermediate Work with User Jobs display instead of the basic Work with Signed-On Users display.

Figure 3.15 is an example of the Work with Signed-On Users display. For each user, the name of the display station to which he or she is signed on and the activity the user is doing is shown.

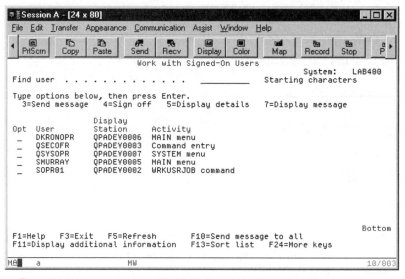

Figure 3.15: An example of the Work with Signed-On Users display.

Complete the following steps to access online help to find a list of possible activities:

1. Position your cursor on the Activity column.

2. Press F1.

3. On the Activity—Help display, page down.

4. Press Enter on the hyperlink entitled "List of Activities."

5. Page up and down the list to view descriptions of various user activities.

Finding Signed-on Users and Sorting the User List

If there are several users signed on, and you need to find a specific user, type the first few characters of the user's name in the *Find user* field and press Enter. The list is positioned at the first user matching the characters you typed.

The list is initially sorted by user name and shows the activities of each user. To sort the list by user name or display station name, press F13 (Sort list). You can show certain information about signed-off users from this display as well. Use F14 (Select other users and display stations). F14 displays the window shown in Figure 3.16.

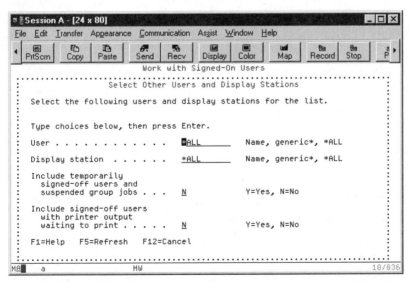

Figure 3.16: The Select Other Users and Display Stations display from the Work with Signed-On Users display.

Users who are temporarily signed off are not included in this list. To include them, type a *Y* in the *Include temporarily signed-off users and suspended group jobs* field. You might also need to display signed-off users who have output waiting to be printed.

Finding Additional Information about Signed-on Users

There are two ways you can display additional information about the users currently signed on to the system:

- For a single user listed, select option 5 (Display details). This shows the user description and display station description in addition to what you already see on the Work with Signed-On Users display.

- For all users listed, press F11 (Display additional information). This displays a pop-up window where you can select which type of information you want to see in the third column of the Work with Signed-On Users display: activities, display station descriptions, or user descriptions.

Sending Messages to Signed-on Users

From the Work with Signed-On Users display, you can send messages to one, several, or all users signed on to the system. Use these steps to send a message:

1. Select option 3 for each user to send a message to one or several signed-on user. Or, to send a message to all signed-on users, press F10 (Send message to all).

2. Type your message in the *Message text* field on the Send a Message display.

3. Press F10 (Send) on the Send a Message display to send the message. (For details about messages, see chapter 4.)

Note: The Send a Message display is set up to interrupt the user or users to whom you're sending the message. If you do not want to interrupt them, change the value in the *Interrupt user* field to *N*.

Signing Users off the System

Signing a user off interrupts their interactive job in the middle of processing, removes it from the system, and signs the user off. You might use this function to sign off users who have forgotten to sign off.

Warning: Use caution when signing a user off the system. Ending a user's interactive job in the middle of processing might interrupt job or file updates.

To sign a user off the system:

1. Use option 4 (Sign off) for the user or users you want to sign off the system, and press Enter.

2. On the Confirm Sign Off display, press Enter again to sign users off the system, or press F12 (Cancel) to leave the user signed on.

The Work with Signed-On Users display is refreshed, no longer showing the user(s) you signed off the system.

DISPLAYING ACTIVE JOB STATISTICS

System operators often monitor AS/400 performance. System administrators or security officers are typically the only people who can actually modify the system. However, it is the job of the system operator to inform the system administrator that changes may be needed. Although this topic does not go into details on monitoring and measuring system performance, it is necessary to introduce a display that allows you to work with job activity.

The Work with Active Jobs display, shown in Figure 3.17, allows you to monitor a job's CPU usage. If users are experiencing slow response times, it is likely that a certain job is demanding a lot of processing time to complete. Because programmers tend to have higher system priority and use more resources when they are compiling or testing applications, other users' jobs could get slowed, or users' display stations could even lock up.

To access the Work with Active Jobs display, do one of the following:

- Select option 2 (Work with all active job statistics) on the Jobs (JOB) menu, and press Enter.

- Enter the command WRKACTJOB.

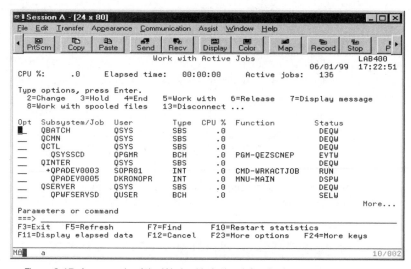

Figure 3.17: An example of the Work with Active Jobs display.

Notice the *Active Jobs* field in the upper-right of the display. It shows the total number of jobs currently running on the AS/400—jobs that have been started, but have not yet ended. This total includes both user and system jobs. Some jobs are system jobs that you see all the time, even when you're the only user on the system.

> **Tip:** To quickly determine how many jobs are active in a subsystem, enter the command WRKSBS. On the Work with Subsystems display, press F11 (Display system data). The number of active jobs in each subsystem is indicated in the Active Jobs column.

Also notice that jobs that run in a subsystem—such as interactive and batch jobs—are indented under the subsystem in which they are associated. Subsystem monitors (e.g., QBATCH, QINTER) and system jobs, on the other hand, are not indented. This is one way you can tell a user job from a subsystem monitor and system job. With the Type column, you can determine specifically what kind of job is running.

Finally, notice that you can perform job control just like you can on the Work with User Jobs display and Work with Subsystem Jobs display. Jobs can be changed, held, released, ended, and so forth.

Note: Use the Work with Active Jobs display rarely, otherwise system response time for other jobs suffers significantly. If you are just searching for active jobs—not monitoring their performance—consider using the following commands instead:

- WRKUSRJOB (Work with User Jobs), which displays jobs by user profile name.
- WRKSBSJOB (Work with Subsystem Jobs), which displays jobs by subsystem name.

These commands, and their associated displays, are discussed in the topics "Working with User Jobs" and "Displaying Jobs in a Specific Subsystem" earlier in this chapter.

EXERCISE 3: SUBMITTING JOBS AND WORKING WITH THOSE JOBS

Procedures

1. Submit two jobs to the job queue you created in chapter 2.

2. Display all job queues on the system and find yours.

3. Display jobs in your job queue.

4. Hold a job.

5. Move a job to a different job queue.

6. End a job.

7. Search for jobs by your user name.

8. Release a job and determine if it completed.

9. Display signed-on users.

10. Work with signed-on users.

Submit Two Jobs to the Job Queue Created in Chapter 2

1. Sign on with a user ID that has system operator authorities.

2. Access the Command Entry display. On a command line:

   ➤ Enter CALL QCMD.

3. Access the Submit Job (SBMJOB) display. On the Command Entry display:

   ➤ Type SBMJOB and press F4.

4. Submit a job to send a message to yourself. On the Submit Job (SBMJOB) display, do the following:

   a) For the *Command to run* parameter, type SNDMSG and press F4. On the Send Message (SNDMSG) display:

      ✓ In the *Message text* area, state briefly what you hope to learn from this course.

      ✓ In the *To user profile* field, type your user ID.

✓ Press Enter to return to the Submit Job display. You will see a command string similar to the following:

```
SNDMSG MSG('I hope to learn more about AS/400 operations') TOUSR(SOPR01)
```

b) For the *Job name* parameter:

➤ Type *xxx*JOB1 (where *xxx* is your initials).

c) For the *Job queue* parameter:

➤ Type *xxx*JOBQ for the job queue and *xxx*LIB for the library (where *xxx* is your initials).

d) Press Enter to submit the job. You will see a message confirming that the job was submitted. The message includes the qualified job name.

✓ What is the job number?   _____

✓ What is the user ID?   _____

✓ What is the job name?   _____

You can use these values to find this job by its qualified name by entering the WRKJOB command. For example, you might use WRKJOB JOB(021839/SOPR01/STMJOB1).

5. Submit a second job to send a message to yourself:

a) On the Command Entry display, retrieve the SBMJOB command and then prompt it.

➤ Press F9 and then F4.

b) On the Submit Job (SBMJOB) display, for the Command to run parameter:

➤ Change the MSG text to read: 'This is fun'.

   c) For the Job name parameter:

       ➢ Change *xxx*JOB1 to *xxx*JOB2 (where *xxx* is your initials).

   d) Press Enter to submit the job. You will again see a message confirming that the job was submitted. The message includes the qualified job name.

       ✓ What is the job number?   _____

       ✓ What is the user ID?   _____

       ✓ What is the job name?   _____

You now have two jobs that you can work with in the following tasks.

Display All Job Queues on the System and Find Yours

   1. On the Command Entry display:

       ➢ Enter WRKJOBQ.

   2. On the Work with All Job Queues display, find your job queue. Page down if you don't see your job queue on the first page. You are looking for *xxx*JOBQ, where *xxx* is your initials.

   3. Look at the Jobs and Subsystem columns for your job queue. (See Figure 3.5 for an example of the Work with All Job Queues display.)

The Jobs column should show that your job queue contains at least two (2) jobs. The Subsystem column should be empty for your job queue. When there is no subsystem name, the queue is not associated with an active subsystem. Therefore, if you are wondering why the jobs you submitted are not processed yet, this is why. A job cannot be processed if the job queue in which it is waiting is not assigned to a subsystem.

However, don't worry about job queue entries here. The job queue you created is sufficient for this exercise. Later in this exercise, you actually move one of your jobs to a job queue that is attached to a subsystem so that the job can run.

> **Tip:** After creating a job queue, you must add a job queue entry to assign a job queue to a subsystem. Use the command ADDJOBQE.

Display Jobs in Your Job Queue

1. On the option line next to your job queue:

   ➤ Type 5 and press Enter.

2. On the Work with Job Queue display, you should see the two jobs you submitted.

Hold a Job

1. On the option line next to job *xxx*JOB1 (where *xxx* is your initials):

   ➤ Type 3 and press Enter.

2. Refresh the display:

   ➤ Press F5.

Notice that the status of *xxx*JOB1 changes to HLD and it gets bumped below *xxx*JOB2 in the queue. An example of this action is shown in Figure 3.18. All jobs with a status of RLS (released and ready to go) are processed before held jobs.

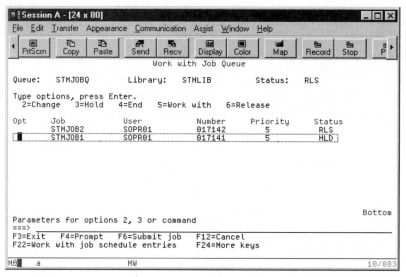

Figure 3.18: An example of changing a job's status to HLD.

Move a Job to a Different Job Queue

1. On the option line next to job *xxx*JOB1 (where *xxx* is your initials):

    ➤ Type 2 and press Enter.

2. On the Change Job (CHGJOB) display, do the following:

    a) Press F10 to see additional parameters.

    b) Type QBATCH for the job queue and QGPL for the library.

    c) Press Enter.

3. On the Work with Job Queue display, the status of job *xxx*JOB1 changes to *CHG. Refresh the display:

    ➤ Press F5.

    What happens? _____

End a Job

1. On the option line next to job *xxx*JOB2 (where *xxx* is your initials):

    ➤ Type 4 and press Enter.

2. On the Confirm End of Job display:

    ➤ Press Enter.

    You are predictably made aware of what you just did. An example of the message that appears as a result of this action is shown in Figure 3.19.

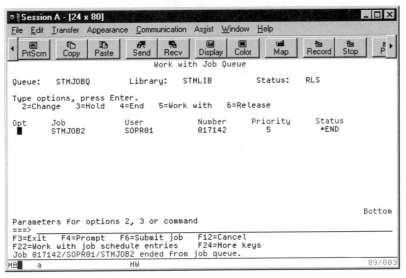

Figure 3.19: An Ending a Job message.

3. Refresh the display:

    ➤ Press F5.

    What happens? _____

4. Return to the Command Entry display:

    ➤ Press F3.

Search for Jobs by Your User Name

1. On the Command Entry display:

    ➤ Enter WRKUSRJOB.

    When you enter this command, only those jobs initiated by your user profile are displayed. What menu can you use to work with jobs?

    _____

2. On the Work with User Jobs display, find the job you held in the task above. Page down if you don't see your job on the first page.

    Hint: Look at the Status column.

An example of a Held job is shown in Figure 3.20.

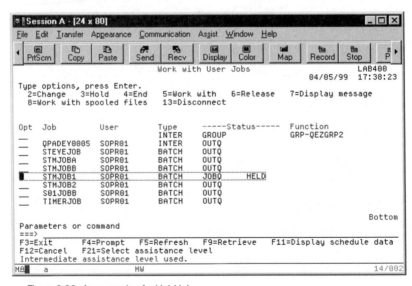

Figure 3.20: An example of a Held job.

Release a Job and Determine If It Completed

1. On the option line next to your held job:

    ➤ Type 6 and press Enter.

    Notice that the status of *xxx*JOB1 changes to RLS, meaning the job is re-
    leased and ready to be processed in the subsystem, which is QBATCH in
    this case.

2. Refresh the display:

    ➤ Press F5.

    What happens? _____

    You might be asking yourself, "Well, I released the job, how do I know
    if it ran?" Good question! Let's check subsystem QBATCH to see if your
    job is out there.

3. On the command line:

    ➤ Enter WRKSBS.

4. On the Work with Subsystems display, on the option line next to
    QBATCH:

    ➤ Type 8 and press Enter.

    On the Work with Subsystem Jobs display, if the job you released is not
    listed, it means it has completed. There may not be any jobs listed.

    If the job you released is listed under other jobs, it means the job is wait-
    ing for the jobs ahead of it to complete. Continue to press F5 (Refresh)
    until your job disappears from the list, meaning it has been processed.

    If your job is listed along with various other jobs, and the list doesn't
    seem to be changing, it may mean that there are some long jobs being
    processed, or the QBATCH queue may be held. If the queue is held, see
    your system administrator.

Let's say your job is complete, and since you know the job you submitted was a message to yourself, go find your message.

5. On the command line:

➤ Enter DSPMSG.

The Display Messages display appears, as shown in Figure 3.21. Voilà! You should now see the message you included within a submitted job in the first part of this exercise.

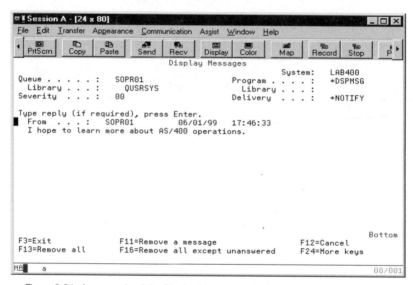

Figure 3.21: An example of the Display Messages display.

6. Return to the Command Entry display:

➤ Press F3 repeatedly.

Display Signed-On Users

1. On the Command Entry display:

➤ Enter go MANAGESYS.

2. On the Manage Your System, Users, and Devices menu:

   ➤ Select 12 and press Enter.

   The Work with User Jobs display appears.

3. Change the assistance level of this display to basic:

   ➤ Press F21, type 1 (Basic), and press Enter.

   The Work with Signed-On Users display appears. You see all users currently signed on to the system and what they're doing.

   Tip: On keyboards with one row of function keys, F21 is the same as pressing Shift and F9. Hold down the Shift key and press F9.

Work with Signed-On Users

1. Find a specific user. In the *Find user* field:

   ➤ Type the first few characters of their user ID and press Enter.

   Tip: You can type *TOP to go to the beginning of the list and *BOT to go to the end of the list.
   ---

2. Find a description of a user. On the option line next to that user:

   ➤ Type 5 and press Enter.

3. Return to the Work with Signed-On Users display:

   ➤ Press Enter.

4. Display descriptions of users:

   a) Press F11.

   b) In the Display Additional Information window, type 3 (User descriptions) and press Enter.

   What happens? _____

5. Display signed-off users with printer output waiting to print:

   a) Press F24 to see other function keys.

   b) Press F14.

   c) In the Select Other Users and Display Stations window, tab to the *Include signed-off users with printer output waiting to print* field.

   d) Type Y and press Enter.

6. Display activities of users again:

   a) Press F11.

   b) In the Display Additional Information window, type 1 (Activities) and press Enter.

   You can easily distinguish between those users who are actively signed on and those who are signed off with print jobs pending.

7. Send a message to a user. On the option line next to that user:

   ➢ Type 3 and press Enter.

8. On the Send a Message display:

   a) In the *Message needs reply* field, type *Y*.

   b) In the *Message text* area, tell the user you want to buy them lunch and ask the user for a time and favorite restaurant.

   c) In the *Send to* field, add names of any other users you wish to ask to lunch.

   d) Press F10 to send the message.

Since you kept the default of *Y* for the *Interrupt user* field, this message automatically pops up on their display station, interrupting their current activity if they're signed on. (You will learn more about AS/400 messaging in chapter 4.)

9. Sign yourself off. On the option line next to your user ID:

    ➤ Type 4 and press Enter.

    What happens? _____

MANAGING MESSAGES

This chapter includes sections on the following topics:

- Identifying characteristics of messages and message queues

- Sending messages

- Displaying messages

- Removing messages

- Handling system and error messages

- Displaying message queue attributes

- Changing message queues

IDENTIFYING CHARACTERISTICS OF MESSAGES AND MESSAGE QUEUES

Messages provide the means of communication between the system and its users. When you ask the system to do something, the system might respond with messages indicating the status of your request. You can also communicate with other users of the system through messages that are sent via the system. In addition, each application program (such as RPG) can have a set of messages to communicate with the user.

Message Sources

There are three different sources for messages on the AS/400:

- System—The system generates messages, such as when you attempt to perform operations that cannot be performed.

- Application—Applications produce messages that are specifically concerned with the application program.

- User—Any message that comes from another user of the system, including the system operator, is a user message.

You can think of messages as mail sent from one point in the AS/400 to another.

Message Types

Two common types of messages are sent on the AS/400: *informational* and *inquiry*. Informational messages don't require a reply from the receiver. For example, last night, before you left work, you sent a big job to the printer. This morning when you signed on to the system, you were notified that your job had been printed. You received this message:

```
Job Inventory List Completed.
```

As the system operator, you often send informational messages to warn users of system shutdown. For example, when you need to load and apply new PTFs from

IBM, you must shut down the system. Therefore, you need to notify users what you are about to do so that they can sign off.

Inquiry messages request a reply. For example, the system operator might receive the following message from the system:

```
System cannot call controller Q1PCTL. No lines available. (C R)
Reply . . .
```

In this case, you are prompted to select from the options provided (C R). System messages are discussed in detail later in this chapter.

Messages are sent to either the system operator message queue (QSYSOPR), a user message queue, or the workstation message queue. Also, users may send you messages to your own user message queue.

Message Queues

A message queue is similar to a mailbox for messages; it receives and holds messages for you that you display when you want. Message queues are assigned to users or workstations. It is important to think about where you are assigning messages and how these assignments differ.

Each user has a message queue with the same name as the user profile name (or user ID). With user message queues, you can deliver a message to any user without needing to know where they are working. When a user signs on to the system for the first time, the system automatically creates a user message queue. A system operator who uses the user profile QSYSOPR has a message queue named QSYSOPR. Printer messages are sent to the QSYSOPR message queue by default. Moreover, the QBATCH subsystem usually sends all system operator messages to this message queue. When the system is configured for the first time, the system operator queue is created.

Each workstation has a message queue with the same name as the workstation device name. A workstation device name is shown on the sign-on screen in Figure 4.1. In this example, QPADEV0003 is the name of the workstation. This is the name you would use for the message queue in order to send a message to this workstation. You can send a message to any workstation regardless of who is working on it. When a workstation is connected to the system for the first time, the system automatically creates a workstation message queue.

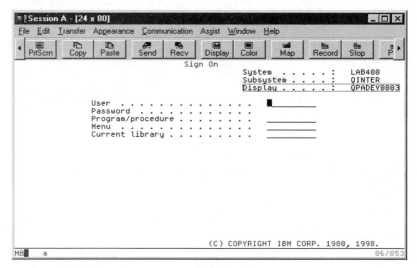

Figure 4.1: A sign-on screen with a workstation device name.

Keep in mind the following tips when working with message queues:

- A message-waiting status indicator (such as the code *MW*) appears at the bottom of the display station when a new message appears in a message queue. If the display station is equipped for sound, a short alarm might sound.

- The message-waiting status indicator is turned off after you have viewed the message queue.

- When you display messages for your workstation, you see the workstation message queue only if it contains messages.

- The user message queue is displayed whether or not it contains messages.

- Once you review your messages, like incoming mail, you can decide to keep or discard them.

- Messages remain in a message queue until someone deletes them; since messages take up space on the system, it is important to clean up message queues periodically. Remove messages of limited value as you encounter them.

- During an interactive session, messages sent from other users and messages sent by the system are usually placed in the interactive user's message queue.

See the topics "Display Message Queue Attributes" and "Changing Message Queues" for more details about message queue characteristics.

SENDING MESSAGES

You can send messages to users and workstations. To send messages, do one of the following:

- Follow a menu path:

    1. On the AS/400 Main menu (MAIN), type 3, General system tasks, and press Enter.

    2. On the General System Tasks menu (SYSTEM), type 4, Messages, and press Enter.

    3. On the Messages menu (MESSAGE), type 1, Send a message, and press Enter.

    > *Hint:* Take a fast path to the MESSAGE menu by entering the command GO MESSAGE.

- Interrupt your current job; start an alternative interactive session:

    1. If you're using a non-programmable terminal, press and hold the Shift or Alt key (depending on the keyboard), and then press the

System Request (Sys Req or Sys Rq) key. An entry line appears at the bottom of the display. If you're using a PC with 5250 display session emulation, as found in Client Access/400, you might need to use an alternative method to access the system request line. In Client Access/400, for example, right-click the mouse to display a keypad and click the SysRq button.

2. Press Enter on the system request entry line to display the System Request menu.

3. Type 5, Send a message, and press Enter.

> **Tip:** You do not need to display the System Request menu. You can enter the option number for the task you want to perform directly on the system request entry line and press Enter. To interrupt your current job to send a message, for example, just type 5 on the line and press Enter.

- Type the SNDMSG command and press F4. The Send Message (SNDMSG) display appears, as shown in Figure 4.2.

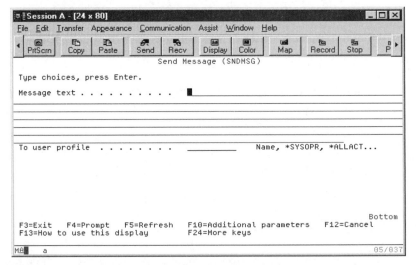

Figure 4.2: An example of the Send Message (SNDMSG) display.

Sending Informational Messages to Users

To send an informational message to a user using the Send Message display, you would simply type the message, specify the user who should receive the message, and press Enter.

Tip: To send a message to all signed-on users, type *ALLACT in the *To user profile* field.

Sending Informational Messages to Workstations

To send an informational (or non-break) message to a workstation (or display station), you need to first press F10 to see the additional parameters on the Send Message display. Then, for the *To message queue* parameter, you must specify the name of the workstation device where you want to send the message. Figure 4.3 shows an example of preparing to send a message to a workstation message queue.

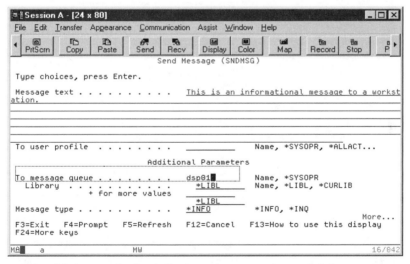

Figure 4.3: An example of preparing to send a message to a workstation message queue.

You can specify the name of any message queue to send a message to. However, the *To user profile* and *To message queue* parameters are mutually exclusive. Only one of these parameters can be used per message.

> **Note:** When sending an informational message, you can send to a
> maximum of 50 message queues at a time.

Sending Inquiry Messages

To send an inquiry message, you need to first press F10 to see the additional parameters on the Send Message display. Then, for the *Message type* parameter, you must specify *INQ. Figure 4.4 shows an example of preparing to send an inquiry message. Notice that the default value for sending a message is *INFO (Informational).

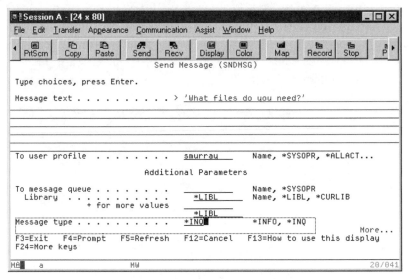

Figure 4.4: An example of preparing to send an inquiry message.

> **Note:** When sending an inquiry message, you can send to only one user
> or workstation at a time. By default, the reply comes back to the message
> queue of the workstation sending the message.

Sending Break Messages to Workstations

To send a break (immediate) message to a workstation or multiple workstations, type the command SNDBRKMSG and press F4. The Send Break Message display appears. An example of a break message about to be sent to all workstations is shown in Figure 4.5.

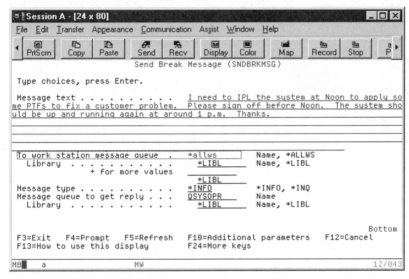

Figure 4.5: An example of a break message about to be sent to all workstations.

A break message appears on a workstation screen as soon as it is received. It does not get stored in a message queue. Because break messages are immediately displayed, they can only be sent to workstation message queues. Also, even though both informational and inquiry messages are allowed, inquiry messages cannot be sent to multiple workstations.

As a system operator, you often send break messages. The example in Figure 4.5 is a typical situation in which you would want to send a break message. When you need the immediate attention of users to inform them of critical system events (such as system shut down), and have a specific request for them (such as sign off), send a break message.

Sending Messages Using an Alternative Display

From time to time, you might come across a different-looking display than the ones discussed so far for sending messages. For example, consider the Send a Message display shown in Figure 4.6.

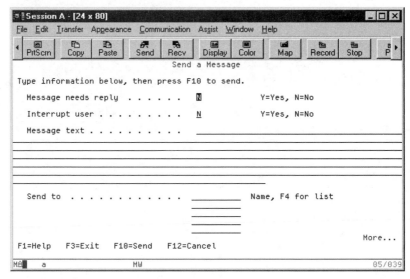

Figure 4.6: The Send a Message display.

This display does not allow you to send messages to workstation message queues, but it simplifies the process of sending messages to users. You can send both non-break (Interrupt user = N) and break (Interrupt user = Y) messages to users from this one display. You can access this display in one of two ways:

- From the AS/400 Operational Assistant (ASSIST) menu, select 4, Send messages.

- From the Work with Signed-On Users display, select 3, Send message.

The Send a Message display uses the basic assistance level, whereas the Send Message (SNDMSG) and Send Break Message (SNDBRKMSG) displays use the intermediate assistance level. (See chapter 1 for details about choosing assistance levels.)

DISPLAYING MESSAGES

You can display messages in user and workstation message queues. Messages can be displayed using either the basic or intermediate assistance level. To display messages, do one of the following:

- Follow a menu path:

    1. On the AS/400 Main Menu (MAIN), type 3, General system tasks, and press Enter.

    2. On the General System Tasks (SYSTEM) menu, type 4, Messages, and press Enter.

    3. On the Messages (MESSAGE) menu, type 3, Display messages, and press Enter.

- Interrupt your current job; start an alternative interactive session:

    1. If you're using a non-programmable terminal, press and hold the Shift or Alt key (depending on the keyboard), and then press the System Request (Sys Req or Sys Rq) key. An entry line appears at the bottom of the display. If you're using a PC with 5250 display session emulation, as found in Client Access/400, you might need to use an alternative method to access the system request line. In Client Access/400, for example, right-click the mouse to display a keypad and click the SysRq button.

    2. Type 4 on the system-request entry line and press Enter. Option 4 on the System Request Menu allows you to display your messages.

- Type DSPMSG and press F4. The Display Messages (DSPMSG) prompt
  screen appears, as shown in Figure 4.7.

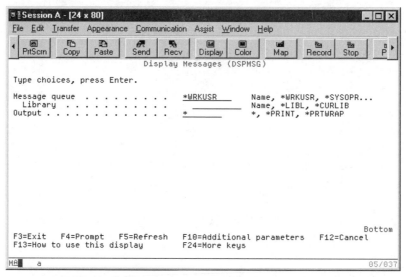

Figure 4.7: The Display Messages (DSPMSG) prompt screen.

The default value *WRKUSR for the Message queue parameter means that messages are shown from your workstation's message queue if there are any messages on it. Therefore, if you accept the default values and press Enter, your
workstation message queue display is shown, as long as you have messages. Figure 4.8 is an example of messages in a workstation message queue.

When you press Enter on that display, messages are shown from your (user profile) message queue. If there are no messages on the workstation's message
queue, only the messages from the user profile message queue are shown. Figure
4.9 is an example of messages in a user message queue.

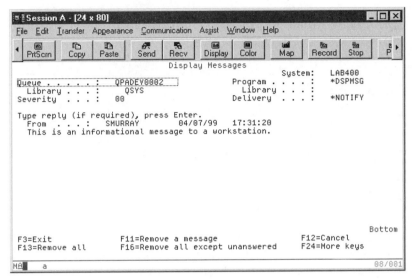

Figure 4.8: An example of messages in a workstation message queue.

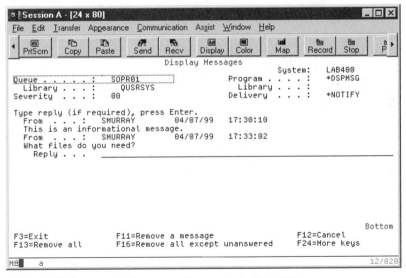

Figure 4.9: An example of messages in a user message queue.

> **Tip:** To directly access your workstation or user message queue, just type either DSPMSG or WRKMSG and press Enter.

Replying to Inquiry Messages

All inquiry messages, including break messages that interrupt a user, provide a reply line after the message. Just type your reply on this line and press Enter. The answer is sent back to the source of the message. You can always reply at a later time.

Displaying Messages
Using Basic and Intermediate Assistance Levels

The previous two examples used the intermediate assistance level for displaying messages. However, you can choose to use a basic assistance level for this display. To change from intermediate to basic assistance level, follow these steps:

1. Press F24 to see more function keys.

2. Press F21 to select the assistance level. The Select Assistance Level window appears, as shown in Figure 4.10.

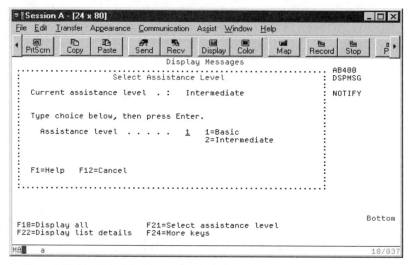

Figure 4.10: The Select Assistance Level window.

3. Select 1 (Basic), as shown in Figure 4.10, and press Enter. The Work with Messages display appears, as in Figure 4.11.

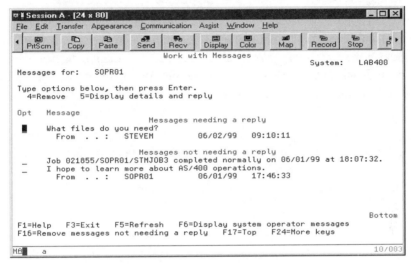

Figure 4.11: An example of the Work with Messages display.

The Work with Messages (basic) display shows all user and workstation messages on the same display, whereas the Display Messages (intermediate) display separates user and workstation messages on different displays. Using the Work with Messages display, you must take some extra steps to determine which messages have been sent to the user message queue, and which have been sent to the workstation message queue. To make these determinations, follow these steps:

1. Type 5 (Display details and reply) next to the message and press Enter.

2. On the Additional Message Information display, press F9 (Display message details). On the Display Message Details display, the *To message queue* parameter shows the name of the workstation or user message queue where the message has been sent.

The Work with Messages display categorizes inquiry and informational messages, with inquiry messages always listed first. This is helpful if there are several messages listed, and you want to quickly find those you need to answer. (See the next topic for a comparison of the Work with Messages and Display Messages displays when viewing the QSYSOPR message queue.)

To reply to a message using the Work with Messages display, type 5 (Display details and reply) next to the inquiry message, and press Enter. A reply line is then provided at the bottom of the Additional Message Information display, which gives you more detailed information about a message. Among the information shown is the date and time sent, the message text, and a cause and recovery if applicable.

In general, as with all displays that offer a choice of assistance level (look for F21), the level is set for that display once you change it. When you exit that display, or sign on again, your assistance level remains the same. Therefore, you can use the basic assistance level for some displays and the intermediate assistance level for other displays.

> **Tip:** Select the assistance level with which you feel most comfortable working and which allows you to get your work done efficiently. However, you will find that the intermediate assistance level gives you more flexibility in working with the AS/400, especially when managing spooled files and devices.

Displaying System Operator Messages

You can work with system operator messages exactly as you would any other messages. When signing on to the system, the message queue defined in your user profile is put into the delivery mode specified in your user profile. The system operator using the user profile QSYSOPR is assigned the message queue QSYSOPR, unless it has been changed. If you do not sign on as QSYSOPR, you can still display messages in the QSYSOPR message queue by doing one of the following:

- Press F6 (Display system operator messages) on the Work with Messages display using basic assistance level.

- Type DSPMSG QSYSOPR or WRKMSG QSYSOPR on any command line. You can optionally specify the ASTLVL keyword with a value of *BASIC or *INTERMED.

- Select 3 (Display system operator messages) on the General System Tasks (SYSTEM) menu.

- Select 4 (Display system operator messages) on the Messages (MESSAGE) menu.

- Select 6 (Display system operator messages) on the System Request menu.

- Select other menus from which you can display system operator messages, such as the TECHHELP and MANAGESYS menus.

Note: As described in the topic "Sending Messages" earlier in this chapter, a system request interrupts your current job to start an alternative interactive session.

For comparison purposes, Figure 4.12 shows the Display Messages display (intermediate assistance level) with system operator messages, while Figure 4.13 shows the Work with Messages display (basic assistance level) with system operator messages.

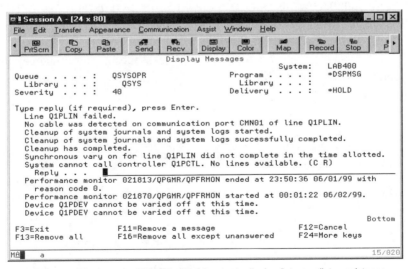

Figure 4.12: An example of the Display Messages display (intermediate assistance level) with system operator messages.

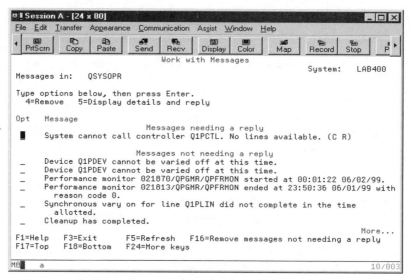

Figure 4.13: An example of the Work with Messages display (basic assistance level) with system operator messages.

The system operator message queue typically contains several system messages, and of those, inquiry messages are common. For this purpose, the Work with Messages display might be more efficient than having to "surf" the Display Messages display to find messages that need a reply. However, the advantage with the Display Messages display is that it lists the messages in chronological order, which is more helpful for problem solving. Prior messages might give more information about which system event triggered a recent message.

REMOVING MESSAGES

It is important to remove messages from user and workstation message queues for these reasons:

- Messages sent to a queue remain there until they are removed.

- Messages remaining in a queue take up disk space on the AS/400.

Leaving messages in your message queue is a sensible thing to do because messages provide information about past activity. However, as messages accumulate in a message queue, they occupy increasing amounts of system storage that could be used for other purposes. Remove messages of limited value when you first encounter them. You can choose to remove individual messages, all messages in a queue, or all messages that do not need a reply.

Keep in mind that once you remove a message from your message queue, you cannot recover it. Also, when you remove an unanswered inquiry message, a default reply is sent by the operating system.

> **Caution:** Be careful about deleting messages from the QSYSOPR message queue, even messages that don't require a reply. QSYSOPR messages provide an audit trail for system activity. The information in the messages helps you, as the system operator, to review actions taken earlier that might have caused the current problem.

Removing Individual Messages

To remove a single message using the intermediate assistance level (Display Messages display), follow these steps:

1. Position the cursor anywhere on the message you want to delete.
2. Press F11 (Remove a message).

To remove a single message using the basic assistance level (Work with Messages display), follow these steps:

1. On the option line next to the message you want to delete, type 4 (Remove).
2. Press Enter.
3. On the Confirm Remove of Messages display, press Enter.

Removing All Messages in a Queue

To remove all messages at once, using the intermediate assistance level, press F13 (Remove all). Cursor position has no bearing on this function; F13 empties the entire message queue.

At the basic assistance level, type 4 next to each message and press Enter. This could be a tedious task; therefore, it would be easier to use the intermediate display and just press F13.

Removing All Messages Not Needing a Reply

To remove all messages except those that haven't been answered, press F16. This works like F13, except any unanswered inquiry or sender copy messages in the message queue are saved. All other messages are deleted, just as if you had pressed F13. The use of F16 is available at both the basic and intermediate assistance levels.

HANDLING SYSTEM AND ERROR MESSAGES

You are sure to receive a variety of system messages that indicate conditions ranging from simple typing errors to problems with system devices or programs. You might receive any one of the following:

- An error message on your current display.

- A message regarding a system problem that is sent to the system operator message queue.

- A message regarding a system problem that is sent to the message queue specified in a device description.

- A message regarding a potentially severe system condition that is sent to the system operator message queue and other message queues specified by the users.

One of the first things you want to do when you encounter a system or error message that you don't understand is to get more information about it.

Getting Help on a Message

Let's say you're looking at system operator messages in the QSYSOPR message queue, and you come across a strange message requesting a reply, such as this one:

```
System cannot call controller Q1PCTL. No lines available. (C R)
Reply . . .
```

To obtain additional information about this message (if you are displaying messages at the intermediate assistance level), complete the following steps:

1. Place the cursor anywhere on the message.

2. Press F1 (Help).

An Additional Message Information display similar to Figure 4.14 is shown, giving you more information about the message.

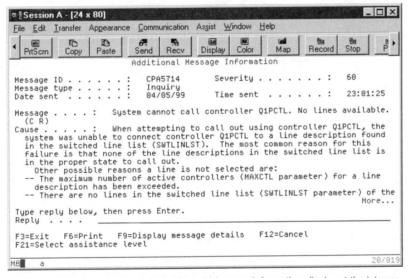

Figure 4.14: An example of the Additional Message Information display at the intermediate assistance level.

Usually, one of the causes listed helps you identify the problem. However, be aware that the suggested solutions might not correct the problem. The listed causes are only probable reasons why the error is getting triggered.

Message Identifiers

Notice the words "Message ID" in the upper-left corner of Figure 4.14. Message identifiers or message IDs are used to distinguish one system message from another in the message file. The first three letters indicate the message category. Message categories and their explanations are shown in Table 4.1.

Table 4.1: Message categories and explanations.

Category	Explanation
CPA – CPZ	Messages from the operating system
CBE – CBX	COBOL messages
CSC	COBOL language syntax checker
LBE – LSC	COBOL messages
MCH	Licensed Internal Code messages
QRG	RPG language messages
RPG – RXT	RPG language messages
SBX – SSC	COBOL messages
SQL	Structured Query Language (SQL) messages

Tip: You can display or print information about the messages in a message file. The system message file is QCPFMSG. The descriptions of specific messages, or a range of messages in one message file, can be specified by their identifiers. Also, all messages in one message file can be specified. Use the Display Message Description (DSPMSGD) command. For example, to display all message descriptions in QCPFMSG, enter the command DSPMSGD *ALL.

To work with all message descriptions in QCPFMSG, enter the command WRKMSGD.

Severity Codes

Notice the severity code in the upper-right corner of Figure 4.14. Message severity codes are associated with different system message types. Codes are made up of two digits, ranging from 00 to 99. The higher the value, the more severe the condition. To get a list of the message types associated with severity codes, follow these steps:

1. Place the cursor on the Severity field.

2. Press F1 (Help).

3. Press Enter on the hypertext phrase "Message severity codes."

The range of severity codes is generally categorized into these three severity levels:

- Information messages.

- Warning messages.

- Severe or termination messages.

Other Types of Error Messages

You can also get help on an error message that appears at the bottom of a menu or other display, or on a program error message. Position your cursor on the message and press F1. The Additional Message Information display appears in all cases. Figure 4.15 is an example of an application or program error message.

> **Note:** If you press Enter on a reply message without typing a reply, the system uses a default reply. In the error shown in Figure 4.15, C (to cancel or stop the program) is the default entry.

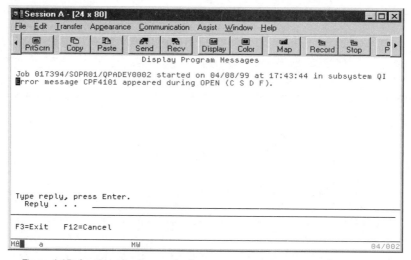

Figure 4.15: An example of an application or program error message.

Replying to System and Error Messages

Message reply choices are typically one-character codes. The choices are displayed within parentheses at the end of the message and explained in the recovery section on the Additional Message Information display.

After paging through the cause and recovery for a message and determining what action to take, type your reply on the line provided, and press Enter.

Printing Messages

To print a single message, press F6 (Print) on the Additional Message Information display. This prints all the information about the message. The output is sent to a spooled file, and the output can be viewed or printed from the output queue.

Occasionally, a problem seems to grow as efforts are made to correct it. When problem resolution becomes lengthy, printing out the sequence of error messages is one of the best things you can do to help resolve it. Rather than print each individual message, you can easily print the entire message queue. For example, to print all messages in the QSYSOPR message queue, enter this command:

```
DSPMSG MSGQ(*SYSOPR) OUTPUT(*PRINT)
```

To access the spooled file containing the messages, enter this command:

```
WRKSPLF
```

On the Work with All Spooled Files display, find the spooled file at the end of the list. You can then display the file or send it to your printer of choice. (See chapter 5 for details about printing and working with printer output, also known as spooled files.)

DISPLAYING MESSAGE QUEUE ATTRIBUTES

When you display messages at the intermediate assistance level, you see certain attributes of the message queue at the top of the Display Messages display. These attributes include the message queue name, severity level, and delivery mode. Regardless of whether you are displaying messages at the basic or intermediate assistance level, F22 (Display list details) is available. This function key shows all attributes of the message queue. Pressing F22 while displaying messages in your message queue shows a display similar to that in Figure 4.16. Similarly, if you are displaying messages in your workstation message queue, F22 shows the attributes of the workstation message queue.

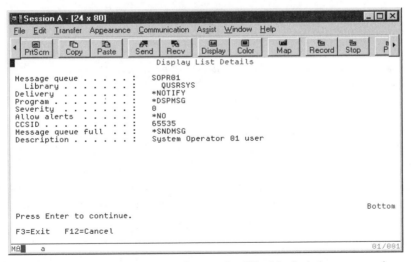

Figure 4.16: An example of display after pressing F22 while displaying messages in your message queue.

As always, you can press F1 to find out more information about a field. The Delivery, Program, and Severity fields are of particular interest, and are discussed next.

Delivery

Delivery refers to the method by which messages are transferred. As the operator, you will frequently need to change the delivery mode. Common delivery values are as follows:

- *NOTIFY—When you receive a message, your work is not interrupted. You are notified that a message has arrived by the workstation message waiting light and an alarm (if your workstation has one) that sounds. You can use either the Display Messages (DSPMSG) command or Work with Messages (WRKMSG) command to see the message.

- *BREAK—When you receive a message, your work is interrupted, and a separate message display containing the message is shown. This value can be overridden if a program has been specified to handle the message. For example, the *BREAK value can be used when you, as the system operator, need to shut down the system. The "shut down" message interrupts all interactive users and allows them time to close their jobs and sign off.

- *HOLD—You are not notified when a new message arrives. The message queue retains the messages until you request them using the Display Messages (DSPMSG) or Work with Messages (WRKMSG) command. This is the default Delivery value for the QSYSOPR message queue.

Program

Program is more appropriately called the "break-message handling program." This field names a program that the system calls if a message of sufficient severity arrives in a message queue that is in *BREAK (interrupt) mode. The program may activate an error-correction sequence, stop the job stream, or call a message program. The programmer usually defines the severity value. The default value is *DSPMSG, to use the system-supplied message display program.

Severity

You can use the severity code in *BREAK mode to filter messages that interrupt the user's work. For example, if the message severity code is 40 (which is the default severity code for the QSYSOPR message queue), the system interrupts the user's work only if messages with codes of 40 or greater are detected. Any message with a severity code of less than 40 is sent to the message queue, and the message waiting symbol is turned on, assuming that the Program value is *DSPMSG.

In *NOTIFY mode, if the message severity code is 40, the system notifies the user of any messages that have a severity code of 40 or greater. The message waiting symbol appears, and an alarm is sounded (if the display station has one). Any message with a severity code of less than 40 is sent to the message queue, but the message waiting indicator does not appear. The message is saved until the user reads and deletes it. (See the topic "Handling System and Error Messages" for more information about the severity codes associated with certain message types.)

CHANGING MESSAGE QUEUES

You can change the way a message queue notifies you of messages, change the message queue severity level, change the break-handling program, and more. To change message queue attributes, type the command CHGMSGQ and press F4. The Change Message Queue (CHGMSGQ) prompt display appears, as shown in Figure 4.17.

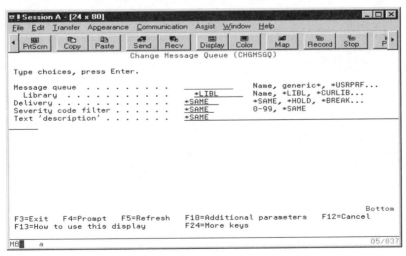

Figure 4.17: An example of the Change Message Queue (CHGMSGQ) prompt display.

Specify the name of your message queue, which is typically the same name as your user profile. Any changes you make to a message queue are reflected the next time that a message is delivered. For example, changing Delivery from *NOTIFY to *BREAK for your message queue forces your work to be interrupted every time a message is sent to you. Press F10 to see additional parameters for this display. (See the topic "Displaying Message Queue Attributes" for details about parameters of particular interest on this display.)

Tip: To work with all workstation and user message queues, just type the command WRKMSGQ *ALL. The Work with Message Queues display shown in Figure 4.18 allows you to create, change, delete, and clear message queues. Be aware that several restrictions apply to the options available on the Work with Message Queues display. For example, you need certain authorities to clear (remove) messages in a message queue.

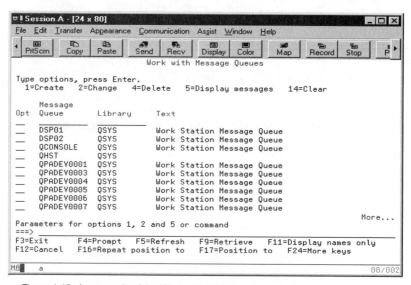

Figure 4.18: An example of the Work with Message Queues display.

EXERCISE 4: WORKING WITH USER AND SYSTEM MESSAGES

Note: Make sure your message delivery value is set to *NOTIFY for this exercise. To check, just enter DSPMSG and look for the Delivery value in the upper part of the display. To change this value if it isn't *NOTIFY, see the previous topic, "Changing Message Queues."

Procedures

1. Send a message to yourself.

2. Display your messages and note the delivery mode.

3. Change your message queue to use *BREAK delivery.

4. Send another message to yourself.

5. Change your message queue to use *NOTIFY delivery.

6. Send a break message to your workstation message queue.

7. Send an inquiry message to the QSYSOPR message queue.

8. Display system operator messages and send a reply.

9. Remove all messages in your workstation and user message queues.

10. Get help on a system inquiry message in the QSYSOPR message queue.

Send a Message to Yourself

1. Sign on with a user ID that has system operator authorities. From the Sign-On screen:

    a) Write down your workstation (display station) device name. You will need this when sending a break message later in this exercise.

    _____

    b) Specify QCMD as the program to display the Command Entry display after you sign on.

2. On the Command Entry display:

    ➤ Type SNDMSG and press F4.

3. On the Send Message (SNDMSG) display:

    a) Type your message, such as "This is an informational message."

    b) Type your user ID in the *To user profile* field.

    c) Press Enter.

Were you notified that you have new messages? How can you tell?

_____

Display Your Messages and Note the Delivery Mode

1. On the Command Entry display:

    ➤ Enter DSPMSG.

What is the name of your user message queue?

_____

What is the delivery mode of your messages? What does it mean?

Note: Do not delete this message.

---

2. Return to the Command Entry display:

➤ Press F3.

Change Your Message Queue to Use *BREAK Delivery

1. On the Command Entry display:

➤ Type CHGMSGQ *<your user ID>* and press F4.

2. On the Change Message Queue (CHGMSGQ) display, shown in Figure 4.19:

a) Type *BREAK in the *Delivery* field.

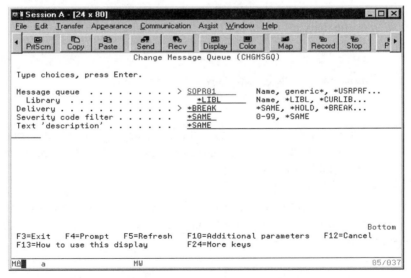

Figure 4.19: An example of the Change Message Queue (CHGMSGQ) display.

b) Press Enter.

If you have any messages in your message queue, they will appear. If that happens, just press Enter to return to the Command Entry display.

Send Another Message to Yourself

1. On the Command Entry display:

   a) Put your cursor on the SNDMSG command string and press F9 to bring it to the command line, for example:

   ```
   SNDMSG MSG('This is an informational message.') TOUSR(SOPRO1)
   ```

   b) Change the message (MSG) text if you wish, or just leave it.

   c) Press Enter.

   What happened?

   _____

   Does the delivery mode indicate *BREAK on the Display Messages display? _____

2. Remove the message. On the Display Messages display:

   ➢ Press F11.

   You are returned to the Command Entry display. If you leave your message queue in *BREAK mode, every message you receive will interrupt your work like the second message did.

Next, you will change your message queue to use *NOTIFY delivery mode once again. Anyone who wants to interrupt you can still do so by sending a break message (SNDBRKMSG).

Change Your Message Queue to Use *NOTIFY Delivery

1. On the Command Entry display:

    a) Press F9 repeatedly to retrieve the previous CHGMSGQ command string, for example:

    ```
    CHGMSGQ MSGQ(SOPRO1) DLVRY(*BREAK)
    ```

    b) Change the string as follows:

    ```
    CHGMSGQ MSGQ(SOPRO1) DLVRY(*NOTIFY)
    ```

    c) Press Enter.

Send a Break Message to Your Workstation Message Queue

Scenario: You're a system operator, and you need to send an urgent message to all workstations telling everyone to sign off at a certain time. Because you're practicing here, and you really don't want to send this message to all workstations, think of yourself as the system operator, but just send the message to your workstation message queue.

1. On the Command Entry display:

    ➤ Type SNDBRKMSG and press F4.

2. On the Send Break Message (SNDBRKMSG) display:

    a) Type a message similar to the following: "Please sign off in 20 minutes. I need to shut down the system to apply some PTFs."

    b) Type your workstation device name in the *To work station message queue* field, as shown in Figure 4.20.

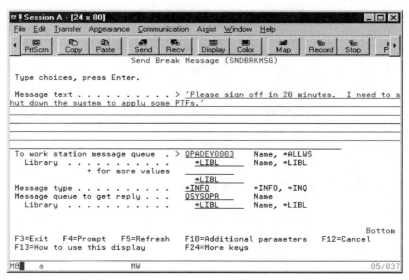

Figure 4.20: An example of the Send Break Message (SNDBRKMSG) display.

c) Press Enter.

You should have received the message. If not, make sure you entered your workstation device name. To get the name of your workstation device, do a System Request and enter 7 on the system request entry line. On the Display Work Station User screen, note your workstation name and re-send the break message using that name.

What is the name of the message queue? _____

Is this a user or workstation message queue? _____

What is the delivery mode of the messages? _____

If the delivery mode is *NOTIFY, then how could you have received a break message? Doesn't the delivery mode of the message queue have to be *BREAK?

_____

Note: Do not delete this message.
---

3. Return to the Command Entry display:

   ➤ Press F3.

Send an Inquiry Message to the QSYSOPR Message Queue

Scenario: You're an AS/400 user in the Payroll department. You're trying to get the checks out, and therefore really can't afford time to be off the system. You decide to prompt the system operator for more information on when the system will be ready again. Pretend you are an AS/400 user now, and send an inquiry message to the system operator.

1. On the Command Entry display:

   ➤ Type SNDMSG and press F4.

2. On the Send Message (SNDMSG) display:

   a) Type a message like, "When can I use the computer again?"

   b) Type *SYSOPR in the *To user profile* field.

   c) Press F10 to display additional parameters.

   d) Type *INQ in the *Message type* field, as shown in Figure 4.21.

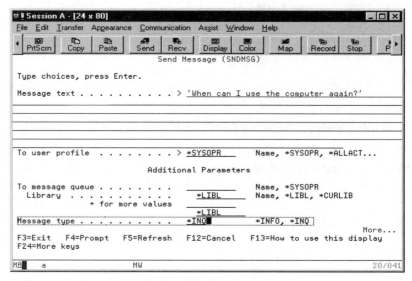

Figure 4.21: An example of the Send Message (SNDMSG) display.

e)   Press Enter.

Write out the entire CL command string (including all keywords and values) that was returned on the Command Entry display:

_____

_____

Display System Operator Messages and Send a Reply

Scenario: You're a system operator, and you decide to display messages in the QSYSOPR message queue. While you're scanning the messages, you notice several inquiry messages sent from users regarding your note to sign off. Find the inquiry message you sent to the QSYSOPR message queue, and reply to the message from the system operator's viewpoint.

1.   On the Command Entry display:

➤ Enter DSPMSG QSYSOPR.

2. Change the assistance level from intermediate to basic:

    ➤ Press F21, type 1 for Basic, and press Enter.

    The Work with Messages display appears, as shown in Figure 4.22.

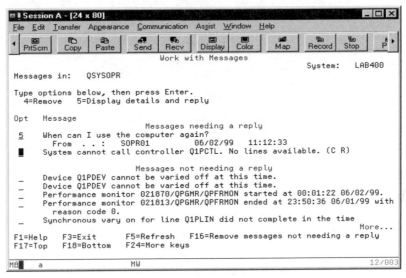

Figure 4.22: An example of the Work with Messages display.

Messages needing a reply are now sorted first. The message you sent is identified by your user profile along with the date and time.

3. Reply to the message. As shown in Figure 4.22, on the option line next to your message:

    a) Type 5 and press Enter.

    b) On the reply line, type a message similar to the following: "The system will be up again in about 1 hour." Figure 4.23 shows an example of replying to the user's message.

Figure 4.23: An example of replying to a message.

c) Press Enter to send the reply.

d) Press Enter to return to the Work with Messages display.

Notice that once you reply to a message using the Work with Messages display, the message is moved to the *Messages not needing a reply* section.

4. Change the assistance level back to intermediate:

    ➣ Press F21, type 2 for Intermediate, and press Enter.

The Display Messages display appears.

5. Return to the Command Entry display:

    ➣ Press F3.

Remove All Messages
in Your Workstation and User Message Queues

1. On the Command Entry display:

   ➤ Enter DSPMSG.

   The messages in your workstation message queue should appear first, and you should see the reply sent from the system operator to your inquiry message.

2. Remove all messages in your workstation message queue:

   ➤ Press F13.

   To delete only those messages that don't require a reply, what function key would you use?

   _____

3. Display the messages in your user message queue. On the Display Messages display showing your workstation messages:

   ➤ Press Enter.

4. Remove all messages in your user message queue:

   ➤ Press F13.

5. Do not exit the Display Messages display.

Get Help on a System Message in the QSYSOPR Message Queue

1. Interrupt your current job to display QSYSOPR messages:

   a) If you're using a non-programmable terminal, press and hold the Shift or Alt key (depending on the keyboard), and then press the System Request (Sys Req or Sys Rq) key. An entry line appears at the bottom of the display. If you're using a PC with 5250 display session emulation, as found in Client Access/400, you might need to use an alternative method to access the system request line. In Client Access/400, for example, right-click the mouse to display a keypad and click the SysRq button.

b) Press Enter on the entry line at the bottom of the display.

c) Type 6 on the System Request menu, shown in Figure 4.24.

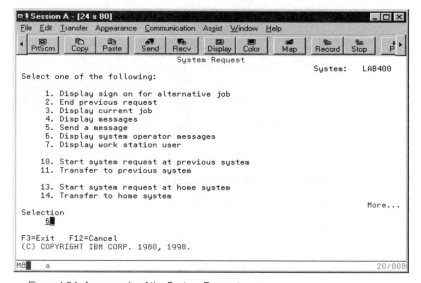

Figure 4.24: An example of the System Request menu.

d) Press Enter.

The system operator messages are listed.

Tip: To quickly display system operator messages, just type 6 on the system request entry line and press Enter. You don't need to display the System Request menu if you know what the menu option number is for the operation you want to do.

What would be a valid reason for using the System Request method to interrupt your job to display QSYSOPR messages versus just entering the DSPMSG QSYSOPR command?

_____

_____

_____

_____

2. Display additional message information about a message you don't understand:

   a) Position the cursor on that message.

   b) Press F1.

3. Return to the Command Entry display:

   ➤ Press F3 repeatedly.

CONTROLLING PRINTER OUTPUT

This chapter includes sections on the following topics:

- Understanding AS/400 printing terms

- Finding printer output

- Managing printer output

- Determining why output is not printing

- Working with local printers

UNDERSTANDING AS/400 PRINTING TERMS

As a system operator, much of your job involves directing and controlling the printing process in a multitasking, multiple-printer environment. Many jobs that run on your AS/400 system create printer output. There are several system components that work together to get output to a printer. Dividing the printing into several different pieces allows you to share printers among multiple users and to take advantage of the many types of printers available for the AS/400.

Spooled Files

AS/400 programs typically do not send data directly to printers. Programs create images of printer output, which are called *spooled files* in AS/400 terminology. With print spooling, multiple users can use the same printer. That is, the system can temporarily stack (or *queue*) several users' print jobs in an output queue where these jobs all wait their turn to print. The spooled file with the highest priority is printed first. When that spooled file finishes, the next priority print job is selected and printed. Job queues process jobs in the same way. By interleaving all the users' print jobs this way, the system ensures that the printer is used to its maximum.

Output Queues

Spooled files are placed on output queues until a printer is available to print them. Like job queues, an *output queue* is a holding area—in this case, of spooled files waiting to print. A single output queue may have spooled files from many different jobs and many different users. In some cases, a single job might place spooled files on more than one output queue.

Printer Writers and Printer Devices

The spooled files on an output queue remain there until a printer writer is started. The *printer writer* is a system program that sends spooled files from an output queue to a physical printer, known as a *printer device*. Normally, you have an output queue and a device description for each printer on your system, and the printer device and output queue have the same name. For example, the PRT01 output queue is associated with the PRT01 printer; likewise, the PRT02 output queue is associated with the PRT02 printer, and so on.

However, you can use the printer writer to assign any output queue to any printer device on the system. For example, the PRT01 output queue could be associated with the PRT02 printer, and the PRT02 output queue could be associated with the PRT01 printer.

Moreover, you can have output queues that aren't assigned to any printer. Spooled files in such an output queue are not printed until you either assign that queue to a printer, or move individual spooled files to a printer associated with an output queue. For example, an output queue may be set aside for all printer output requiring special forms. As the operator, you need to check this queue periodically to decide when to assign reports to a printer and what forms are needed.

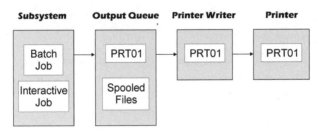

Figure 5.1: Moving a job through an output queue to a printer.

Figure 5.1 shows how a job moves through an output queue to one printer. You can also use multiple printers to print spooled files from the same output queue. Up to ten printer writers can be started per output queue. This allows you to easily balance the printing load among multiple printers. Figure 5.2 shows this multiple-printer approach.

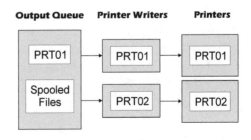

Figure 5.2: Moving a job through an output queue to multiple printers.

With this approach, the AS/400 takes the next available spooled file and prints it on the next available printer. This can be especially helpful if you have several printers in the same room or general vicinity, but not if your printers are on opposite ends of the office building. If your printers are far apart from each other, you would always be guessing about the printer on which the output printed.

Printer Device Files

A job can call any number of programs to run. If your job requires some printing, it needs the printer device file. The *printer device file* contains information such as the printer to be used, output queue, font, and number of lines per inch. Format information is typically stored separately (in the printer device file) from the program that creates the report. This allows you to change certain aspects of a report format before the report is printed, such as the number of copies, pages to print, and what form type to use.

FINDING PRINTER OUTPUT

You can view information about the printer output (spooled files) waiting to print on your system in several different ways. You can view the information sorted by one of these categories:

- User
- Job
- Output queue
- Printer

> **Note:** To view or change printer output created by other users, you need either spool control (*SPLCTL) or job control (*JOBCTL) special authority in your user profile. As the system operator, you should already have either or both of these special authorities. You can easily view your user profile by entering the following command:
>
> ```
> DSPUSRPRF <your user ID>
> ```
>
> It is important to remember that though you may have created the output, the spooled file may actually be listed under some other user if the job that created the spool file ran under another user profile.

Displaying Printer Output for a User

The Work with All Spooled Files display is by far the most powerful and flexible means available to find and manage printer output for a certain user or all users. You can also use this method to work with printer output associated with a particular printer. To find the Work with All Spooled Files display, do one of the following:

- Follow a menu path:

  1. On the AS/400 Main Menu (MAIN), type 3, General system tasks, and press Enter.

  2. On the General System Tasks (SYSTEM) menu, type 8, Device Operations, and press Enter.

  3. On the Device Operations (DEVICE) menu, type 3, Printer, and press Enter.

  4. On the Printer (PRINTER) menu, type 1, Work with spooled output files, and press Enter.

Hint: Take a fast path to the Printer menu by entering the command GO PRINTER.

- Type the WRKSPLF command and press F4.

The Work with Spooled Files (WRKSPLF) entry display appears, as shown in Figure 5.3.

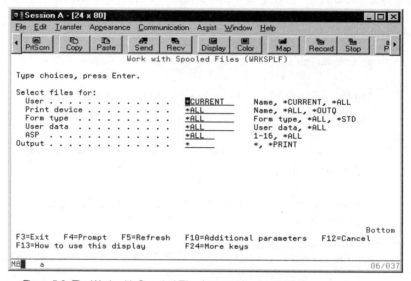

Figure 5.3: The Work with Spooled Files (WRKSPLF) entry display.

Notice the first and second parameters on this display. The *User* parameter defaults to *CURRENT, meaning you see only your spooled files. You can specify a particular user's name as it appears in the user profile. In this case, you see only the spooled files for that user. Alternatively, you can specify *ALL to see the spooled files for every user in the system.

> **Caution:** If there are many spooled files on the system, or during peak usage times, select a user ID instead of typing *ALL for this parameter. Displaying all user spooled files may adversely affect the performance of other jobs.

The *Print device* parameter defaults to *ALL, meaning you see the print output on all printer and user-created output queues on the system. You can specify a particular print device name. In this case, you see only the spooled files waiting to print on that printer. Alternatively, you can specify *OUTQ to see only those spooled files on all output queues not currently assigned to any printer.

Tip: To quickly display your spooled files, type WRKSPLF on a command line and press Enter, or enter WRKSPLF *<user ID>* to display the spooled files for a particular user. This bypasses the display shown in Figure 5.3.

To see if you have any spooled files waiting to print, press Enter on the display shown in Figure 5.3, taking the default entries, or enter WRKSPLF on a command line. The Work with All Spooled Files list display appears. An example of this display is shown in Figure 5.4.

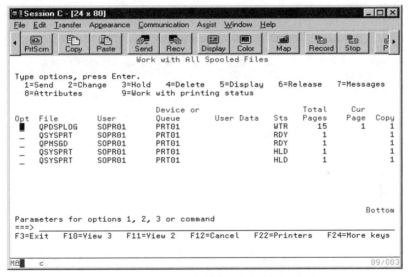

Figure 5.4: An example of the Work with All Spooled Files list display.

Any print jobs for your user profile are listed. The status (Sts) column reveals the condition of the print job. For example, a status of WTR indicates that the file is currently being printed, while other spooled files are ready to print (RDY), or are held (HLD). To learn what a status code means, position your cursor anywhere on the Sts column and press F1 for online help. (See the topic "Managing Printer

Output," later in this chapter, for details about the options available on the Work with All Spooled files display.)

As you might have already guessed, the Work with All Spooled files display is at the intermediate assistance level. To see what this display looks like at the basic assistance level, follow these steps:

1. Press F21 (Select assistance level).

2. In the Select Assistance Level window, type 1 for Basic, and press Enter.

A different screen called Work with Printer Output appears, as shown in Figure 5.5.

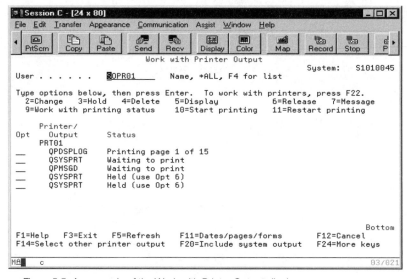

Figure 5.5: An example of the Work with Printer Output display.

Notice the status of each of the print jobs. Instead of just listing a status code, as on the Work with All Spooled Files display (Figure 5.4), this display explicitly shows you what's happening with each print job. In some cases, you are even told what to do, as in the case of held output ("use Opt 6").

Initially, only your own printer output is displayed. To see the printer output for a different user, type the user ID in the User field and press Enter.

> **Tip:** If you do not know the user ID, press F4 (for List) to select a user ID from a list of all users on the system on the Select a User display. You can also use a generic name in the *User* field. For example, if you want to see output for all the user IDs that start with "AR," type AR* in the *User* field. If you want to see the printer output for all users, type *ALL in the *User* field.

The printer output on this display is sorted by printer, with the output assigned to that printer indented under the printer name. Some printer output may have a status of "Not assigned to a printer." This printer output appears last in the list on your display.

There is another view of the Work with Printer Output display that shows when printer output was created, the number of pages in the job, what form types are used, and how many copies to print. To see this view of the display, shown in Figure 5.6, Press F11 (Dates/pages/forms).

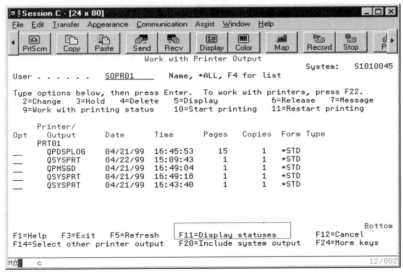

Figure 5.6: An example of a secondary view of the Work with Printer Output display.

Keep in mind that with any basic assistance display, your options are limited. This is certainly true when working with spooled files and print writers. For example, more parameters are available at the intermediate assistance level when changing attributes of spooled files, which is discussed later in the "Managing Printer Output" topic. Therefore, it is recommended that you use the intermediate assistance level.

Displaying Printer Output by Job

To work with all spooled files created by a particular job, use the Work with Job Spooled Files display. To find this display, use the command WRKUSRJOB. The Work with User Jobs display appears, as shown in Figure 5.7. On this display, select 8, Work with spooled files, next to the job that produced the spooled file(s) that needs to be controlled. Now, you see the Work with Job Spooled Files display, as shown in Figure 5.8.

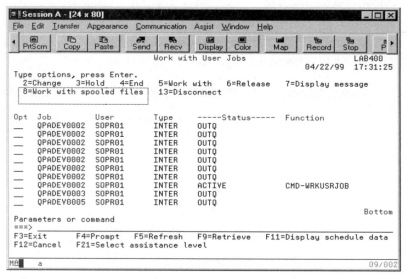

Figure 5.7: An example of the Work with User Jobs display.

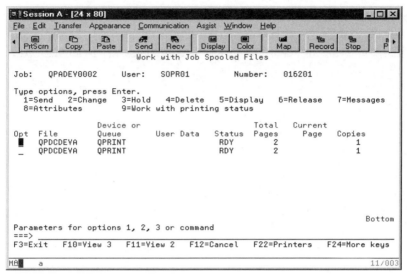

Figure 5.8: An example of the Work with Job Spooled Files display.

From this list display, you can easily change the hold, release, delete, and display attributes for one or more of a job's spooled files. The same options on the Work with All Spooled Files (WRKSPLF) display (Figure 5.4) are available on the Work with Job Spooled Files (WRKUSRJOB, option 8) display.

Displaying Printer Output by Output Queue

You can see how many spooled files are on all output queues, and you can work with spooled files on a particular output queue.

Working with All Output Queues

To display all output queues in all of the libraries to which you are authorized, use this command:

```
WRKOUTQ
```

Figure 5.9 is an example of the Work with All Output Queues display.

```
Session C - [24 x 80]                                        _ □ ✕
File  Edit  Transfer  Appearance  Communication  Assist  Window  Help

  ◄   □       □       □       □       □       □       □       □       □      ◄ ►
    PrtScrn   Copy    Paste    Send    Recv   Display  Color    Map    Record  Stop   P
                         Work with All Output Queues

Type options, press Enter.
   2=Change    3=Hold       4=Delete    5=Work with   6=Release   8=Description
   9=Work with Writers    14=Clear

Opt    Queue        Library      Files   │ Writer    │   Status
  _    QDKT         QGPL             0    │           │   RLS
  _    QPFROUTQ     QGPL             0    │           │   RLS
  _    QPRINT       QGPL             0    │           │   RLS
  _    QPRINTS      QGPL             0    │           │   RLS
  _    QPRINT2      QGPL             0    │           │   RLS
  _    TPIZEL       QGPL            23    │           │   RLS
  _    VERNO        QGPL            57    │           │   RLS
  _    QTY          QTY              0    │           │   RLS
  _    PC2S1        QUSRSYS          0    │           │   RLS
  _    PRTOFFICE    QUSRSYS          0    │ PRTOFFICE │   RLS
  _    PRT01        QUSRSYS          8    │ PRT01     │   RLS
  _    PRT010200    QUSRSYS          2    │ PRT010200 │   RLS
                                                           More...
Command
===>
F3=Exit    F4=Prompt    F5=Refresh    F12=Cancel    F24=More keys

MA█    c                                                      06/002
```

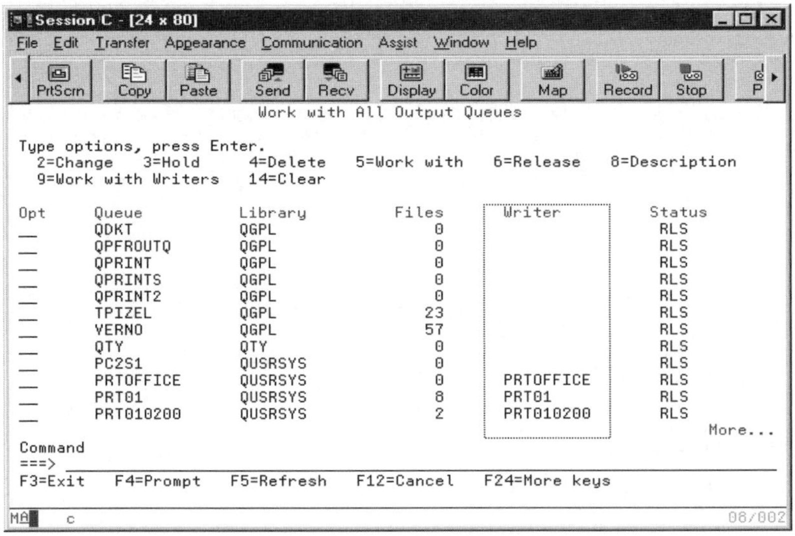

Figure 5.9: An example of the Work with All Output Queues display.

You can perform many of the same functions on output queues as you can on job queues (which are discussed in chapter 3). For example, the options to hold, delete, work with, and release output queues are the same whether you're working with job queues or output queues.

Notice the Writer column. If this field is blank, there is no writer started to this queue, and therefore, no output can be produced. If the writer name has an asterisk (*) in front of it, it means that more than one writer is started to that output queue.

Find the name of the output queue you created in the exercise for chapter 2. You might need to page down. Are there currently any spooled files in your queue? You can tell quickly by looking at the Files column on this display.

The number in the Files column is the number of spooled files currently in the output queue. This number increases as spooled files enter and decreases as spooled files are printed. The numbers on the screen indicate the number of spooled files that are in the queue only at the exact instant the display is requested. Press F5 (Refresh) to determine in real-time how many spooled files are coming in and going out of a queue.

Working with One Output Queue

To work with spooled files on a certain output queue, do one of the following:

- Select option 5 (Work with) for the designated output queue on the Work with All Output Queues display.

- Use the command WRKOUTQ *<output queue name>*, for example, WRKOUTQ PRT01 from the command line.

When you use either method, a display similar to the one in Figure 5.10 appears.

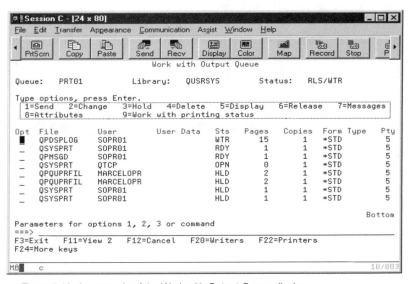

Figure 5.10: An example of the Work with Output Queue display.

The type of information displayed and the options available should look quite familiar by now. In prior examples, you viewed spooled files for only one user and one job, here you see all spooled files on a specific output queue, regardless of which user or job produced the output.

Displaying Printer Output by Printer

Recall that an output queue exists for each printer on the system. Often, output queues have the same name as the printers on the system. Therefore, you can work with the spooled files associated with a particular printer by accessing the printer's output queue. There are three methods available to work with printer output by printer:

- Prompting the command WRKSPLF and specifying a printer for the *Print device* parameter. This is described earlier in the "Displaying Printer Output for a User" topic.

- Entering the command WRKOUTQ to work with all output queues and selecting option 5 (Work with) for the designated output queue. This is described earlier in the "Displaying Printer Output by Output Queue" topic.

- Entering the command WRKWTR to work with all printers and selecting option 8 (Work with output queue) for the designated printer.

  An example of the Work with All Printers display is shown in Figure 5.11. (See the "Working with Local Printers" topic, later in this chapter, for details about the options available on the Work with All Printers display.)

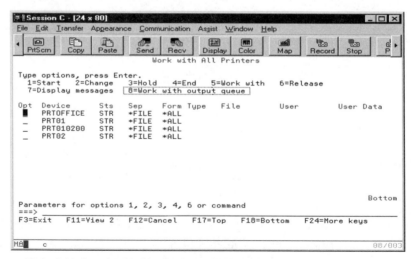

Figure 5.11: An example of the Work with All Printers display.

MANAGING PRINTER OUTPUT

As a system operator, you use the Work with All Spooled files display to inspect the flow of spooled print jobs as they proceed to the printer. You also use this display to determine if a user's print job is doing one of the following:

- Currently printing.
- Waiting in line to be printed.
- Waiting for a response to a message.

You might find this display helpful in determining some of the following things:

- The total number of pages in a report.
- The priority of a print job.
- The date and time the report was created.

In this section, you will learn about the options and information available on the Work with All Spooled files display.

Exploring Different Views of Printer Output

The Work with All Spooled files display has various views, each providing you with slightly different information. The default view is shown in Figure 5.12.

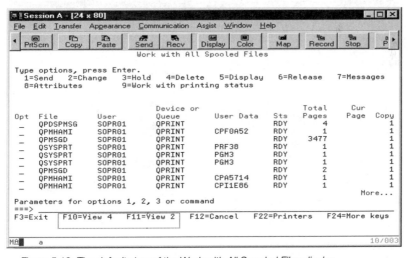

Figure 5.12: The default view of the Work with All Spooled Files display.

Here, you see information such as the output queue where the spooled output is located, the printing status, total pages, and number of copies to be printed. This view lists the spooled files in the order they are to be printed, assuming that all the spooled files have the same priority.

For the *Device or Queue* column, remember that the name here may be the same as the name of the printer that prints the report.

The *User Data* field contains information that users can specify to identify a spooled file. For example, a user can put a report name here or a personal code. Depending on how the programmer sets up the job, this column can contain any of the following items:

- The name of the procedure that created the file.
- The name of the application program that created the file.
- Blanks, or any other value you choose.

Notice keys F10 and F11. These keys enable you to see more columns of information about the spooled files. F11 displays the views in sequence—from the first view to the last view. F10 displays the views from the last view to the first view.

To see view 2, as shown in Figure 5.13, press F11.

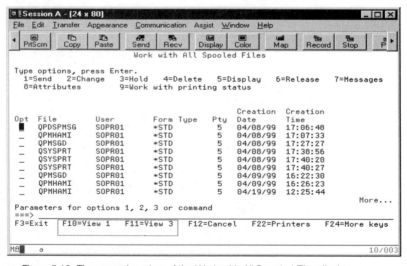

Figure 5.13: The secondary view of the Work with All Spooled Files display.

Here, you see several new pieces of information. The Form Type states what kind of paper is to be used for the printing process. Notice in this figure that all the spooled files are requesting standard forms. For example, the standard forms at your company might be 8½-by-11-inch paper. Nonstandard forms may be preprinted documents, such as checks and invoices.

The priority of the spooled file may be assigned from a high of one to a low of nine. In this display, since all of the jobs have the same priority, the spooled files print in the order displayed.

Date and Time fields are updated whenever a spooled file is created. Suppose a user ran a program again because the first report had some errors. Now there are two files with the same information, except for the time. In this case, the user may be able to delete the file with the earlier time and print the file with the later time.

To see view 3, as shown in Figure 5.14, press F11.

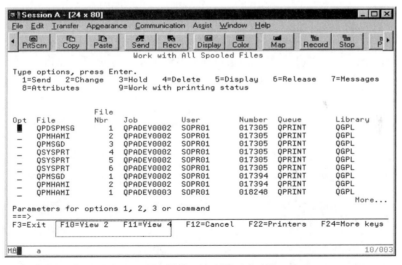

Figure 5.14: The third view of the Work with All Spooled Files display.

Here, you see the name of the job that produced the spooled file, along with the user name and job number. This is referred to as the qualified job name (e.g., 017305/SOPR01/QPADEV0002), as discussed in chapter 3.

The *Job* column shows the name given to the batch job when it is submitted, or for interactive jobs, this is the name of the workstation where the user started the job. Identifying the workstation can immediately distinguish two files with the same name.

The *Queue and Library* columns indicate the name of the output queue that contains your file and the name of the library that contains this output queue. Your spooled files might be all in one queue, or they might be in several different queues.

Press F10 or F11 to explore other views. If you do not understand what any particular column of information means, just put your cursor on that column and press F1 to read the online help.

Displaying the Contents of Printer Output

Displaying spooled files is helpful to review long reports before printing them. In fact, you should encourage users to review their reports before they print, in case the user only needs to print certain pages. Then, hopefully, if an error occurs, they can delete the spooled file, correct the input that caused the error, and rerun the job—without requiring that you be involved in the process at all.

You can display a spooled file, as shown in Figure 5.15, in one of two ways:

- Select option 5 (Display) on the Work with All Spooled Files display, for the file you want to see.

- Use the command DSPSPLF and press F4 to specify the spooled file and any additional parameters.

The rule line marks where the actual data will appear on the printed output. Use the *Control* and *Find* fields at the top of the display to locate information. To easily go to the bottom of a long report, type *B* in the *Control* field. Likewise, if you're at the bottom and want to go straight to the top, type *T*. You can use the *Find* field to locate any text you type with an exact match in the spooled file. (Read the online help for more details about these fields, or about the display in general.)

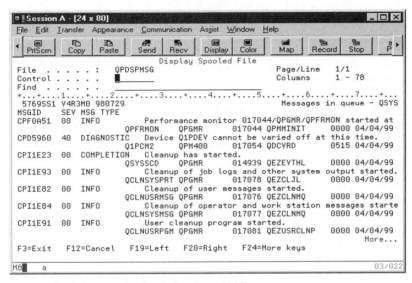

Figure 5.15: An example of a displayed spooled file.

Holding Printer Output

The Hold option on the Work with All Spooled Files display enables you to suspend a print job. When you put a hold on a print job, you prevent it from allowing the spooled file to print until you release it. You might want to hold a spooled file if you want to move it to another queue, change its priority, or change other attributes.

If a file is currently printing, and a higher priority file enters the queue, OS/400 does not stop the printing process to allow a higher priority file to access the printer. However, you can hold the lower priority file, which suspends it from printing and allows the higher priority file to begin printing.

> *Tip:* When you hold a spooled file that is currently printing, and later release the file, the file begins printing from the first page.

You can hold a spooled file in one of two ways:

- Select option 3 (Hold) on the Work with All Spooled Files display, for the file or files you want to hold. Once you hold a spooled file, *HLD appears in the Status column. Press F5 (Refresh), and the file is moved to the bottom of the queue.

- Use the command HLDSPLF and press F4 to specify the spooled file and any additional parameters. With this command, you can specify when to hold a spooled file that's currently printing—immediately or at the end of the page.

Tip: You might want to hold spooled files that print on special forms or for very long reports, instead of routing them to a separate output queue. You can release the files when it is convenient to print them.

Releasing Printer Output

The Release option on the Work with All Spooled Files display enables you to free a held print job. Once released, the job is sequenced according to its priority. If the job was held while it was printing, the printing starts over at the first page. You can release a spooled file in one of two ways:

- Select option 6 (Release) on the Work with All Spooled Files display, for the file or files you want to release. Once you release a spooled file, *RLS appears in the Status column. Press F5 (Refresh), and the file changes to RDY status. Alternatively, the status may be WTR if the file is in the process of being sent to a print writer, or SND if the file is being sent to a remote printer. A remote printer can be any printer that is not directly attached to the AS/400. For example, a local area network (LAN) printer could be configured to handle AS/400 print output.

- Use the command RLSSPLF and press F4 to specify the spooled file and any additional parameters.

Changing the Attributes of Printer Output

The Change option on the Work with All Spooled Files display enables you to assign spooled output to a printer, and to change other attributes of the printed output.

You can change attributes of a spooled file in one of two ways:

- Select option 2 (Change) on the Work with All Spooled Files display, for the file you want to change.

- Use the command CHGSPLFA and press F4 to specify the spooled file and any changes you want to make.

Figure 5.16 shows the Changed Spooled File Attributes (CHGSPLFA) display after F10 (Additional parameters) has been pressed.

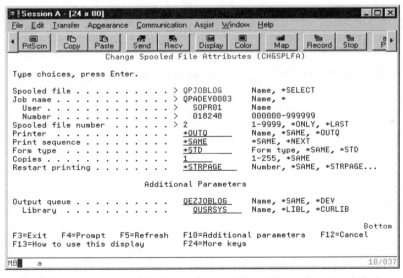

Figure 5.16: An example of the Change Spooled Files Attributes (CHGSPLFA) display.

Let's examine some of the attributes you can change on the first page of the Change Spooled File Attributes (CHGSPLFA) display.

Printer Field: Specify the device name of a printer to use to print a report. Use this field to assign a printer to a report that has not been assigned, or to move a report from one printer to another.

Form Type Field: If a report requires a nonstandard form, specify the name of that form here. This field can also be useful during application testing. For example, you may want to test programs, such as check or invoice printing on ordinary paper.

Copies Field: Specify how many copies of the report you want to print.

Output Queue Field: If you need to move a report to a different output queue, such as one that's not assigned to a printer, specify the name of that output queue here. If you have reports that you're not sure you should delete, you can move them to an unassigned output queue. This way, those reports don't get printed, and you don't have to clutter up an active output queue by putting them on hold.

There are many other parameters you can change for a spooled file. When you press F10 to display additional parameters (as shown in Figure 5.16) and then page down, more parameters appear, as shown in Figure 5.17.

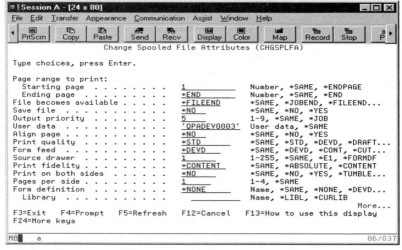

Figure 5.17: Additional parameters for the Change Spooled File Attributes (CHGSPLFA) display.

Let's examine some of the attributes you can change on the second page of the Change Spooled File Attributes (CHGSPLFA) display.

Page range to print field: If you don't want to print the entire report, specify the page that this report should begin printing on, along with the ending page number. This page range is helpful, for example if you need to reprint part of a report that has been damaged by a paper jam.

Save file field: If you want to save a report after it is printed, type *YES in this field. Normally, you would want printer output deleted to avoid cluttering up your system. However, for output that prints on special forms, you might want to save it. If you discover an alignment problem after the output has printed, you can reprint without having to rerun the program.

Output priority field: If you need to move a report to the front of the queue for printing, specify a higher priority (with 1 being the highest) here. The user who owns the spooled output has authority to make this change. As system operator, you can also make these changes if you have *SPLCTL special authority. Your user profile specifies the highest priority available to you when changing printer output. When you change priority, the printer output is placed with other reports with the same priority and forms type. Higher priority print jobs are printed first.

Print on both sides field: If you have a printer capable of printing on both sides of the paper, you can specify the type of duplex printing you want to do. This is helpful at large companies if paper conservation is an issue.

> **Note:** If the printer output you want to change is currently printing, you can only change the Copies and Save file fields. If you want to change any other fields, hold the printer output, make your changes, and then release the printer output.

Changing the Same Attribute on Multiple Printer Jobs

Sometimes you might need to move more than one print job to the same printer. For example, you might have 20 print jobs that need to be moved to the same printer. These jobs are currently on the same output queue. If you use the Change option on the Work with All Spooled Files display, you would have to type 2 next to one job, press Enter, and specify the printer or output queue. Then, you would need to repeat this process 19 additional times. This could become a very time-consuming process, especially if you need to do it regularly. A much easier method is available by making changes to the Work with All Spooled Files display, as shown in Figure 5.18.

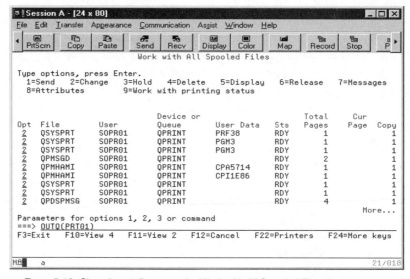

Figure 5.18: Changing attributes on the Work with All Spooled Files display.

Recall that on any list display, you can specify any parameter on the command line for the options listed. On the Work with All Spooled Files display, you can take advantage of this flexibility for the parameters in options 1 (Send), 2 (Change), or 3 (Hold).

Continuing the printing scenario, you simply type 2 next to each print job and then enter the CHGSPLFA command parameter OUTQ(<*printer name*>) on the command line. After you press Enter, the selected spooled files are moved to the specified output queue.

DETERMINING WHY OUTPUT IS NOT PRINTING

The Work with All Spooled Files (WRKSPLF) display (Figure 5.4) is helpful in determining why a report is not printing. Once you have found the printer output on this display, follow these steps to determine why it is not printing:

1. Check the Status column. The Status column usually gives you enough information to solve the following scenarios:

   - If the output has a held status (HLD), release it using option 6 (Release).

   - If the output has messages requiring a reply (MSGW), answer them using option 7 (Messages).

   - If the status is ready (RDY), but the spooled file does not print, see step 2.

2. Use option 9 (Work with printing status) to get more detailed information on what to do next.

Working with Printing Status

The information on the Work with Printing Status display can be helpful in solving any printer problems that you might encounter. An example of the Work with Printing Status display is shown in Figure 5.19. You can get to this display by doing one of the following:

- Select option 9 (Work with printing status) on the Work with All Spooled Files display.

- Prompt the command WRKPRTSTS and specify the spooled file and any other parameters.

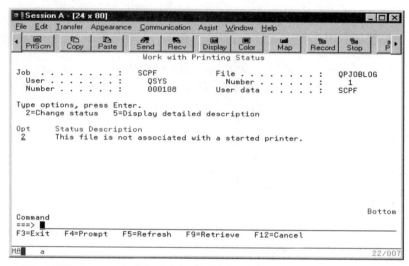

Figure 5.19: An example of the Work with Printing Status display.

Selecting option 2 (Change status) on a message prompts you for the action to take. For example, changing the status on this message prompts you to select a printer, as shown in Figure 5.20.

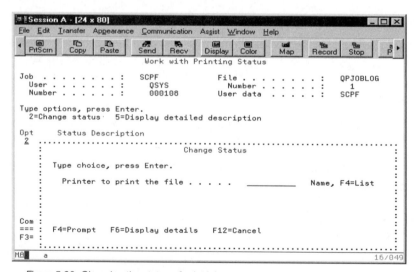

Figure 5.20: Changing the status of print job.

If you're not sure which printer to use, press F4 to select from a list of printers. Once you select a printer, you are then asked if you want to move the file to the output queue of the printer writer or change the printer writer to use the output queue of the file.

The Work with Printing Status display may have more than one status message for the output, as shown in Figure 5.21.

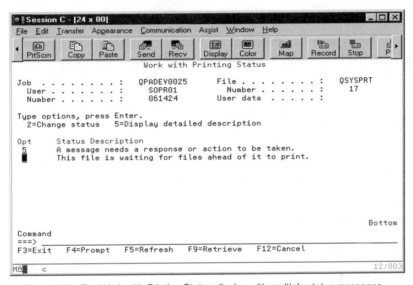

Figure 5.21: The Work with Printing Status display with multiple status messages.

Selecting option 5 (Display detailed description) on a message gives you an explanation of the status and a list of alternative actions.

Displaying Completed Printer Output

If the system administrator or security officer configured the AS/400 to save information about completed printer output, you can audit what has been printed. For example, if users insist that certain reports have printed (because they displayed their spooled files and saw the status of those being written), but they can't find the reports on the printer, you can check to be sure that the reports did indeed print. If so, it could be that someone mistakenly grabbed the printouts, or perhaps the output printed on another printer.

If this feature is configured, F6 (Completed printer output) is available on the Work with Printer Output display (Figure 5.5). Recall that this display is set at the basic assistance level.

Investigating Other Reasons Why the Output Isn't Printing

To further investigate why the printer isn't printing, gather information about the job and the output. You might look for information about the job name and find one of the following:

- The output was created interactively, and the job name is the name of the workstation the person was using.

- The output was created by a batch job, and the job name is assigned on the Submit Job (SBMJOB) command, with the default name being QDFTJOBD.

Also, consider these questions:

- What user ID was used to create the output?

- Where does it usually print (which printer)?

- Does it print on special forms?

- How many pages is it?

- What is the output name?

- When was the job run?

Table 5.1 lists some of the most common problems that prevent or delay output from printing and some suggested solutions. For technical details on printing problems, use option 9 (Work with printing status) on the Work with All Spooled Files display.

Table 5.1: Common Printing Problems and Solutions.

Problem	Solution
Printer messages are unanswered.	WRKSPLF and option 7 (Messages)
Printer is not started.	WRKWTR and option 1 (Start)
Printer output is not assigned to a printer.	To assign a spooled file to a printer: WRKSPLF and option 2 (Change) or 9 (Work with printing status) To assign the entire output queue to a printer: STRPRTWTR
Printer output has form type that has not been started for the printer.	WRKWTR: End the printer (option 4), then start it (option 1) with the desired form type
Printer output has value of *JOBEND in the Schedule field and the job has not finished.	To change this field to *FILEEND: CHGSPLFA
Printer output held.	WRKSPLF and option 6 (Release)
Nothing is printing on any printers on the system.	Check to see if the QSPL subsystem is started. If not, start it either by starting a printer or by using the Start Subsystem (STRSBS) command. Look for messages relating to the QSPL subsystem (DSPMSG QSYSOPR).
Printer status says MSGW, but you can't find the message.	WRKWTR and option 7 (Display messages)

What Determines Where Output Prints?

The user profile is the best place to start to determine where printed output will go. (Refer to Exercise 5 for additional information on output.) Specifically, you want to look at the *Print device* and *Output queue* parameters, as shown in Figure 5.22. To see these parameters, follow these steps:

1. Type CHGPRF and press F4 to change your user profile.

2. Press F10 for additional parameters.

3. Page down.

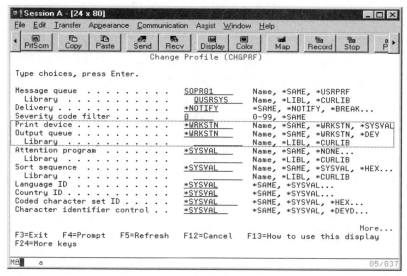

Figure 5.22: The values for printer parameters on the Change Profile (CHGPRF) display.

The default value for both the *Print device* and *Output queue* parameters is
*WRKSTN, which points to the user's workstation to determine where printer out-
put should go. However, this value can be changed to a specific output queue so
that, regardless of the workstation at which a user is working (that is, wherever
the user signs on), the user's spooled files go to the same output queue.

The printer device—the name of the physical printer where output is printed—is
specified in the user profile. A default printer is automatically assigned at the
time a user signs on. To change the default printer for a user, specify one of the
following values for the *Print device* parameter in the user's profile:

- A specific printer name (for example, PRT03).

- The value *WRKSTN (the printer assigned to the user's workstation).

- The value *SYSVAL (the printer assigned for the whole system). Note:
  *SYSVAL points to the printer specified for the QPRTDEV system value.

The output queue, where a user's print output should go, is also specified in the
user profile. The output queue for the default printer is automatically assigned at

the time a user signs on. To change the default output queue for a user, specify one of the following values for the Output queue parameter in the user's profile:

- A specific output queue name (for example, STEVEOUTQ).

- The value *WRKSTN (the output queue assigned to the user's workstation; default).

- The value *DEV (the output queue with the same name as the printer specified on the *Print device* parameter).

> **Note:** You can change these parameters for your own profile whether or not you have any special authorities. Just prompt (F4) the CHGPRF command. However, you must have *SECADM special authority to create or change profiles. For a list of special authorities and what each offers, prompt the command CHGUSRPRF *<your user ID>*. Press F10, page down, and then press F1 on the *Special authority* parameter.

WORKING WITH LOCAL PRINTERS

You can manage all the printers that are physically connected to the system via the Work with All Printers display. This display includes information about the writers started to the printers. Recall that printer writers send spooled files from an output queue to a printer for printing. To find the Work with All Printers display, do one of the following:

- Follow a menu path:

  1. On the AS/400 Main Menu (MAIN), type 3, General system tasks, and press Enter.

  2. On the General System Tasks (SYSTEM) menu, type 8, Device operations, and press Enter.

  3. On the Device Operations (DEVICE) menu, type 3, Printer, and press Enter.

4. On the Printer (PRINTER) menu, type 2, Work with printers, and press Enter.

> **Hint:** Take a fast path to the PRINTER menu: Enter the command go printer.

- Press F22 (Printers) on the Work with All Spooled Files display (Figure 5.4).

- Enter the WRKWTR command.

The Work with All Printers display appears, as shown in Figure 5.23.

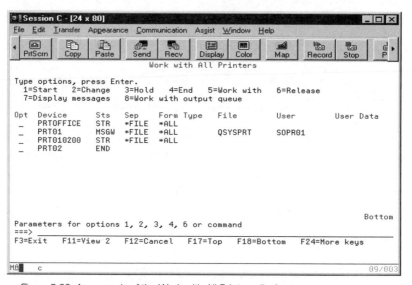

Figure 5.23: An example of the Work with All Printers display.

The status (Sts) column reveals the condition of the printer. An STR indicates that the printer writer is started, meaning spooled files can be printed on the associated print device. MSGW indicates that a printer message must be answered before the print device can be used for printing again. END indicates that the printer writer is stopped, meaning no spooled files can be printed on the associated print device until the writer is restarted. To find the meaning of other status codes, position your cursor anywhere on the Sts column and press F1 for online help.

To see view 2, as shown in Figure 5.24, press F11.

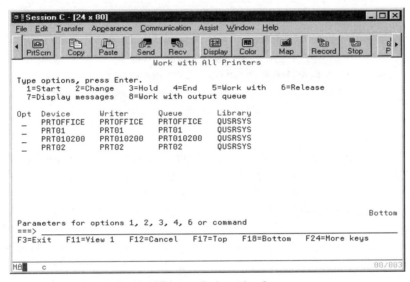

Figure 5.24: The Work with All Printers display—view 2.

The *Writer* column indicates whether there is a writer started to the printer device. If this field is blank, there is no writer started, and therefore, no output can be produced.

The *Queue* column indicates the output queue the writer uses to process spooled files. In this example, each printer is configured to use the output queue having the same name as the printer, which is the default. However, you can specify that the printer print files from any output queue.

Starting a Printer Writer

The Start option on the Work with All Printers display enables you to start a printer writer with a status of END. You can start a printer writer in one of two ways:

- Select option 1 (Start) on the Work with All Printers display, for the printer or printers you want to start.

- Use the command STRPRTWTR and press F4 to specify the printer and any additional parameters.

Tip: When you start a printer writer, it might take a few seconds for the system to process the request. Just press F5 to refresh the screen until the status changes to STR. Sometimes when you start a printer, the status changes to MSGW, which typically means there is a forms-alignment message. (See the "Answering Printer Messages" topic later in this chapter for details about this common message.)

By default, a writer is started for the output queue with the same name as the printer. When you start a writer, however, you can do things like assign it to a different output queue and specify a special message queue for the printer. To start a printer writer and change these parameters, complete the following steps:

1. Prompt the Start option or the STRPRTWTR command. The Start Printer Writer (STRPRTWTR) display appears, as shown in Figure 5.25.

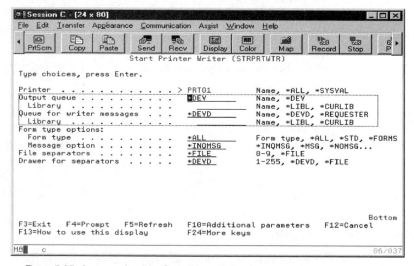

Figure 5.25: An example of the Start Printer Writer (STRPRTWTR) display.

2. Specify the name of a valid output queue for the *Output queue* parameter. *DEV means that the output queue with the same name as the printer is used.

3. Specify the name of a valid message queue for the *Queue for writer messages* parameter. *DEVD means that printer messages are sent to the message queue in the printer's device description. To see the device description for a printer, enter the command DSPDEVD PRT01.

All printer messages typically go to the QSYSOPR message queue. However, you may find the volume of messages in this queue to be quite large. If so, separate the messages for each printer to a different message queue, especially if the printers are in remote locations.

Note: Changing the message queue when starting a printer writer is a temporary solution. To permanently change where printer messages are located, use the Work with Device Description command:

```
WRKDEVD <printer name>
```

For example, enter WRKDEVD PRT01 and change the PRT01 printer device to use a message queue other than QSYSOPR. (For more information about messages and message queues, see chapter 4. For more information about working with device descriptions, see chapter 6.)

Ending a Printer Writer

The End option on the Work with All Printers display enables you to end (stop) a printer writer with a status of STR. This means that the printer stops printing, even though the printer might still be powered up. You might end a printer writer for one of the following reasons:

- The printer needs repair.
- A paper jam occurred.
- The printer can't be active after regular hours for security reasons.
- You need to load different forms on the printer.

You can end a printer writer in one of two ways:

- Select option 4 (End) on the Work with All Printers display, for the printer or printers you want to stop.

- Use the command ENDWTR and press F4 to specify the printer and any additional parameters.

The default is a controlled end, at the end of the spooled file currently being printed. However, you might have a very long report printing, but you can't wait for it to finish before the end takes effect. For example, you might need to stop printing because the individual has arrived to repair your printer, and your company gets charged for all the time this person spends on the premises.

When you end a writer, you can specify to end it immediately or at the end of the current page. Just prompt the End option or the ENDWTR command, and the End Writer (ENDWTR) display appears, as shown in Figure 5.26.

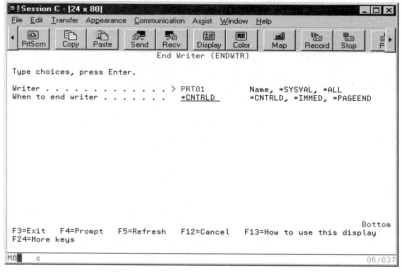

Figure 5.26: An example of the End Writer (ENDWTR) display.

Holding and Releasing a Printer Writer

Options 3 (Hold) and 6 (Release) on the Work with All Printers display enable you to interrupt and restart the printing of a report by holding and releasing the printer writer. When you release the writer, you can specify the page on which printing is to start, or simply have the writer start printing plus or minus some number of pages from where it was printing when held.

To change the default for when to hold the writer, prompt the Hold option or the HLDWTR command. The Hold Writer (HLDWTR) display appears, as shown in Figure 5.27.

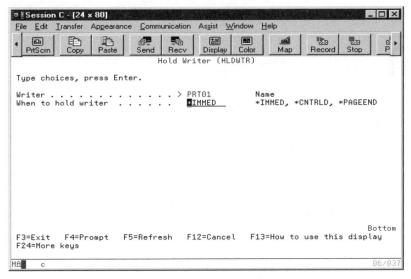

Figure 5.27: An example of the Hold Writer (HLDWTR) display.

The following values are available for the *When to hold writer* parameter:

- *IMMED—Holds the writer immediately (default).

- *CNTRLD—Holds the writer at the end of the spooled file currently being printed.

- *PAGEEND—Holds the writer at the end of the current page.

To change the default for when to resume printing, prompt the Release option or the RLSWTR command, and the Release Writer (RLSWTR) display appears, as shown in Figure 5.28.

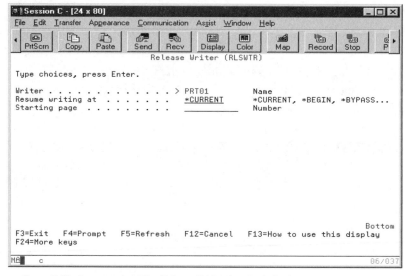

Figure 5.28: An example of the Release Writer (RLSWTR) display.

You can specify any one of the following values for the *Resume writing at* parameter:

- *CURRENT—Resumes printing at the point the writer was held (default).

- *BEGIN—Resumes printing at the beginning of the current spooled file.

- *BYPASS—Resumes printing at the beginning of the next spooled file.

- *INTEGER—Resumes printing at a specific number of pages ahead of or back from the point where the spooled file was held.

Alternatively, you can specify to resume printing on a specific page of the current spooled file for the *Starting page* parameter.

> **_Tip:_** Option 11 (Restart) on the Work with Printers display combines the functions of hold and release available when using the intermediate assistance level. To access this display, enter WRKWTR ASTLVL(*BASIC); this is the basic assistance level for the intermediate Work with All Printers display. If you need to stop printing a report and restart on another page, or if you have a paper jam and need to reprint part of a report, the Restart option may simplify the task.
>
> Another alternative is to just hold and release files on the output queue, rather than working directly with the printer writer. To work with all spooled files waiting in the output queue assigned to the printer, select option 8 (Work with output queue) on the Work with All Printers display. However, you cannot specify where you want to resume writing when you release a spooled file (RLSSPLF) as you can when you release a writer (RLSWTR).

Answering Printer Messages

Option 7 (Display messages) on the Work with All Printers display enables you to view and respond to printer messages, where the status is MSGW. You frequently see one of the following messages:

- Load form type... (Message ID CPA3394 or CPA3395).
- Verify alignment on printer... (Message ID CPA4002).

These messages might appear when printing restarts. Once you have displayed the message causing the writer to wait, you can respond to it. The reply you choose determines whether the writer continues printing. Specific information about how to answer the message is provided.

The entire *Verify alignment on printer* message is shown in Figures 5.29, 5.30, and 5.31 for you to examine.

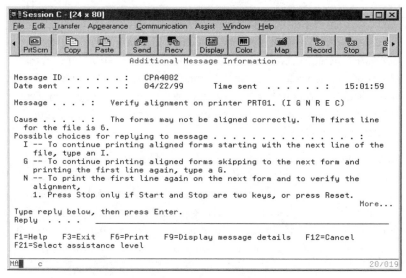

Figure 5.29: The Verify alignment on printer message, part 1 of 3.

Notice the word "More..." in the lower-right corner. This indicates that more information is available. Page down to continue.

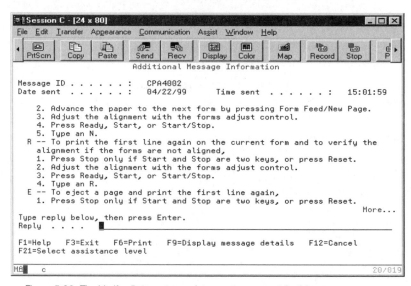

Figure 5.30: The Verify alignment on printer message, part 2 of 3.

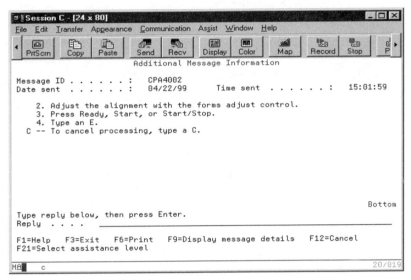

Figure 5.31: The Verify alignment on printer message, part 3 of 3.

Printer messages are sent to the message queue specified in the printer's device description, or to a message queue you specify when you start a printer writer. The default message queue for printer messages is QSYSOPR. (For more details, see the subheading "Starting a Printer Writer" earlier in this chapter.)

EXERCISE 5: WORKING WITH SPOOLED FILES

Note: This exercise is based on printing to an IBM-compatible printer that is directly attached to the AS/400, as opposed to a remote printer (such as a LAN printer configured to handle AS/400 printer output.).

Procedures

1. Change your user profile to use the output queue you created in chapter 2.

2. Do several print screens to generate spooled files.

3. Find and display your spooled files.

4. Determine why your spooled files have not printed.

5. Check if a printer writer is attached to your output queue.

6. Hold the first and last spooled files you generated.

7. Move both spooled files to an output queue associated with a started printer writer.

8. Find your held spooled files on the printer's output queue.

9. Change the number of copies of your first held spooled file to 2.

10. Release this spooled file and get the copies on the printer.

11. Delete your other spooled file that's held on the printer's output queue.

12. Clear your output queue of any remaining spooled files.

Change Your User Profile
to Use the Output Queue You Created in Chapter 2

1. Sign on with a user ID that has system operator authorities.

2. Issue the Change Profile command. On the command line:

   ➤ Type CHGPRF and press F4.

3. On the Change Profile (CHGPRF) display, do the following:

   a) Press F10 to display additional parameters.

   b) Record the name of the job description that your profile uses.

When anything is printed, the printer file first determines routing. If the printer file defaults—DEV(*JOB) and OUTQ(*JOB)—have been used, the printer file points to the job description.

The job description then decides where your printer output goes because your user profile tells which job description to use when you sign on, which starts the interactive job. If your user profile specifies QDFTJOBD, this job description typically points right back to the user profile to determine where printer output goes.

By default, QDFTJOBD contains the value of *USRPRF for the *Printer device* and *Output queue* parameters. Entering the command DSPJOBD QDFTJOBD produces the Display Job Description display, as shown in Figure 5.32.

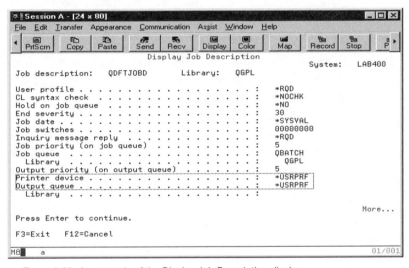

Figure 5.32: An example of the Display Job Description display.

If your user profile is using a job description other than QDFTJOBD, and the printer device and output queue values in that job description are not *USRPRF, then by default your printer output is spooled to the output queue specified in that job description. If this is the case, change the *Job description* parameter in your user profile to QDFTJOBD in library QGPL so that you can complete this exercise. After the exercise, you can change this value back to what it was.

Note: It is strongly recommended that objects starting with Q (which are IBM-supplied) not be changed or deleted. QDFTJOBD is one such object that comes with your AS/400. With the correct authority, you can copy Q objects and change any value in the duplicate object.

233

c) Page down.

d) Specify your output queue, and the library where you created it (see chapter 2 for your library's name), for the *Output queue* parameter:

➤ Type *xxx*OUTQ and *xxx*LIB for the library (where *xxx* is your initials).

All print output is spooled to this output queue, which is not associated with a printer writer. This way, you can practice working with spooled files without having to worry about them printing. The spooled files you generate remain in your output queue until you either move them to an output queue that's associated with a started printer writer or specify that an active writer grab spooled files from your output queue.

e) Press Enter to accept the changes. You will see a message confirming that your user profile has been changed.

5. Sign off. On the command line:

➤ Type SIGNOFF and press Enter.

You have to sign off, and then sign back on for the change you made to your profile to take effect.

6. Sign on. Call the Command Entry display directly from the Sign On screen. After you type your user ID and password:

a) Place the cursor on the *Program/procedure* field.

b) Type QCMD and press Enter.

Do Several Print Screens to Generate Spooled Files

Caution: "Print screen" refers to the AS/400 print screen function, which generates a spooled file and displays the message "Print operation complete to the default printer device file." Do not confuse this with your workstation printer's screen print. If you have a non-programmable terminal, use the Print key. If you have a PC, you might be able to use the Print Screen key on your keyboard if it is mapped correctly. Otherwise, ask someone for the system print-screen key.

Tip: If you're using a PC with a 5250 display session emulation tool such as found in Client Access/400, that tool might contain a method to print AS/400 screens. In Client Access/400, for example, right-click the mouse to display a keypad, change from Pad 1 to Pad 2, and click the HostPrn button.

---

1. Print the list of objects in your library:

   a) Enter WRKLIB *<your library name>* on the Command Entry display, where *<your library name>* is the name of the library you renamed in chapter 2 (e.g. STMLIB).

   b) Type 5 and press Enter to display the objects in your library.

   c) Print the screen. You should receive a message stating that the print operation is complete to the default printer device file. Does this mean the list actually printed? Why or why not?

   _____

   d) Press the Reset key (or left Ctrl key) to clear the message and unlock the keyboard.

   e) Press F3 to return to the Work with Libraries display.

2. Print the list of spooled file commands available on the system:

   a) Enter GO CMDSP* to search for a menu containing spooled file commands.

   Tip: Just enter this command at the bottom of the Work with Libraries display.

   ---

b) Select CMDSPLF and press Enter. The Spooled File Commands menu appears, as shown in Figure 5.33.

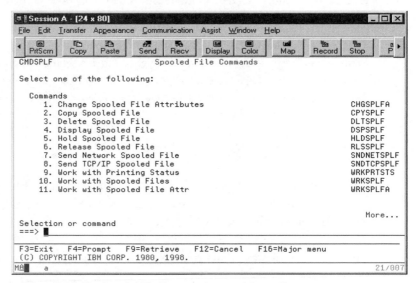

Figure 5.33: The Spooled File Commands menu (screen 1).

c) Print the first screen of spooled file commands.

d) Press the Reset key (or left Ctrl key) to clear the message and unlock the keyboard.

e) Page down. The second screen of the Spooled File Commands menu appears, as shown in Figure 5.34.

3. Print a list of related spooled file commands:

a) Select an option to explore any of the related-command menus.

b) Print the screen of the selected menu.

c) Press the Reset key (or left Ctrl key) to clear the message and unlock the keyboard.

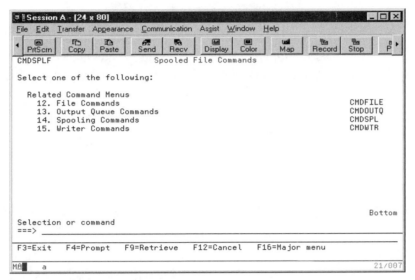

Figure 5.34: The Spooled File Commands menu (screen 2).

4. Print additional message information for a message on the QSYSOPR message queue:

   a) Enter DSPMSG QSYSOPR at the bottom of the menu that's currently displayed.

   b) Find a message you don't understand, preferably a reply message prompting you to take action.

   c) Press F1 on that message to get more information about it. For a message requiring a reply, the Additional Message Information display lists and explains the options you can choose to resolve the problem. You might have to page down to view all the information.

   d) Press F6 to print all the information about the message. This is different from doing a print screen. A print screen just captures the current display. The F6 print function, on the other hand, captures the information on all displays of the message and spools it to the default output queue. Also, the system message "Printer output created" that gets returned is different. The spooled file for this print request is identified with a different name than the spooled files for your print screens. You will see this when you find your print output.

5. Return to the Command Entry display:

    ➤ Press F3 repeatedly.

6. Display the commands you already entered in the previous steps:

    ➤ Press F10.

    Even though you didn't enter the commands GO CMDSP* and DSPMSG QSYSOPR on the Command Entry display, F10 (Include detailed messages) enables you to retrieve them so that you have a history of all commands you entered since signing on—regardless of where you entered them. If you press F10 again (Exclude detailed messages), only those commands you entered using the Command Entry display are shown.

Find and Display Your Spooled Files

1. Use the command that allows you to work with all your spooled files. On the Command Entry display:

    ➤ Enter WRKSPLF.

    The Work with All Spooled Files display appears, with an example shown in Figure 5.35.

    You should see at least four spooled files, which are those you just generated. If you have several spooled files listed, the four you generated in this exercise are at the bottom of the list. You will be working with these spooled files later.

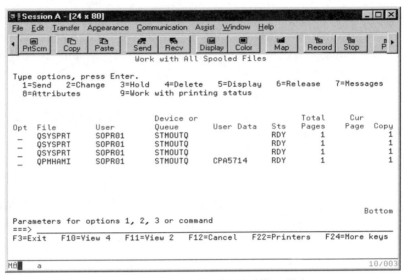

Figure 5.35: An example of the Work with All Spooled Files display.

2. Without actually displaying them, list a few ways you can tell which spooled files you want to work with:

_____

_____

_____

> **Hint:** What does the Device or Queue column tell you? What sort of information can you derive from the F10 and F11 keys?

3. List the names of each of your four spooled files, along with the date and time they were created, for example:

QSYSPRT   4/30/99   10:06:2

_____   _____   _____

_____   _____   _____

_____   _____   _____

_____   _____   _____

If a spooled file is just sitting in an output queue (as is the case here), or waiting its turn to be printed, you can view the contents before it prints. After viewing a file, you might decide that you don't need to print it after all.

4. Display the spooled file for the additional message information you printed. On the option line next to the file:

➤ Type 5 and press Enter.

Did you notice the User Data column for this spooled file? It should contain a description (the message ID in this case) to further identify the spooled file. An example spooled file display is shown in Figure 5.36.

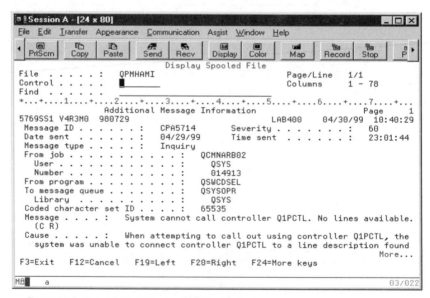

Figure 5.36: An example of the spooled file display.

5. View the text not shown on the right, then scroll back to the left:

➤ Press F20 and then press F19.

6. If there is more information, quickly jump to the end of the file. In the *Control* field:

    ➤ Type *B* and press Enter.

7. Quickly jump back to the beginning of the file. In the *Control* field:

    ➤ Type *T* and press Enter.

Note: The *Control* field allows you to control several paging options. Just press F1 to access online help on a field you don't understand.

---

8. Return to the Work with All Spooled Files display:

    ➤ Press F12.

Determine Why Your Spooled Files Haven't Printed

1. Notice the status of the four spooled files you generated. They should each have a status of RDY.

2. Find out the definition of RDY:

    a) Position the cursor on the Sts column.

    b) Press F1.

    Upon reading the definition, and based on the knowledge of your output queue, why do you suppose none of your files have printed? The screen says they're ready, and it doesn't appear that they're waiting for files ahead of them to print.

    _____

    _____

3. Exit online help:

    ➤ Press F12.

4. Check the printing status for one of your spooled files. On the option line next to the file:

   ➢ Type 9 and press Enter.

   What does the Work with Printing Status display tell you?

   _____

5. Display additional details about the status. On the option line next to the status description:

   ➢ Type 5 and press Enter.

   This should help clarify the action you must take in order to print the file.

   ═══
   Warning: Do not take any action at this time! You will get the
   chance to print later.
   ═══

6. Return to the Work with All Spooled Files display:

   ➢ Press F12 repeatedly.

Check If a Printer Writer Is Attached to Your Output Queue

1. Use the command to work with all output queues. On the Work with All Spooled Files display:

   ➢ Tab to the command line and enter the command WRKOUTQ.

2. Find your output queue (the one you created).

   Does the name of a printer writer appear in the Writer column for your output queue? Why or why not?

   _____

   _____

3. Find an output queue with a writer attached.

If you move your spooled files to this output queue, will they print?

_____

> **Warning:** Do not move any spooled files now. You will do this later.

How can you tell if multiple writers are attached to an output queue?

_____

_____

See the first topic in this chapter, "Understanding AS/400 Printing Terms," for a scenario in which several printer writers could be grabbing spooled files from the same output queue.

Explain the difference between a printer writer and a printer:

_____

_____

_____

4. Return to the Work with All Spooled Files display:

    ➤ Press F12.

Hold the First and Last Spooled Files You Generated

1. On the option line next to your first spooled file, or the one containing a print screen of the list of objects in your library:

    ➤ Type 3 (but do not press Enter yet).

2. On the option line next to your fourth spooled file, or QPMHAMI, the one containing additional information about a QSYSOPR message:

    ➤ Type 3 (but do not press Enter yet).

3. Now press Enter. The status should have changed to *HLD for both spooled files.

4. Refresh the display:

    ➤ Press F5.

Notice that the status of these spooled files changes to HLD and they get bumped below the other files in the queue. All print jobs with a status of RDY will be processed before held jobs when a print writer is attached to the output queue.

Move Both Spooled Files
to an Output Queue Associated with a Started Printer Writer

1. Find the printers on your system. On the Work with All Spooled Files display:

    ➤ Press F22.

2. Find a started writer to use. On the Work with All Printers display:

    ➤ Look for a status of STR.

    If there isn't a printer with a status of STR, check to see if there is a printer with a message waiting (MSGW).

    What option can you take to display printer messages?

    _____

3. Display the message and respond to it given the information.

    If all printers on your system are either held or ended, find out why, and then make sure it is okay to release or start one for your use in this exercise.

    What option can you take to start a printer writer?

    _____

4. Find the name of the output queue for the started writer. On the Work with All Printers display:

   ➤ Press F11.

   Record the name of the queue.

   _____

5. Return to the Work with All Spooled Files display:

   ➤ Press F12.

6. On the option line next to your first HLD spooled file, or the one containing a print screen of the list of objects in your library:

   ➤ Type 2 (but do not press Enter yet).

7. On the option line next to your second HLD spooled file, or QPMHAMI, the one containing additional information about a QSYSOPR message:

   ➤ Type 2 (but do not press Enter yet).

8. Specify the output queue to move these files to. On the command line:

   ➤ Type OUTQ(*<name>*), where *<name>* is the name of the output queue you recorded in step 4 previously.

   > **Note:** Make sure you type parentheses around the value for OUTQ.

9. Now press Enter.

   Notice that the name in the Device or Queue column changes to show to which output queue these print jobs now belong.

10. Refresh the display:

    ➤ Press F5.

Find Your Held Spooled Files on the Printer's Output Queue

1. Find the printers on your system. On the Work with All Spooled Files display:

    ➤ Enter the command WRKWTR or press F22.

2. Work with the printer's output queue. On the option line next to the printer:

    ➤ Type 8 and press Enter.

    How else could you have accessed this display?

    _____

3. Find your spooled files:

    ➤ Look for your user profile under the User column.

Change the Number of Copies
of Your First Held Spooled File to 2

1. On the option line next to your first HLD spooled file, or the one containing a print screen of the list of objects in your library:

    ➤ Type 2 and press Enter.

2. On the Changed Spooled File Attributes (CHGSPLFA) display, as shown in Figure 5.37:

    a) Type 2 for the *Copies* parameter.

    b) Press Enter.

    You are returned to the Work with Output Queue display. The status of the spooled file is *CHG.

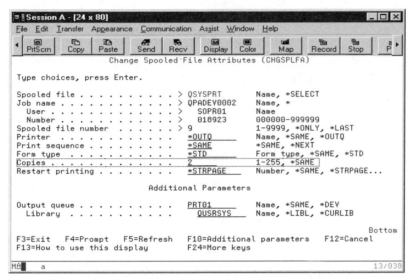

Figure 5.37: An example of Changed Spooled File Attributes (CHGSPLFA) display.

3. Refresh the display. On the Work with Output Queue display:

➤ Press F5.

Release the Spooled File and Get the Copies on the Printer

1. On the option line next to your first HLD spooled file, or the one containing a print screen of the list of objects in your library:

➤ Type 6 and press Enter.

The status should have changed to *RLS.

2. Refresh the display:

➤ Press F5.

If your spooled file is at the top of the list, it is currently being printed with a status of WTR. The spooled file might have been bumped out of the queue so quickly that you don't even see this status.

If your spooled file is waiting for files ahead of it to print, its status is RDY.

> **Note:** Once a spooled file has printed, it leaves the output queue, unless you specify to save it, in which case it remains in the queue after it has printed. Keep in mind that spooled files take up disk space, so save them sparingly. See the "Changing Attributes of Printer Output" topic for details about the *Save file* parameter, which dictates whether a spooled file is to be saved after printing.

3. If the two copies of your spooled file have printed:

   ➤ Skip to step 5.

   If the two copies of your spooled file have not yet printed:

   ➤ Continue with step 4.

4. Continue to refresh the display to see where your spooled file is waiting on the queue:

   ➤ Press F5 repeatedly.

   If you are in doubt about whether any spooled files are printing, what option can you use to check on printing status?

   _____

5. Once the two copies of your spooled file have printed:

   a) Grab both copies on the printer.

   b) Keep one copy for yourself.

   c) Give the other copy to your instructor/supervisor or a coworker/student and brag about the objects you created on the AS/400!

Delete Your Other Spooled File
Held on the Printer's Output Queue

Tip: Delete spooled files that don't need printing to avoid cluttering up the output queue.

---

1. On the option line next to your second HLD spooled file, or QPMHAMI, the one containing additional information about a QSYSOPR message:

   ➤ Type 4 and press Enter.

2. Confirm that you want to delete this spooled file. On the Confirm Delete of Spooled Files display:

   ➤ Press Enter.

Clear Your Output Queue of Any Remaining Spooled Files

Tip: If an output queue contains spooled files that don't need printing, clear the queue. Spooled files that aren't intended to be printed waste disk space.

---

1. Work with all output queues:

   ➤ Enter the command WRKOUTQ.

2. Find your output queue (that which you created).

3. On the option line next to your output queue:

   ➤ Type 14 and press Enter.

4. Confirm that you want to clear this output queue so no more spooled files remain. On the Confirm Clear of Output Queues display:

    ➤ Press Enter.

5. Refresh the Work with All Output Queues display:

    ➤ Press F5.

    The Files column for your output queue should now read zero.

MANAGING DEVICES

This chapter includes sections on the following:

- Working with device status

- Varying devices on and off

- Displaying device messages

- Determining the controller to which a device is attached

- Displaying all devices attached to a controller

- Varying controllers on and off

- Displaying all controllers attached to a line

WORKING WITH DEVICE STATUS

Note: This chapter does not describe how to attach and configure devices on the AS/400. It describes how to maintain those devices once they are attached and configured on the system.

A system operator is typically responsible for managing the various states of AS/400 devices. The AS/400 supports a number of hardware devices, including workstations, printers, tape drives, and CD-ROM drives. Devices can be turned on or off, disconnected from the system to be repaired, or upgraded.

The AS/400 is a very stable system that rarely fails. However, there are times when something goes wrong with normal system operations. When a problem occurs, you need to check the status of a device to see whether or not the device is available for use. Once you have determined that there is a problem with a device, you need to fix the problem, and then change the status to make the device available for use.

In this section, the following activities are discussed:

- How to display all devices on your system.

- How to interpret the status of various devices.

Details on how to change the status of devices are a part of the "Varying Devices On and Off " topic that appears later in this chapter.

Displaying All Devices on Your System

The Work with Configuration Status display is to managing devices what the Work with All Spooled Files display is to controlling printer output. Not only can you use this display to work with device status, but you can also use it to work with other configuration types, such as controllers and communication lines. For now, use the Work with Configuration Status display to list all devices. To find this display using a menu path, follow these steps:

1. On the AS/400 Main Menu (MAIN), type 3, General system tasks, and press Enter.

2. On the General System Tasks (SYSTEM) menu, type 8, Device operations, and press Enter.

3. On the Device Operations (DEVICE) menu, type 1, Work with device status, and press Enter.

Hint: Take a fast path to the Device Operations menu by entering the GO DEVICE command.

The Work with Configuration Status (WRKCFGSTS) entry display appears, as shown in Figure 6.1.

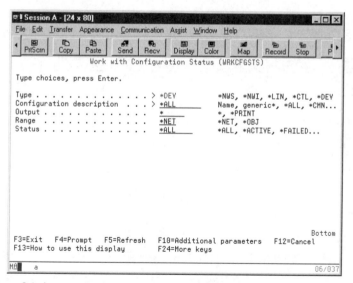

Figure 6.1: An example of the Work with Configuration Status (WRKCFGSTS) entry display to show all devices.

The *Configuration description* parameter defaults to *ALL, meaning you see a list of all devices to which you have authority that are configured on the system. You can specify to display a particular device configuration description, such as one of the following:

- *DSP—Workstations.

- *PRT—Printers.

- *TAP—Tape drives.

- *OPT—CD-ROM drives.

In this case, you see only the devices for that configuration description. Prompt (press F4) this field to view a list of all possible values, as shown in Figure 6.2, or access online help. Not all of these values apply, since the values depend upon the configuration type. For example, certain values are only valid for devices, while other values only pertain to controllers, and still others to lines only. On-line help describes which values apply to which configuration types.

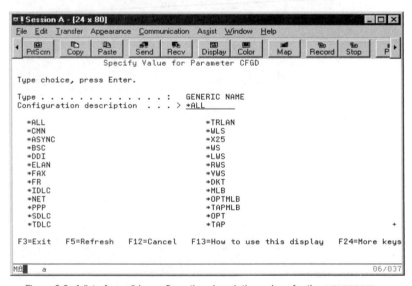

Figure 6.2: A list of possible configuration description values for the WRKCFGSTS command.

To quickly find all devices configured on the system, enter WRKCFGSTS CFGTYPE
(*DEV) on a command line. Or, using positional notation, just enter WRKCFGSTS
*DEV.

> ***Caution:*** If there are a large number of devices configured on the system,
> or during peak usage times, select a particular configuration description
> instead of accepting the default of *ALL for this parameter. Displaying all
> devices might adversely affect the performance of other jobs. If you enter
> the command WRKCFGSTS *DEV *DSP, for instance, the Work with
> Configuration Status display appears, listing all workstation devices. An
> example of this display is shown in Figure 6.3.

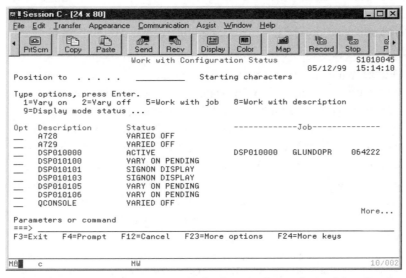

Figure 6.3: An example of the Work with Configuration Status display, listing all workstation devices.

Device status and options 1 and 2 on the Work with Configuration Status display
are described in the next two topics.

Interpreting the Status of Devices

The Status column on the Work with Configuration Status display describes the current availability of each device listed. The more common status types for workstations, printers, and tape drives are explained. However, to learn about any status code, just position your cursor anywhere on the Status column, and press F1 for online help.

Workstation Devices

Workstation devices can consist of the system console, non-programmable terminals, PCs with display emulation, and remote workstations. A device with the name of DSP01 is typically the IBM default name for the system console. The DSP prefix typically identifies non-programmable display stations, which are directly attached to the AS/400 via twin axial cable. These types of display stations are also affectionately known as "dumb" terminals, "dumbheads," or "dumb" tubes.

> **Note:** When devices are autoconfigured (QAUTOCFG=1), system value QDEVNAMING dictates how a workstation or printer or media device is named. The default value is *NORMAL, which names, for example, a workstation DSP01, a printer PRT01, a tape drive TAP01, and so forth. The second value is *S36, which is a hold over from the System/36, and the device names are similar to W1 (workstation), P1 (printer), T1 (tape drive), and so forth. The last value is *DEVADR, which concatenates the abbreviation of workstations and printers (DSP or PRT) with the local workstation controller number, port number, and switch setting of the device. A workstation could be named DSP010103; a printer could be named PRT010302. Looking at the parts of a workstation name might clarify this a bit more. If the workstation name of DSP010103 is broken apart, you have DSP for the workstation device, 01 for the local workstation controller, the next 01 for the port, and the 03 for the address (switch setting).

Table 6.1 shows different status types for local workstations (such as DSP010000). Local workstations (*LCL) are attached to the AS/400 via cable and a local workstation controller (*LWS) card.

Table 6.1: Local Workstation Status.	
Status	**Meaning**
SIGNON DISPLAY	The device is available, and a sign-on screen is displayed. When a user has signed off but has left the terminal powered on, this is the status that appears.
VARY ON PENDING	The system is attempting to make the device available or is waiting for the device to start. The device is available for use, but there is a blank screen; the device might be powered off.
VARIED OFF	The device is not available, and there is a blank screen. Use option 1 to make it available for use.
ACTIVE	The device is currently being used.

Workstation devices with a status of ACTIVE are identified by a qualified job name. When a user is signed on to a workstation, which is an interactive job, the Work with Configuration Status display includes the following three columns of information under the Job heading:

- Workstation device name in the first column.

- User ID in the second column.

- System-assigned job number in the third column.

Figure 6.4 shows a status of ACTIVE for three virtual workstations (such as QPADEV0005). Virtual workstations (*VRT) perform display emulation. If you are using Client Access/400, for instance, you have virtual workstations because you are using a PC to emulate AS/400 displays. You can also have virtual printers (*VRTPRT) that perform print emulation on the AS/400.

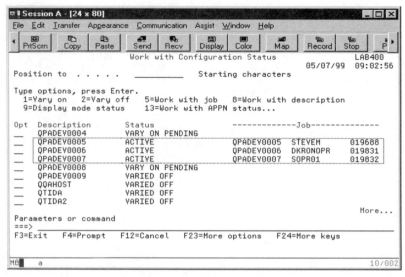

Figure 6.4: The ACTIVE status for three virtual workstations on the Work with Configuration Status (WRKCFGSTS) display.

There are many types of workstation devices available on the AS/400, depending on how a device is configured. In this topic, you have worked with only a sample of local and virtual workstation devices.

Printer Devices

There might be a variety of printers connected to your AS/400—from local to virtual to remote types. Figure 6.5 shows a list of local printers (*LCL) attached to the AS/400.

Tip: To display only printer devices attached to the AS/400, enter the command WRKCFGSTS CFGTYPE(*DEV) CFGD(*PRT). You can also filter the list within a particular device. For example, to display only remote printers, using positional notation, enter the command WRKCFGSTS *DEV *RMTPRT.

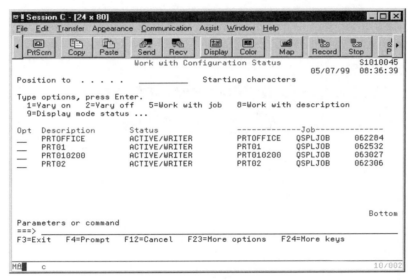

Figure 6.5: A list of local printers attached to the AS/400.

Common status types for printer devices are shown in Table 6.2.

Table 6.2: Printer Device Status.

Status	Meaning
ACTIVE/WRITER	The device is available, and a printer writer has been started for the device.
VARY ON PENDING	The device is available, but is powered off, or a printer writer has not been started for the device.
VARIED OFF	The device is not available; use option 1 to make it available for use.

Tape Devices

Like other devices on the AS/400, tape devices must be varied on or made available for use. Tapes are typically used to back up AS/400 objects. (See chapter 7 for details on how to run a backup to tape.) Figure 6.6 shows the status of a tape drive. VARIED ON is the normal status for tape and diskette devices. It simply means the device is available to use.

Tip: To display only tape drives on the AS/400, enter the command
WRKCFGSTS CFGTYPE(*DEV) CFGD(*TAP).

Figure 6.6: The tape drive status.

VARYING DEVICES ON AND OFF

Options 1 (Vary on) and 2 (Vary off) on the Work with Configuration Status display (WRKCFGSTS *DEV) allow you to make a device available (VARIED ON) or unavailable (VARIED OFF). You can also use the VRYCFG (Vary Configuration) command if you know the name of the device to vary on or off.

VARIED ON could be further described as the condition in which the AS/400 is ready to listen and respond to the device. Once the device status is ACTIVE, then communication between the AS/400 and the device is actually occurring.

Likewise, VARIED OFF could be further described as the condition in which the AS/400 is not ready to listen and respond to the device. The device could be powered on, but if it is VARIED OFF, then the AS/400 isn't communicating with that device.

When Would You Need to Vary On or Vary Off a Device?

You might use these options to enhance security. For example, you can vary off a device in a public place so that it cannot be accessed during off-shift hours. Then, you need to vary on the device in the morning to make it available again.

For another reason to use these options, consider the scenario in which a user calls and reports that a terminal named DSPJIM is down. The user forgot the password and tried four different passwords. Because trying several incorrect passwords violates security, the operating system makes the device unavailable by varying the terminal offline. In this case, once the user is assigned a new password, you would need to vary on the user's terminal. (You might or might not have the authority to assign new passwords, which requires changing user profiles.)

> **Note:** In the previous scenario, the QMAXSIGN system value might be set to 3, which indicates that a maximum of three invalid sign-on attempts is allowed. Any attempts after the third try might vary off the device, disable the user profile, or vary off the device and disable the user profile. You can check the setting for any system value by entering the command WRKSYSVAL and selecting option 5 (Display) for the system value. You need special authorities beyond system operator authorities to change certain system values.

Why Can't You Vary Off a Device with an ACTIVE Status?

When a device is ACTIVE, the AS/400 and that device are currently conversing. You can interrupt a conversation or decide not to speak any longer when in a conversation, but you cannot force other people to stop talking with each other if they don't want to. The same is true when an AS/400 and devices on the system are "talking." For example, if you try to vary off an active printer, you receive the following message:

```
Device PRT01 not varied off. Error occurred.
```

If you press F1 on this message, you'll see the top reason for why you couldn't vary off this printer: "The device is active." Figure 6.7 shows this message.

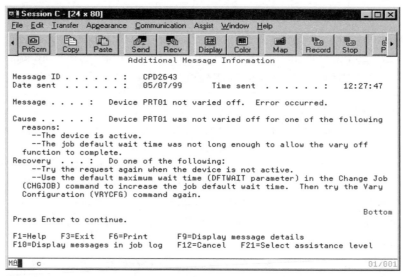

Figure 6.7: An error message that is displayed when trying to vary off an active device.

The AS/400 and printer are saying, "We're doing business right now." In the case of an active printer device, if you need to vary it off (or end the two-way conversation), you must do the following, in order:

1. End the printer writer, which silences the printer's side of the conversation. This changes the status of that device to VARIED ON. However, the AS/400 still wants to talk to that printer, even though the printer is not listening.

2. Vary off the printer device. The AS/400 and printer know that each other still exists, but they aren't talking.

If the AS/400 and a VARIED OFF printer are to resume talking, follow the reverse sequence:

1. Vary on the printer device.

2. Start the printer writer.

The Vary on and Vary off options might take time to complete. Therefore, the system displays the VARY ON PENDING or VARY OFF PENDING message until the device status has changed. Press F5 to refresh the display.

If you try to start the printer writer before varying on a VARIED OFF printer, a printer message is issued, as shown in Figure 6.8. (See chapter 5 for more on how to start and end printer writers.)

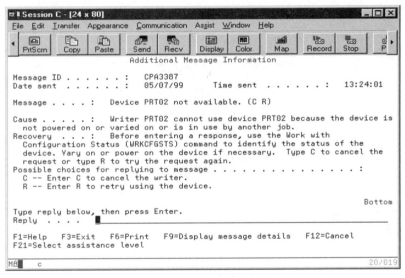

Figure 6.8: An error message that is displayed when trying to start the writer for a printer device that has been varied off.

Isn't it a relief to know that even if you try to put the cart before the horse, the AS/400 stops you and helps you rectify the problem? Replying with *C* in this case cancels, or ends, the printer writer.

Tip: To display a printer message, select option 7 on a printer list display or access the message queue where printer messages are sent. By default, this is the system operator (QSYSOPR) message queue. (See chapter 4 for more on how to display and work with message queues.)

DISPLAYING DEVICE MESSAGES

The QSYSOPR message queue alerts you to situations that need your attention with devices. Monitoring this queue is the simplest way to monitor devices. Examples of device messages are shown in Figure 6.9.

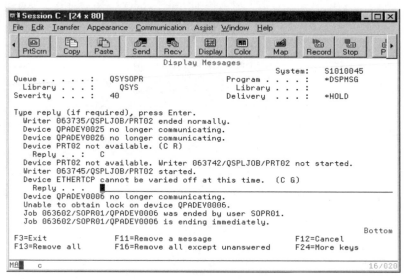

Figure 6.9: Some examples of device messages.

Most of the messages in the QSYSOPR message queue have to do with a device that is not communicating. These types of messages are typically triggered when the device has been powered off or has lost a connection to the AS/400. If you are not sure what a message means, position the cursor on it, and press F1 to display additional message information.

DETERMINING THE CONTROLLER TO WHICH A DEVICE IS ATTACHED

Workstation and printer devices are connected to the AS/400 via a hardware card called a *controller*, which can be local, remote, or virtual. It is helpful to know the name of the controller to which a device is attached when you need to troubleshoot problems with a device. For example, if a workstation will not vary on, the controller might not be active. The controller must be active for the devices attached to it to function.

> **Note:** Tape, diskette, and optical (CD-ROM) drives are not attached to a controller. They are typically part of the AS/400 unit and are identified by a special address called a *resource name*.

To find the controller to which a workstation or printer device is attached, complete these two steps:

1. On the Work with Configuration Status display, as described earlier in the topic "Working with Device Status," press F14 (Work with devices).

2. On the Work with Device Descriptions display, as shown in Figure 6.10, type 8 (Work with status) next to the device and press Enter.

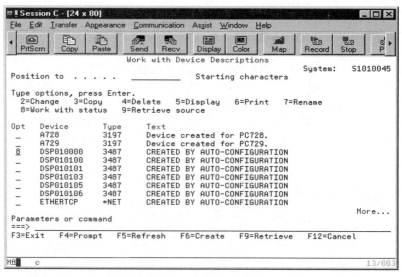

Figure 6.10: An example of selecting a device to find the controller to which it is attached.

The Work with Configuration Status display appears, as shown in Figure 6.11.

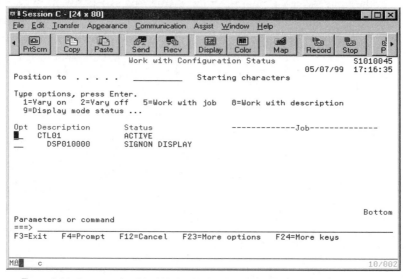

Figure 6.11: An example of the Work with Configuration Status display.

This version of the Work with Configuration Status display is slightly different than the examples described under the subheading "Working with Device Status" earlier in this chapter. The controller is listed, with the device indented under the controller. Notice that the status of the controller is ACTIVE.

> **Tip:** Another way to find the controller to which a device is attached, which might be quicker for you, is to enter WRKCFGSTS CFGTYPE(*DEV) CFGD(<*name of device*>) on a command line. Or, using positional notation, just enter WRKCFGSTS *DEV <*name of device*>. The Work with Configuration Status display appears with the device indented under its controller (Figure 6.11).

DISPLAYING ALL DEVICES ATTACHED TO A CONTROLLER

There are times when you need to find a list of controllers on the AS/400 so that you can see all the devices that are attached to a controller. For example, if you receive a call that all workstations in a department are down, the problem might be related to the controller to which those workstations are attached. Similar to using the Work with Configuration Status display to view a list of all devices, you can also use this display to view a list of all controllers with their devices. To find this display using a menu path, follow these steps:

1. On the AS/400 Main Menu (MAIN), type 3, General system tasks, and press Enter.

2. On the General System Tasks (SYSTEM) menu, type 9, Communications, and press Enter.

3. On the Communications (CMN) menu, type 1, Communication status, and press Enter.

4. On the Communications Status (CMNSTS) menu, type 2, Work with controller status, and press Enter.

> **Hint:** Take a fast path to the Communication Status menu by entering the command GO CMNSTS.

The Work with Configuration Status (WRKCFGSTS) entry display appears, as shown in Figure 6.12.

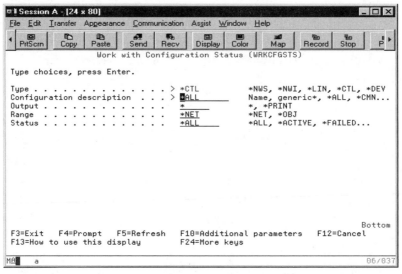

Figure 6.12: An example of the Work with Configuration Status (WRKCFGSTS) entry display, requesting controllers status.

The *Configuration description* parameter defaults to *ALL, meaning you see a list of all controllers to which you have authority that are configured on the system. You can specify to display a particular controller configuration description. Some descriptions you might want to specify are the following:

- *BSC—Bisynchronous controllers
- *LWS—Local workstation controllers
- *VWS—Virtual workstation controllers
- *RWS—Remote workstation controllers
- *WS—All workstation controllers

In this case, you see only the controllers for that configuration description. Prompt (press F4) this field to view a list of all possible values. You can also access online help (press F1) to get a list of values along with a short description of each value.

Tip: To quickly find all controllers configured on the system, enter WRKCFGSTS CFGTYPE(*CTL) on a command line. Or, using positional notation, just enter WRKCFGSTS *CTL. When you enter this command, the Work with Configuration Status display appears. An example of this display is shown in Figure 6.13.

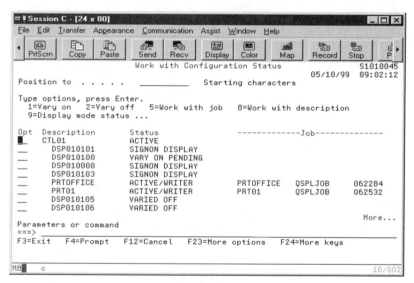

Figure 6.13: An example of the Work with Configuration Status display, listing all controllers.

In Figure 6.13, CTL01 is the controller. All of the display and print devices attached to this controller are indented under the controller. Notice that the status of the controller is ACTIVE, meaning it is functioning properly. If any devices on that controller are malfunctioning, then you could conclude that the problem has to do with the device or perhaps a cabling issue.

Because the word "More..." appears in the lower-right of the display, you can page down to see if there are any other devices attached to this controller. Figure 6.14 shows two other devices, printers PRT010200 and PRT02, connected to controller CTL01.

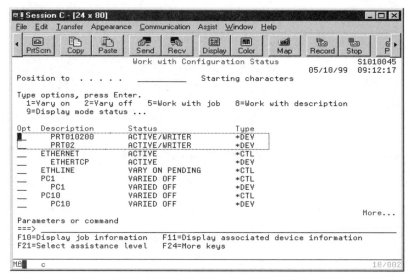

Figure 6.14: Two printer devices attached to a specified controller.

VARYING CONTROLLERS ON AND OFF

Options 1 (Vary on) and 2 (Vary off) on the Work with Configuration Status display (WRKCFGSTS *CTL) allow you to make a controller available (VARIED ON) or unavailable (VARIED OFF). You can also use the VRYCFG (Vary Configuration) command if you know the name of the controller to vary on or off. (See the "Varying Devices On and Off" topic for more details about the meanings of VARIED ON and VARIED OFF, since the same principle applies to both devices and controllers.)

If you need to vary on or vary off several workstation and printer devices that are all attached to the same controller, it may be more efficient for you to start at the controller level versus the device level. For instance, when you try to vary off a controller, all non-ACTIVE devices on that controller are varied off. Non-ACTIVE devices include those with a status such as SIGNON DISPLAY (for workstations), VARY ON PENDING, and VARIED ON. If there are ACTIVE devices, the controller is not varied off—that is, it remains ACTIVE, since it still needs to support the devices in use.

Perhaps you need to vary off controller CTL01, and then vary it back on again to reset the controller and all of its attached devices. Look again at Figure 6.13; it shows what the display looks like before you attempt to vary off CTL01. When you choose option 2 and press Enter to vary off the controller, Figure 6.15 shows the results.

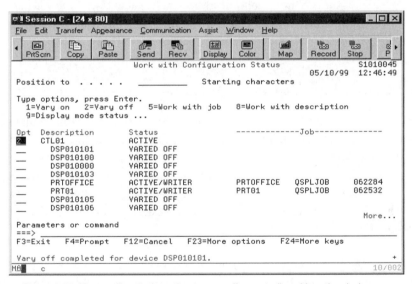

Figure 6.15: The results of attempting to vary off a controller with active devices.

CTL01 does not get varied off. Its status is still ACTIVE, just as it was before the "vary off." However, notice that the status of the first four display terminals under CTL01 (DSP010101, DSP010100, DSP010000, and DSP010103) did change. Earlier, their status is either SIGNON DISPLAY or VARY ON PENDING. The last two display terminals (DSP010105 and DSP010106) were already varied off. Finally, since the printers (PRTOFFICE and PRT01) are ACTIVE, they could not be varied off while in that state. (See the "Varying Devices On and Off" topic for reasons why devices in an ACTIVE condition cannot be varied off. Also, see the "Interpreting the Status of Devices" topic for meanings of common device statuses.)

On the Work with Configuration Status display for a list of controllers, the options and functions can also be used on individual devices attached to the controller. Therefore, if you need to vary on or vary off a device, you can do so right from the controller/device (WRKCFGSTS *CTL) list rather than resorting to the device-only list (WRKCFGSTS *DEV).

Tip: Encourage users to sign off before you need to vary the configuration of controllers and devices. This prepares their workstations to be varied off. Make sure you give users plenty of advance notice about what you will be doing and your expectations of them.

DISPLAYING ALL CONTROLLERS ATTACHED TO A LINE

There are times when you need to find a list of lines on the AS/400 so that you can see all the controllers that are attached to a line. Because lines are the first level of connection from the AS/400, it makes sense that you would want to find a list of them. For example, if you receive a call that all workstations in a department are down, and you've determined that the problem is not with any particular workstation or the controller to which those workstations are attached, the next step would be to check the status of the line.

You can use the Work with Configuration Status display to view a list of lines and their controllers. To find this display using a menu path, follow these steps:

1. On the AS/400 Main Menu (MAIN), type 3, General system tasks, and press Enter.

2. On the General System Tasks (SYSTEM) menu, type 9, Communications, and press Enter.

3. On the Communications (CMN) menu, type 1, Communication status, and press Enter.

4. On the Communications Status (CMNSTS) menu, type 1, Work with line status, and press Enter.

Hint: Take a fast path to the Communication Status menu by entering the command GO CMNSTS.

The Work with Configuration Status (WRKCFGSTS) entry display appears, as shown in Figure 6.16.

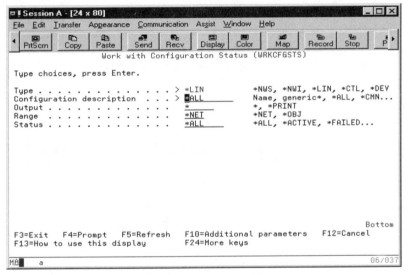

Figure 6.16: An example of the Work with Configuration Status (WRKCFGSTS) entry display, requesting communication lines status.

The *Configuration description* parameter defaults to *ALL, meaning you see a list of all lines to which you have authority that are configured on the system. You can specify to display a particular line configuration description. Some descriptions you might want to specify to display are the following:

- *ELAN—Ethernet
- *FAX—Facsimile

- *SDLC—Synchronous data link control, which is typically used to connect remote systems

- *TDLC—Twin axial data link control, which is a direct link to an AS/400 using twin axial cable

- *TRLAN—Token-Ring

In this case, you see only the lines for that configuration description. Prompt (press F4) this field to view a list of all possible values. You can also access online help (press F1) to get a list of values along with a short description of each value.

> **Tip:** To quickly find all lines configured on the system, enter WRKCFGSTS CFGTYPE(*LIN) on a command line. Or, using positional notation, just enter WRKCFGSTS *LIN. When you enter this command, the Work with Configuration Status display appears. An example of this display is shown in Figure 6.17.

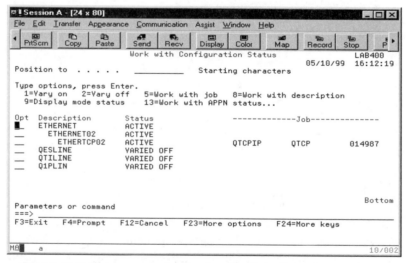

Figure 6.17: Viewing communication lines from the Work with Configuration Status (WRKCFGSTS) display.

You can tell the system represented by Figure 6.17 is using an Ethernet connection. Ethernet or Token-Ring is the typical arrangement in a LAN, where personal computers, printers, fax machines, etc., are attached in a network. ETHERNET02 is the name of the controller that is attached to line ETHERNET, and ETHERTCP02 is a TCP/IP adapter device that is attached to ETHERNET02.

> ***Tip:*** Do not get confused by the name of the Line Description (ETHERNET). This is just a label and could just as easily have been XYZZY instead of ETHERNET. The only way to be certain that you have an Ethernet or Token-Ring network would be to view the description of the line using option 8.

When you're looking at different levels or a hierarchy of information, the OS/400 indents lower-level information. Communication lines are leftmost under the Description column. Controllers are indented two spaces under the lines and devices are indented two spaces under the controllers.

As you come across several levels of data, it might get tricky determining what each level represents, with the line-controller-device hierarchy being a good example. F11 (Display types) indicates what each level means. When you press F11, the Job column changes to the Type column, as shown in Figure 6.18.

> ***Tip:*** You can use a function key even if it's not shown. Whenever you see F24 (More keys), press it to view other available function keys.

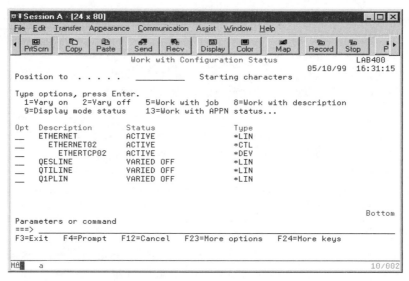

Figure 6.18: Displaying the type of configuration description on the Work with Configuration Status display.

Notice the lines QESLINE and QTILINE. These are used to connect this system directly to IBM. Specifically, QESLINE is used for Electronic Customer Support (ECS) to order program temporary fixes (PTFs) and report problems. QTILINE is used for communications with IBMLINK.

Options 1 (Vary on) and 2 (Vary off) perform similar functions for lines as for controllers and devices. (See the topics "Varying Devices On and Off" and "Varying Controllers On and Off" for details about these options.)

EXERCISE 6: WORKING WITH DEVICES, CONTROLLERS, AND LINES

Procedures

1. Display CD-ROM devices.

2. Display tape devices.

3. Display the workstation device you're using.

4. Try to vary off the workstation device you're using.

5. Sign off your workstation and sign on to a different one.

6. Vary off the workstation at which you signed off.

7. Vary on the workstation you varied off.

8. Display a list of all devices that are varied on.

9. Find the name of the controller to which the workstation you're using is attached.

10. Display all devices attached to this controller.

11. Try to display local workstation controllers using an incorrect CFGD value.

12. Display all lines on the system.

Display CD-ROM Devices

Scenario: You want to know if your AS/400 has a CD-ROM drive, but the system is located on the other end of the large office complex. Without walking over to the machine, determine from your workstation if there is a CD-ROM drive.

1. Sign on with a user ID that has system operator authorities.

2. On the command line:

   ➤ Type WRKCFGSTS and press F4.

3. On the Work with Configuration Status (WRKCFGSTS) prompt screen:

   a) Press F11 to display the keywords.

   b) For CFGTYPE, type *DEV.

   c) On the CFGD parameter, press F4 to prompt a list of values and determine which one best represents CD-ROM. After looking at the list, you believe *OPT to be the best choice, since optical devices include a CD-ROM.

   d) Type *OPT and press Enter.

   e) Press Enter again.

4. Look at the Work with Configuration Status list display:

   If there is a CD-ROM drive, write down its name and status:

   _____

   If the device is varied off, what option will vary it on?

   _____

Display Tape Devices

Scenario: You need to back up a library and its contents to tape. You need to know the name of the tape device to use and whether the tape is in a ready state.

1. Retrieve the WRKCFGSTS CFGTYPE(*DEV) CFGD(*OPT) command string:

   ➤ Press F9.

2. On the command line:

   a) Change the CFGD keyword value to *TAP.

   b) Press Enter.

3. Look at the Work with Configuration Status list display:

   How many tape devices are on your system?

   _____

   Are the tape devices usable? Why or why not?

   _____

Display the Workstation Device You're Using

1. Retrieve the WRKCFGSTS CFGTYPE(*DEV) CFGD(*TAP) command string:

   ➤ Press F9.

2. On the command line:

   a) Change the CFGD keyword value to *DSP.

   b) Press Enter.

3. Look at the Work with Configuration Status list display:

   Write the name of the workstation device you're currently using:

   _____

> **Hint:** Look in the Job column for your user ID.

How many workstations are defined on the system?

_____

> **Hint:** All of the devices listed are workstations, since you filtered the list using a CFGD value of *DSP, which means all display stations.

Try to Vary Off the Workstation Device You're Using

1. On the option line next to the device:

   ➤ Type 2 and press Enter.

   You should have received the following error message:

   ```
   Device <name> not varied off. Error occurred.
   ```

2. Get help on the error message:

   ➤ Position cursor on message and press F1.

3. List the first reason for what might have caused this error.

   _____

4. List the first recommendation to recover from this error.

   _____

5. What action do you need to take before you can vary off your work-station device?

   _____

6. Return to the Work with Configuration Status List display:

   ➤ Press Enter.

7. Clear the "2" on the option line:

   ➤ Press the space bar to space over it, or press the backspace key.

Note: For the next three tasks, "Sign Off Your Workstation and Sign On to a Different One," "Vary Off the Workstation at Which You Signed Off," and "Vary On the Workstation You Varied Off," you need to be able to physically sign on at another AS/400 display. However, if you're using a 5250 display session emulation tool, as found in Client Access/400, just open another 5250 display session.

Sign Off Your Workstation and Sign On to a Different One

1. On the command line:

   ➤ Type SIGNOFF and press Enter.

2. Find another workstation to sign on at, or open a new 5250 display emulation session.

Tip: If you're using locally attached 5250 twin axial workstations, you could use the system console as the other workstation. If you're using a 5250 display session emulation tool, as found in Client Access/400, and cannot create another 5250 display session, check the QAUTOVRT system value. QAUTOVRT may limit the number of virtual devices that can be autoconfigured. When you open a new emulation session, and all the existing virtual devices are currently being used (status is ACTIVE), the system automatically configures a new virtual device for that session. If a new virtual device won't configure, see the system administrator about increasing the QAUTOVRT value, or wait until an existing virtual device becomes available. The system randomly chooses from among available virtual devices. A status of VARY ON PENDING typically indicates that a virtual workstation device is available. Also, you might want to check to see if there are a large number of devices varied off, delete the device descriptions, and the system can recreate them as necessary.

---

3. On the other workstation or emulation session:

> Sign on with a user ID that has system operator authorities.

Tip: Just use the same user ID and password as you did on the workstation or session at which you signed off.

Vary Off the Workstation at Which You Signed Off

Scenario: A user complains that a particular workstation is "hung up" and can't get anything done. You need to vary off the device and vary it back on to reset it. For the purpose of this exercise, you will vary off your own workstation (the one you just signed off from), and then vary it back on using the second workstation or session at which you signed on.

1. On the command line of the second workstation or session:

> Type WRKCFGSTS and press F4.

2. On the Work with Configuration Status (WRKCFGSTS) prompt screen:

a) For CFGTYPE, type *DEV.

b) For CFGD, type *DSP.

c) Press Enter.

d) Press Enter again.

3. On Work with Configuration Status list display:

a) Find the name of the workstation or session device at which you were previously signed on.

> *Hint:* You should have recorded the name of this device in the earlier task called "Display the Workstation Device You're Using." If you didn't record the name, look in the upper-right corner of the Sign-On screen on the previous workstation or session. The name is in the Display field.

b) Look at the Status column for that device. It should say SIGNON DISPLAY.

Can you vary off a device with a status of SIGNON DISPLAY? Go ahead and try it!

> *Warning:* Triple-check to make sure this is the device you were using, so that you don't mistakenly vary off someone else's workstation.

c) On the option line next to that device, type 2 and press Enter.

You should have received the following message:

```
Vary off completed for device <name>.
```

d) If the status reads VARY OFF PENDING, press F5 to refresh the display until the status changes to VARIED OFF.

4. Do not exit the Work with Configuration Status list display.

5. Go to your original workstation or session.

Can you sign on? Why or why not?

Vary On the Workstation You Varied Off

1. Using the second workstation or session device:

    ➤ Make sure the Work with Configuration Status list display is showing the display devices on the system.

2. On the option line next to the device you varied off in the last task:

    ➤ Type 1, and press Enter.

    You should have received the following message:

    ```
    Vary on completed for device <name>
    ```

    The status should now read VARY ON PENDING.

    What does VARY ON PENDING mean?

    _____

3. Refresh the display to see if the status changes:

    ➤ Press F5.

    For local workstations, the status eventually changes to SIGNON DISPLAY, thereby allowing you to sign on to that workstation once again.

    For virtual workstations, the status remains at VARY ON PENDING. Therefore, a blank screen still appears for that device session. Simply close that session. When you open a new 5250 display emulation session, the system can choose to use that device and offer a Sign-On screen.

Display a List of All Devices That Are Varied On

Scenario: You need to vary off all workstation and printer devices. To determine which devices are varied on versus those that are already varied off, you need to filter the list by displaying only those devices that are varied on. This query includes all devices with a status of VARIED ON, VARY ON PENDING, ACTIVE, SIGNON DISPLAY, and so forth.

Warning: Do not attempt to vary off all workstation and printer devices in this exercise.

---

1. On the command line:

   ➤ Type WRKCFGSTS and press F4.

2. On the Work with Configuration Status (WRKCFGSTS) prompt screen:

   a) For CFGTYPE, type *DEV.

   b) For CFGD, leave the default of *ALL.

   c) Press Enter.

   d) On the STATUS parameter, press F4 to prompt a list of values. Use the value of *VARYON.

   e) Type *VARYON and press Enter.

   f) Press Enter again.

3. Look at the Work with Configuration Status List display:

   Examine the various devices, and list three or four status codes that are returned as a result of querying devices that are varied on:

   _____   _____

   _____   _____

   Write the number of devices that have a status of ACTIVE:

   _____

   Steps must be taken before an active device can be varied off. For workstations, users must sign off. For printers, you must end the printer writers.

How can you sign a user off of a workstation?

_____

Hint: See chapter 3.

How do you end a printer writer?

_____

Hint: See chapter 5.

Find the Name of the Controller
to Which the Workstation You're Using Is Attached

1. On the command line:

   ➤ Enter WRKCFGSTS CFGTYPE(*DEV) CFGD(<*name of your workstation device*>).

   Hint: If you don't remember the name of your workstation, use System Request menu option 7 (Display work station user).

2. Write what the WRKCFGSTS command string would look like if you entered it using CL positional notation.

   _____

3. Look at the Work with Configuration Status List display.

   What is the name of the controller?

   _____

4. Do not exit the Work with Configuration Status List display.

Display All Devices Attached to This Controller

Scenario: Your manager just called to inform you that all the display devices in the accounting department are down. You suspect that the problem is related to the device controller for that department. For the purpose of this exercise, pretend that the controller to which your workstation is attached is the suspect controller.

1. Retrieve the WRKCFGSTS CFGTYPE(*DEV) CFGD(<*name of your workstation device*>) command string:

   ➤ Press F9.

2. On the command line:

   a) Change the CFGTYPE keyword value to *CTL.

   b) Change the CFGD keyword value to <*name of your workstation controller*>.

   c) Press Enter.

   Now, all devices connected to this controller are listed.

3. Look at the Work with Configuration Status List display:

   What options allow you to vary on and off a controller?

   _____

   What status is required for a controller to allow a device attached to it to function?

   _____

   What happens if you choose option 2 to vary off an ACTIVE controller?

   _____

   _____

   Warning: Do not attempt to vary off the controller.

Can you vary off an individual device listed under its controller?

Try to Display Local Workstation Controllers Using an Incorrect CFGD Value

Scenario: Sometimes you will enter incorrect values for command parameters. When you do, the AS/400 returns an error message. Understand the power of error-message help.

1. Retrieve the WRKCFGSTS CFGTYPE(*CTL) CFGD(<*name of your workstation controller>*) command string:

   ➤ Press F9.

2. Prompt the command:

   ➤ Press F4.

3. On the Work with Configuration Status (WRKCFGSTS) prompt screen:

   a) Change the CFGD value to *LOC.

   Note: This value is incorrect for a controller, but enter it anyway.
   ---

   b) Press Enter.

   c) Press Enter again.

   You should have received the following error message:

   ```
   Configuration description not valid.
   ```

4. Get help on the error message:

   ➤ Position cursor on message and press F1.

The only CFGD values that are appropriate for a CFGTYPE of *CTL are listed, as shown in Figure 6.19.

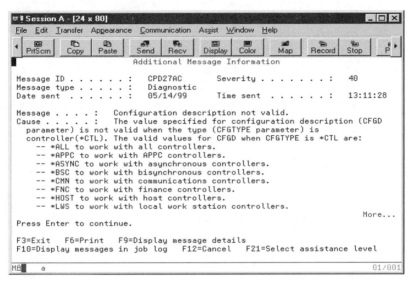

Figure 6.19: Displaying help for error message.

5. Page down to view all possible values.

    What's the correct CFGD to use to work with local workstation controllers?

    _____

    How can you print this whole message—without having to do multiple print screens to capture all the information?

    _____

    If a file hasn't printed on the printer where you expected it to, what command can you use to work with the output?

    _____

    Hint: See chapter 5.

6. Return to the Work with Configuration Status (WRKCFGSTS) prompt screen:

   ➤ Press Enter.

7. On the Work with Configuration Status (WRKCFGSTS) prompt screen, based on your research:

   a) Change CFGD to the correct value for local workstation controllers.

   b) Press Enter twice.

   All local workstation controllers on the system, along with their attached devices, are listed.

8. Do not exit the Work with Configuration Status List display.

Display All Lines on the System

1. Retrieve the WRKCFGSTS CFGTYPE(*CTL) CFGD(*LWS) command string:

   ➤ Press F9.

2. On the command line:

   a) Change the CFGTYPE keyword value to *LIN.

   b) Change the CFGD keyword value to *ALL.

   c) Press Enter.

   Now, all lines on the system are listed.

3. Look at the Work with Configuration Status List display:

   Does a controller control a line?

_____

Briefly describe lines, controllers, and devices, and their relationship to one another.

_____

_____

_____

_____

_____

Hint: Look at the indentation of the configuration objects, or press F11 to display codes for the object types. This helps you determine the hierarchy of configuration objects.

4. Determine what types of lines are connected to your AS/400:

   a) On the option line next to a line, type 8 and press Enter.

   b) Look at the Type column.

   Hint: If you're not sure what the line type code means, position your cursor anywhere on the Type column, and press F1 for online help.

   c) Repeat steps a and b for other lines.

   Based on this information, what is the network configuration? Twin axial? Ethernet? Token-Ring? Other?

   _____

SAVING AND RESTORING

This chapter describes the following activities:

- Understanding OS/400 Save and Restore

- Preparing tapes for a backup

- Running a simple backup

UNDERSTANDING OS/400 SAVE AND RESTORE

> **Note:** This chapter does not discuss backup and recovery strategies or how to perform complex backups, such as a full system save and restore.

Data backup and recovery on the AS/400 are known as *save* and *restore*. Save and restore commands and menus are provided with the operating system. The OS/400 save-and-restore facility allows you to do the following:

- Recover from a program or system failure.

- Exchange information between multiple AS/400s.

- Store infrequently used objects offline.

Normally, objects are frequently saved and infrequently restored.

You can use commands and menu options to save individual objects and groups of objects. You can use some save and restore operations while your system is active. Other save and restore operations require that no other activity is occurring on the system. If your system is busy most of the time, you can use the save-while-active function to reduce the time period that the system is unavailable, while you are performing save operations.

Because the AS/400 supports critical business functions—customer service, sales, order processing, distribution, and manufacturing—your business should have a detailed backup and recovery plan to protect these functions no matter what happens. Planning can mean the difference between business success and business failure.

An AS/400 system operator is typically not responsible for creating backup and recovery procedures and schedules. In most cases, the system administrator puts together the plans for what AS/400 information needs to be saved, how often it should be saved, and where to store the media (such as tape) containing saved information. However, since the operator is responsible for doing the actual backups, this person must have answers to the following questions:

- Why should AS/400 information be saved on a regular basis?
- What can and cannot be saved?
- What media can be used to save data to?
- How can saved information be recovered?

Why You Need to Save Data on the AS/400

The AS/400 is a very reliable business computing system. You might run your system for months or even years without experiencing any problems that cause you to lose information on your system. However, as the frequency of computer problems has decreased, the potential impact of problems has increased. Businesses are more and more dependent on computers and the information stored in them. The information that is in your computer might not be available anywhere else.

Saving the information on your system is time-consuming and requires discipline. So, why should you do it? You need to be prepared in case system failures or losses occur. You can then use backup copies of information to restore all or certain parts of the system when necessary.

Five basic types of failures can occur on a system. Some are more likely to occur than others. In any case, your business should have a save strategy that prepares you to recover from all of them. The five basic types of failures are:

- Disk failure
- System failure
- Power Failure
- Program failure or human error
- Complete system loss

Disk Failure

If a disk unit on your system fails, in most cases the data on that disk unit is destroyed. This requires recovering all the data in the auxiliary storage pool (ASP) that contains the failed unit.

The single-level storage architecture makes the AS/400 system a very productive system to program and to manage. However, the architecture makes recovering from a disk failure somewhat more difficult. The system spreads information across all the disk units in an ASP to provide good performance and storage management. If a unit in an ASP is lost, you cannot determine what data was on that unit because objects are spread across the ASP. You must recover all the data in the ASP.

System Failure

A system failure means that some part of your system hardware fails. Some system failures, such as processor problems, cause your system to stop without warning. This is called an *abnormal end*. When your system ends abnormally, problems can occur. These problems include the following:

- Files might be partially updated.
- Access paths for files might be incomplete.
- Objects that are in use might be damaged.
- Relationships between files might be partially validated.

When you restart (IPL) your system after the failed component is repaired, OS/400 attempts to rebuild access paths, verify file relationships, and synchronize files to transaction boundaries. Essentially, OS/400 tries to return the system to the exact state it was in when it went down. Because DB2/400 is an integral part of the AS/400, many of the tasks that are handled by a system operator are done automatically by the system. The first IPL after the system ends abnormally can take a long time as the system rebuilds itself.

Power Failure

Loss of power also causes your system to end abnormally. You might experience the same types of problems that occur with a system failure. Many systems are equipped with a feature called *System Power Control Network*. This feature provides a function called *Continuously Powered Main Store*. If your system has this feature, a battery provides sufficient power to shut down the system and maintain the contents of memory for up to two days after a power loss. In many cases, this can significantly reduce the amount of time the system requires to perform an IPL after a power loss.

Program Failure or Human Error

Sometimes programs are not adequately tested before they are put into production, or a condition occurs that software developers did not anticipate. A program error can introduce incorrect information in some of your data files.

People using the system can make mistakes, too. An operator might run a month-end program twice. A data-entry person might enter the same batch of orders twice. A system manager might delete a file by mistake.

When these types of errors occur, you need to correct or restore the data that has been damaged.

Complete System Loss

A fire, flood, or other natural disaster could destroy your entire system. To rebuild the system, you should have a complete set of save tapes and documentation stored off-site at a secure, accessible location.

What You Can Save on the AS/400

Any object on the AS/400, whether system-supplied or user-created, can be saved. Some of the information that can be saved is listed here:

- One object in a library.
- A group of objects by generic name.
- A group of objects by generic name and object type.
- One or more entire libraries.
- Office data (document library objects, such as documents, folders, mail, and calendars).
- Objects in directories.
- Objects changed since the last backup.
- System data (QSYS, configuration objects, security data, and licensed internal code).
- All libraries other than the system library.
- All user-created data.
- Security data (such as user profiles).

When an object is saved, more than just the object itself is saved; its attributes are also saved. These include the name and type, save date and time, owner name, storage required in the system, security information, and the textual description of the object.

In essence, you can save data on your system in the following three ways:

- By individual object.
- By library and all of its associated objects.
- By doing an entire system save, which includes all system and user data.

See the subheading Running a Simple Backup for a look at different save commands and options.

Is There Anything You Can't Save?

There is some information on the system that cannot be saved. You cannot save any of the following:

- Contents of job, message, output, and data queues. This means that you cannot back up spooled files or messages; these are not objects. Descriptions of queues can be saved, but not their contents.

  > **Note:** If you need to back up spooled files, use the Copy Spooled File (CPYSPLF) command to copy them to a physical file, which can be saved since it is an object.

- Objects that are damaged.
- Objects in use during the save operation, unless SAVACT (*YES) is specified on a save command. However, even if you choose to save active objects, there is no guarantee that they will be saved.

Media You Can Use to Save Data

You can save and restore objects by using diskette, magnetic tape, or a save file. Tape is the most common media used for save and restore operations. For this reason, an entire topic in this chapter is devoted to preparing tapes to use for offline storage of information. Diskette and tape operations are very similar. For most of the tape commands and functions that are described, there are similar commands and functions for diskettes.

A save file is a special type of file that can be created on the system and which OS/400 treats essentially as a tape. Almost anything that can be saved to tape media can be saved to a save file. Objects and libraries saved to a save file can be restored to disk just as they can from offline media. The whole idea of saving system data offline is to make sure you have a copy of the data offline in case of machine failure. For this reason, for a save to a save file to be complete, it is important that the data in the save file be saved to tape. Saving data to a save file is much quicker than saving to tape because any write operation is faster to disk than to tape. However, you should be aware that save files can take up quite a bit of disk space until the save file contents are transferred to tape.

The AS/400 supports CD-ROM so that you can archive information, but it is not intended to provide backup and recovery capability. It is Read Only. CD-ROM is primarily used to ship the Operating System/400 (OS/400) and the licensed program products (LPPs).

How to Recover Saved Data

Once objects are saved offline, they can be restored back to the system from which they were saved, or restored to another system, at any time. If objects are deleted or damaged, the restore operation takes objects backed up to media (such as tape) and recreates them on the system.

Hopefully, the save and restore process is 99% save and 1% restore, but just in case, the Restore menu provides easy access to all restore commands. Enter the command GO RESTORE to access this menu. For the most part, there is a corresponding restore command for each save command. In other words, you can only restore objects in a certain way. How the objects are saved determines how the restore can be executed.

PREPARING TAPES FOR A BACKUP

The most common media for backing up AS/400 information is tape. The AS/400 supports the following types of tape:

- Quarter-inch tape cartridge and tape unit.
- Quarter-inch mini tape cartridge and tape unit.
- Eight-millimeter tape cartridge and tape unit.
- Half-inch tape cartridge and tape unit.
- Magstar MP tape cartridge and tape unit.
- Half-inch tape reel and tape unit.

It is important to find out the type of tape unit your AS/400 has. However, no matter what type you have, you need to take several steps before information can be saved to tape. You need to choose the correct set of tapes to use, periodically clean the tape unit, and initialize the tapes.

> *Tip:* In the IBM manual *Basic System Operation, Administration, and Problem Handling SC41-5206*, the chapter entitled "What You Need to Know about Your AS/400 System" contains tips and techniques on handling and storing tapes.

Rotating Tapes

An important part of a good save procedure is to have more than one set of tapes. When you perform a recovery, you might need to go back to an old set of save tapes for one of the following reasons:

- Your most recent set is damaged.
- You discover a programming error that has affected data on your most recent save tapes.

Some general rules to observe for tape rotation include the following:

- Keep three complete sets of backup tapes, and rotate through the sets.
  When doing a new backup, use the tapes that contain the oldest backup.
  The following is an example of how to use three sets:

Save 1	Set A
Save 2	Set B
Save 3	Set C
Save 4	Set A
Save 5	Set B
Save 6	Set C

- Keep one backup set offsite and record where sets are kept.

- Keep the job logs with each backup set.

> **Tip:** Immediately after a backup is complete, you can print out the job
> log, which contains any error messages issued during the save. Use the
> command DSPJOBLOG JOB(*) OUTPUT (*PRINT).

- After the backup is complete, put a new backup set where the current set
  was kept and rotate the locations of the other two sets.

- Replace tapes according to the manufacturer's recommendations.

Rotating tapes is just one of many considerations involved in managing tapes and
tape libraries. For more information, read the IBM manual *OS/400 Backup and
Recovery SC41-5304.*

Cleaning Tape Units

Tape drives must be cleaned on a regular basis. The read and write heads collect
dust and other material that can cause errors when reading or writing to tape. In addition to your regular cleaning cycle, you should also clean the tape unit if you are
going to be using it for an extended period of time or you are using new tapes. New
tapes tend to collect more material on the read and write heads of the tape unit. (For
more specific recommendations, refer to your specific tape unit's manual.)

> **Note:** For ¼-inch tape units and ¼-inch mini tape units, tape errors occur during save and restore operations if the tape heads are dirty. In some cases, the errors can be severe enough to cause the system to stop the save or restore process. If tape errors occur as a result of dirty tape heads, you receive a message that the tape device needs to be cleaned. The QIC-5010 and MLR3 tape units also have a cleaning status light that indicates that cleaning is required. It is very important to respond to these cleaning indicators and clean the head using a recommended cleaning method. In the IBM manual *Basic System Operation, Administration, and Problem Handling SC41-5206*, the chapter entitled "What You Need to Know about Your AS/400 System" contains information on how to clean the various tape units, as well as how often to clean each type of tape unit.

Initializing a Tape

Each tape must be initialized before information can be saved to the tape. Initializing a tape is similar to formatting a diskette on a DOS system. When a tape is initialized, any information previously recorded on the tape is erased and written over with the new information. The initialization process creates a *tape label*. To initialize a tape, complete the following steps:

1. Make sure the status of the tape device you are using is VARIED ON. (If the status is ACTIVE, it means the tape device is in use by another job and therefore is not available until that job has ended.) Enter the command WRKCFGSTS CFGTYPE(*DEV) CFGD(*TAP). Make note of the tape device name.

2. Clean the tape drive if necessary. (See the previous topic, "Cleaning Tape Units," for consequences of not regularly cleaning tape drives.)

3. Load the tape in the tape drive.

4. Do one of the following to access the Initialize Tape (INZTAP) display:

   ■ Follow a menu path:

a) On the AS/400 Main Menu (MAIN), type 3, General system tasks, and press Enter.

b) On the General System Tasks (SYSTEM) menu, type 8, Device operations, and press Enter.

c) On the Device Operations (DEVICE) menu, type 4, Tape, and press Enter.

d) On the Tape (TAPE) menu, type 2, Initialize a tape, and press Enter.

Hint: Take a fast path to the Tape menu by entering the command GO TAPE.

- Type the command INZTAP and press F4.

The Initialize Tape (INZTAP) entry display appears, as shown in Figure 7.1.

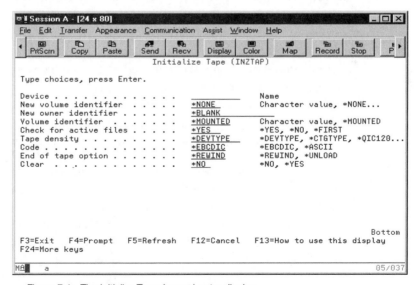

Figure 7.1: The Initialize Tape (INZTAP) entry display.

The most commonly used INZTAP parameters are the following:

- Device

- New volume identifier (Volume ID)

- Check for active files

5. For the *Device* parameter, specify the name of your tape device (for example, TAP01).

6. For the *New volume identifier* parameter, specify a unique volume ID to internally label the tape with a standard label. This identification is recorded on the tape and used by the AS/400 to track information about data that is on the tape. Do not confuse this internal label with the external label, which is a gummed label that appears on the outside of a tape container or the tape itself to help the operator quickly identify what the tape was used for.

A tape can be initialized as either a standard-labeled tape or as a non-labeled tape. Be aware that it is an AS/400 system requirement that tapes used for save and restore operations have *standard labels*. With a standard label, the AS/400 can quickly identify both the tape itself and the information written on it without needing to scan the whole tape. Therefore, this is much faster than if the tape is unlabeled. Standard labels are recommended when using tape for program input or output and for other uses of tape, such as copy, migration, and journaling. Software distribution on tape is always done using standard-labeled tapes.

With *non-labeled tapes*, there is no information displayed about the tape. Non-labeled tape is used to exchange information with another system that does not support standard-label tapes. For example, if you need to send a customer list to a company with an RS/6000, that machine is not able to read an AS/400-labeled tape. So in this case, you would not want to label the tape containing the customer list with a standard label. Unless a non-labeled tape is required for data exchange, standard-labeled tapes should always be used.

If you accept the default of *NONE for *New volume identifier* (NEWVOL), the tape you initialize is an unlabeled tape. If you specify a volume for this parameter, the tape is initialized as a standard-labeled tape.

Tip: Specify a NEWVOL value that identifies the type of save you're going to do. For example, if you are doing a full system save, type SYSTEM for this parameter. You could also specify the date on which you're doing the save, for example, 051899.

---

7. *Check for active files.* An active file has an expiration date that is equal to or later than the current date. Specify one of three options:

    - *YES to check all data files on the tape before the tape is initialized. If an active file is found, the tape is not initialized.

    Note: *YES makes sure you don't overwrite anything accidentally. However, the processing of tapes that have a large file, or tapes that have many files, might take a long time. For example, the initialization of 8-millimeter tapes might take up to three and a half hours.

    - *FIRST to check only the first file on the tape. If this file is active, the tape is not initialized. The processing time depends on the size of the first file on the tape.

    - *NO to initialize the tape immediately without checking for active files. Use *NO for any of the following situations:

        ➢ The tape is new.

        ➢ You are sure you want the tape initialized in the minimum amount of time.

        ➢ The initialization failed when you specified *YES or *FIRST, but you are sure you want the tape initialized anyway.

> **Caution:** Not checking for active files causes the system to overwrite all data that is on your tape. Therefore, make sure the tape is new. If it is not new, be sure that you want the tape initialized regardless of its contents.

8. Press Enter to begin the initialization process. If the initialization process completes successfully, you receive the following message:

```
Volume <name as specified in NEWVOL parameter> prepared for operation
with owner ID *BLANK.
```

Figure 7.2 shows the Initialize Tape (INZTAP) entry display with values for the common parameters.

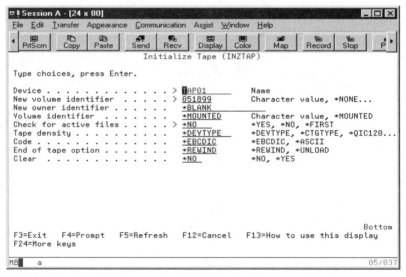

Figure 7.2: The Initialize Tape (INZTAP) entry display with values for the common parameters.

The *Tape density, End of tape option,* and *Clear* parameters are of particular interest. Tape density determines the amount of data recorded per inch of tape. In most cases, use the default value of *DEVTYPE to initialize the tape to the density supported by the tape drive, or specify *CTGTYPE to initialize the tape density supported by the tape cartridge.

If you want the system to automatically unload the tape after initialization is complete, type *UNLOAD for the *End of tape option* parameter. The tape is automatically rewound and unloaded after the operation ends.

The *Clear* parameter defines whether the tape's data should be erased before initialization. Clearing the data takes more time, and the initialization process duplicates this step. For example, specifying CLEAR (*YES) to erase QIC-5010 1/4-inch tapes and 8-mm tapes is not recommended because the process can take hours. Therefore, this parameter is typically *NO.

Displaying Tape Contents

You can find out what data is stored on a tape. You can display just the names of the files on the tape, or if the tape was written by an OS/400 save operation, you can display a list of the saved objects on the tape. To display the contents of a tape, complete these steps:

1. Make sure the status of the tape device you are using is VARIED ON. (If the status is ACTIVE, it means the tape device is in use by another job and therefore is not available until that job has ended.) Enter the command WRKCFGSTS CFGTYPE(*DEV) CFGD(*TAP). Make note of the tape device name.

2. Load the tape in the tape drive.

3. Do one of the following to access the Display Tape (DSPTAP) display:

   ■ Follow a menu path:

     a) On the AS/400 Main Menu (MAIN), type 3, General system tasks, and press Enter.

b) On the General System Tasks (SYSTEM) menu, type 8, Device operations, and press Enter.

c) On the Device Operations (DEVICE) menu, type 4, Tape, and press Enter.

d) On the Tape (TAPE) menu, type 1, Display tape information, and press Enter.

Hint: Take a fast path to the Tape menu by entering the command GO TAPE.

- Type the command DSPTAP and press F4.

The Display Tape (DSPTAP) entry display appears, as shown in Figure 7.3.

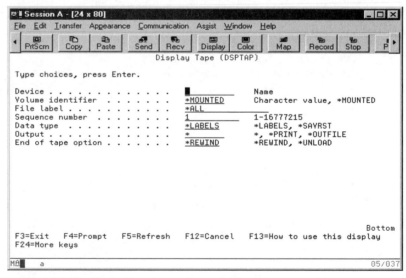

Figure 7.3: The Display Tape (DSPTAP) entry display.

4. Specify the name of your tape device; for example, TAP01.

5. Look at the *Data type* (DATA) parameter. To display just the names of each file on the tape, as well as information such as when each file was created, specify *LABELS. To display a detailed list of the saved objects that exist on the tape, specify *SAVRST.

6. Press Enter to display the requested information. This might take some time to process, depending on how many files are on the tape and how large the files are.

*LABELS Format

The Display Tape Volume Information display appears if you specified DATA(*LABELS) on the DSPTAP command. An example of this display is shown in Figure 7.4.

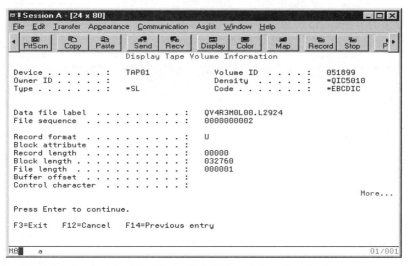

Figure 7.4: An example of the Display Tape Volume Information display.

Note the Type *SL in the upper portion of the display. *SL indicates that this tape was initialized as a standard-labeled tape. Be aware that it is an AS/400 system requirement that tapes used for save and restore operations have standard labels. Since there is a Volume ID (051899), this also indicates that the tape has a standard label. (For more information about standard-labeled versus non-labeled tapes, see the "Initializing a Tape" topic discussed previously.)

Information about the file on the tape appears in the body of the display. As shown in Figure 7.4, the file label QV4R3M0L00.L2924 indicates that this tape was used to save the operating system. You might conclude that there are many more files on this tape, since a save of the operating system is typically done as part of an entire system save (explained briefly later in this chapter under the subheading "Running a Simple Backup" topic).

The AS/400 locates and displays information about one file at a time on the tape. You must press Enter to display information about the next file on the tape. Note the file sequence number as shown in Figure 7.4. It shows the second file on the tape, as indicated by 0000000002.

The word "More..." indicates that additional information about a file can be seen. Use the scrolling keys to page down and up. An example of additional information about a tape volume label is shown in Figure 7.5.

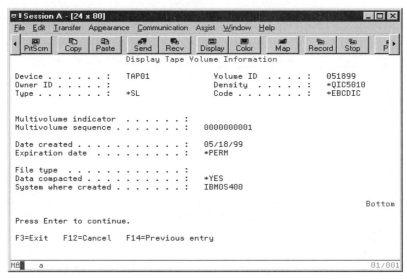

Figure 7.5: An example of additional information about a tape volume label.

The information on this display helps you determine when the file was created and set to expire, among other details.

When *Check for active files* is set to *YES on the Initialize Tape (INZTAP) display, the system looks at the expiration date to determine if a file can be overwritten during tape initialization. If a date is shown, then the file is protected and cannot be overwritten until after that date passes. You can specify a file expiration date on a save command. The default value is EXPDATE(*PERM), which means that the file is protected permanently. However, when *Check for active files* is set to *NO, the file is overwritten during initialization regardless of the expiration date or *PERM.

*SAVRST Format

The Display Saved Objects—Tape display appears if you specify DATA(*SAVRST) on the DSPTAP command. An example of this display is shown in Figure 7.6.

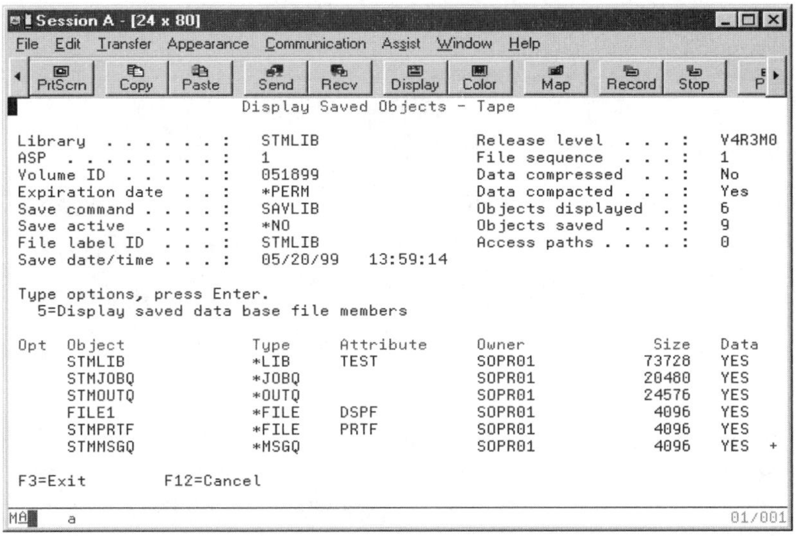

```
Session A - [24 x 80]                                               _ □ ✕
File   Edit   Transfer   Appearance   Communication   Assist   Window   Help
 ◀   PrtScrn   Copy   Paste   Send   Recv   Display   Color   Map   Record   Stop   P ▶
                         Display Saved Objects - Tape
   Library  . . . . . . :   STMLIB          Release level  . . . . :   V4R3M0
   ASP  . . . . . . . . :   1               File sequence  . . . . :   1
   Volume ID  . . . . . :   051899          Data compressed  . . . :   No
   Expiration date  . . :   *PERM           Data compacted . . . . :   Yes
   Save command . . . . :   SAVLIB          Objects displayed  . . :   6
   Save active  . . . . :   *NO             Objects saved  . . . . :   9
   File label ID  . . . :   STMLIB          Access paths . . . . . :   0
   Save date/time . . . :   05/20/99   13:59:14

   Type options, press Enter.
     5=Display saved data base file members

   Opt   Object          Type      Attribute    Owner          Size    Data
         STMLIB          *LIB      TEST         SOPR01        73728     YES
         STMJOBQ         *JOBQ                  SOPR01        20480     YES
         STMOUTQ         *OUTQ                  SOPR01        24576     YES
         FILE1           *FILE     DSPF         SOPR01         4096     YES
         STMPRTF         *FILE     PRTF         SOPR01         4096     YES
         STMMSGQ         *MSGQ                  SOPR01         4096     YES  +

   F3=Exit        F12=Cancel

 MA█    a                                                           01/001
```

Figure 7.6: An example of the Display Saved Objects—Tape display.

Here, the objects saved to the portion of tape indicated by the *File sequence* number (near the upper-right of this display) are listed. As with the DATA(*LABELS) displays, you must press Enter to see if any objects are saved to other parts of the tape. Once you reach the end of all tape files, press Enter on the last tape file to return to the display from which you issued the DSPTAP command.

Notice the Save command value in the upper portion of the display. A value of SAVLIB tells you that a library, and the objects within that library, are saved to this section of tape (File sequence 1). You confirm this by looking at the list in the lower portion of the display.

A plus sign (+) in the lower-right corner of the display indicates that there are more objects in the file sequence. Use the scrolling keys to page down and up.

> **Note:** Displaying a tape interactively might take a long time, if there are a lot of objects on the tape or if the objects are very large. A better alternative is to print the list of objects by specifying OUTPUT(*PRINT) on the DSPTAP command. The output is produced in a spooled file, which you can display if it hasn't already printed.

Handling Tape Errors

When reading from or writing to tape, it is normal for some errors to occur. Here are three types of tape errors that can occur during save and restore operations:

- Recoverable errors—Some tape devices support recovering from media errors. The system repositions the tape automatically and tries the operation again.

- Unrecoverable errors: processing can continue—In some cases, the system cannot continue to use the current tape, but can continue processing on a new tape. The system requests you to load another tape. The tape with the unrecoverable error can be used for restore operations.

- Unrecoverable errors: processing cannot continue—In some cases, an unrecoverable media error causes the system to stop the save process. This type of error might occur if the tape drive needs cleaning. (See the "Cleaning Tape Units" topic earlier in this chapter for information about the importance of regularly cleaning tape drives.)

Tapes physically wear out after extended use. You can determine if a tape is wearing out by periodically printing the error log. Use the Print Error Log (PRTERRLOG) command and specify TYPE(*VOLSTAT) if you have authority to this command. The printed output provides statistics about each tape volume. If you use unique names (volume identifiers) for your tapes, you can determine which tapes have excessive read or write errors and should be removed from the tape library.

If you suspect that a tape has problems and you want to check the integrity of saved information, use the Display Tape (DSPTAP) or the Duplicate Tape (DUPTAP) command. These commands read the entire tape and detect objects on the tape that cannot be read.

> *Tip:* If an error message appears during tape usage, put the cursor on the message, and press F1. Then, follow the instructions in the online help to resolve the problem.

RUNNING A SIMPLE BACKUP

After determining what objects need to be saved offline and initializing a tape as a standard-labeled tape to use for a backup, you can run a simple backup. In this topic, you are learning how to save a library and the objects within that library to tape using the Save Library (SAVLIB) operation. Once the objects are successfully saved, you can confirm that they exist on the tape by displaying the tape's contents. At this point, the objects can be optionally deleted from the system. Whether or not the objects are deleted, you can then restore them from the tape back to the system using the Restore Library (RSTLIB) operation.

This helps you understand the process of backing up data and recovering it, so that you can perform more complex backups—such as full system saves—with confidence. The process of saving your system and restoring it extends beyond the scope of this book. This topic only explains what gets saved with a complete system save and the state at which the system must be before such a save is even possible.

The Save Menu

The simplest place to start any kind of backup is from the Save menu. To find this menu, do one of the following:

- Follow a menu path:

  1. On the AS/400 Main Menu (MAIN), type 3, General system tasks, and press Enter.

  2. On the General System Tasks (SYSTEM) menu, type 6, Save, and press Enter.

- Enter the command GO SAVE.

The Save menu, which consists of three displays, allows you to save just about anything on the AS/400. The three displays are shown in Figures 7.7, 7.8, and 7.9. (See the subheading "Is There Anything You Can't Save?" earlier in this chapter for a list of things that are not saved with any backup.)

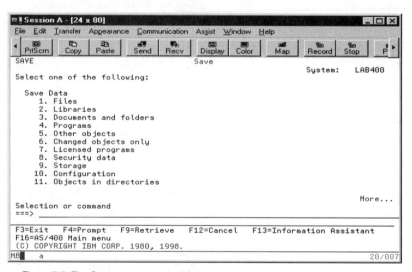

Figure 7.7: The Save menu, part 1 of 3

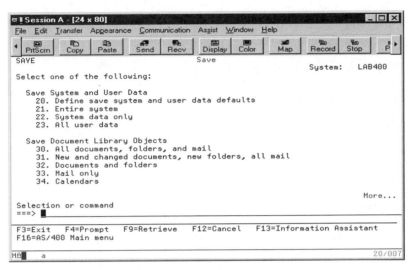

Figure 7.8: The Save menu, part 2 of 3.

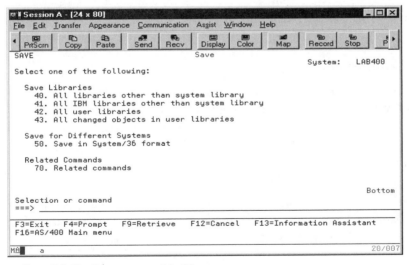

Figure 7.9: The Save menu, part 3 of 3.

Notice that option 21 (Entire system) in part 2 of the Save menu (Figure 7.8) allows you to save the entire system, which includes the following items:

- The Licensed Internal Code (LIC).

- The operating system (OS/400).

- The system library (QSYS).

- The security objects, including user profiles.

- The device configuration objects.

- All IBM-supplied libraries including those containing user data.

- All user libraries including libraries for licensed programs.

- All mail, folders, and documents used with OfficeVision/400.

- All objects in directories.

An entire system save essentially executes a command for each of these items. These commands are described in the next topic.

Save Commands

When you select an option on the Save menu, you are prompted for various save commands. There are several save commands, so you can save only what you need to save, and only when you need to save it. As you become more comfortable working with the AS/400, you might prefer to use these commands rather than the Save menu.

The following is a list of common save commands and a short description of each. Most of these commands are automatically run as part of a full system save (option 21 on the Save menu).

SAVSYS: Saves the system library (QSYS), all security information, all system configuration objects, and the Licensed Internal Code (LIC). The format of this saved data is compatible with the install process. Individual objects cannot be restored from these tapes.

SAVLIB: Saves one or more libraries (up to 300 libraries) and all objects associated with these libraries. When saving to a save file or optical media, only one library can be specified. This command can also be used to save, in one operation, one of the following:

- All libraries on the system other than QSYS (specify a library name of *NONSYS).

- All libraries that normally contain user data.

- All IBM-supplied libraries other than QSYS (as well as other libraries that cannot be saved except by using the command SAVSTG; read the online help for more information).

The command SAVLIB saves the entire library, including the library description and all objects in the library. For job queues, message queues, output queues, data queues, and logical files, only the object definitions are saved, not the contents (such as messages and spooled files).

SAVDLO: Saves documents, folders, and distribution objects (mail) used with OfficeVision/400 in the QDOC library.

SAVOBJ: Saves one or more objects (up to 50 individual objects from the same library) or a group of objects by generic name and/or type from one or more libraries. If *ALL is specified for an object name, objects can be saved from up to 300 libraries. When saving to save file, only one library can be specified.

SAV: Saves one or more directories or objects within directories. This command must be used to save the AS/400 Integrated File System (IFS). Directories are found on the system when the AS/400 is providing server support for attached PCs or LANs. If you're using Client Access/400, for instance, this program creates objects in AS/400 IFS directories. While SAV could be used to save all objects on the AS/400, it cannot produce a SAVSYS tape suitable for IPL (restart of the AS/400) or an install of OS/400.

SAVCHGOBJ: Saves only those named objects that have changed since the last complete save of a library. Both specific and generic names are valid. If *ALL is specified for an object name, objects can be saved from up to 300 specified libraries. When saving to a save file, only one library can be specified.

SAVSAVFDTA: Saves to tape objects that have been saved to a save file.

SAVSECDTA: Saves one or more user profiles or all security information, including profiles, authorization lists, and authority holders. The AS/400 does not have to be in a restricted state to run this command. (See the next topic, "Restricting Access to the System," for details about this condition.)

SAVCFG: Saves all configuration and system resource management information without requiring that the AS/400 be in a restricted state. SAVCFG eliminates having to perform frequent save system (SAVSYS) operations, when changes are made only to configuration objects (such as line, controller, and device configurations).

SAVSTG: Saves a copy of the Licensed Internal Code (LIC) and contents of auxiliary storage (except unused space and temporary objects) to tape. SAVSTG is essentially a dump of the disk to tape and is typically used to provide recovery from a disaster, such as a fire or flood. Be aware that tapes produced by this command can only be used to install the entire system, and then only during a manual IPL (restart of the AS/400). You cannot selectively restore individual libraries and other objects from these tapes. To restore on an object-by-object basis, use the SAVSYS command.

Note that there are limitations to the number of related objects that can be saved in a single save operation. Refer to the IBM manual *OS/400 Backup and Recovery SC41-5304*, for details about these and other save considerations.

Restricting Access to the System

The following save options place the system in a restricted state:

- Option 9—Storage.
- Option 21—Entire system.
- Option 22—System data only.
- Option 23—All user data.
- Option 40—All libraries other than the system library.

A system is in a *restricted state* when all subsystems, except the controlling subsystem (typically QCTL), are ended and therefore no longer active. When the AS/400 is in a restricted state, users cannot log on and use the system. Only the system console is active in the controlling subsystem so that the operator can perform the backup. In other words, you can only use the system console to perform backups requiring a restricted state.

For the listed options, the command ENDSBS SBS(*ALL) OPTION(*IMMED) is issued at the start of the save, and when the save is complete, the command STRSBS SBSD(*<controlling subsystem>*) is issued. At this point, users can log on to the AS/400 again.

In general, restricting access to the system when you are performing saves is a good practice. It ensures that the save contains the most current object a user might be using. If any user has an update or lock on a particular object while you run your backups, the object cannot be saved. So even if the save option doesn't place the system in a restricted state for you, you can use the ENDSBS or ENDSYS command to end all subsystems except the controlling subsystem.

Whenever you need to do a restricted backup and users are signed on to the system, send all users a break message (SNDBRKMSG) telling them to sign off. Specify the time the system is to be taken down and when users can expect the system to be available again. (See chapter 4 for details on break messages.)

Saving and Restoring a Library Using Tape

The following procedure allows you to run a simple backup of a library to tape. Once the library has been saved to tape, you can delete the library off the system and then restore it back to the system from tape. In the exercise at the end of this chapter, you do a similar Save and Restore, but instead of using tape, you create a save file for your backup.

Save a Library

1. Choose a user library that contains some objects. For example, use the library (*xxx*LIB, where *xxx* is your initials) to which you moved and copied objects in the exercise in chapter 2.

> **Warning:** Do not use a system library—libraries starting with Q—for this task.

2. Initialize a tape that's compatible with your system's tape device. The tape must be initialized as a standard-labeled tape. (Follow the procedure in the "Initializing a Tape" topic.)

3. Access the Save Library (SAVLIB) display by doing one of the following:

   - Enter GO SAVE, and then choose option 2 (Libraries) on the Save menu.

   - Type SAVLIB on a command line, and press F4.

4. On the Save Library (SAVLIB) display, do the following:

   a) Specify the following parameters:

      - LIBRARY = the name of the user library to back up (for example, STMLIB).

      - DEVICE = the name of the tape device (for example, TAP01).

   b) Press Enter.

   c) Keep the default values for the other parameters. Figure 7.10 shows example values for the *Library* and *Device* parameters and the other values you should have.

      > **Note:** A volume identifier of *MOUNTED uses the new volume identifier you specified when you initialized the tape.

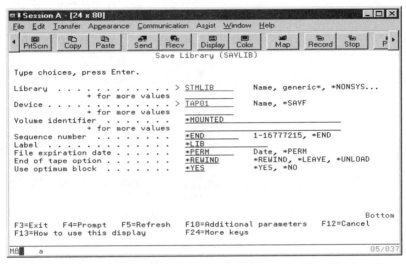

Figure 7.10: Example values for the Library and Device parameters on the Save Library (SAVLIB) display.

d) Press Enter. After a few moments, you should receive a message stating how many objects were saved from the library, similar to this example:

```
4 objects saved from library STMLIB
```

This number includes the library object itself, plus the objects in the library.

Display the Tape's Contents

Now that the library and its objects have been saved to tape, confirm that those objects are really on the tape. To do this, complete the following steps:

1. Access the Display Tape (DSPTAP) display. (Follow the procedure in the "Displaying Tape Contents" topic.)

2. On the Display Tape (DSPTAP) display, do the following:

    a) Specify the following parameters:

        ■ DEVICE = the name of the tape device (for example, TAP01).

        ■ DATA TYPE = *SAVRST.

    Figure 7.11 shows the values you should have for this display.

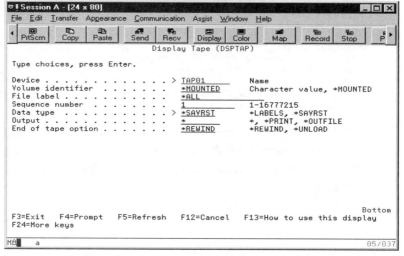

Figure 7.11: An example of values that should be entered on the Display Type (DSPTAP) display.

    b) Press Enter. After a few moments, the Display Saved Objects—Tape display appears with the list of objects you saved via the SAVLIB operation.

4. On the Display Saved Objects—Tape display:

    a) Examine the list to make sure all of the objects in the library you saved are on the tape. If a plus sign appears in the lower-right corner of the display, page down to see more objects.

b) Take a look at the other information on the display, and if there is anything you don't understand, read the online help. Just press F1.

c) Press F3 to exit.

> **Note:** Displaying a tape interactively might take a long time if there are a lot of objects on the tape or if the objects are very large. A better alternative is to print the list of objects by specifying OUTPUT(*PRINT) on the DSPTAP command. The output is produced in a spooled file, which you can display if it hasn't already printed.

Delete the Library

Now that you're sure the library and its objects exist on the tape, you can delete them from the AS/400. This frees up disk space. Deleting a library also deletes the objects in that library. This is an optional step.

> **Note:** If you are not the owner of the library or the owner of the objects in that library, you must have enough object authority to delete an object. If the library you saved is one which you created, and if you created the objects in the library, you are the owner and are able to delete the library.

To delete the library, complete the following steps:

1. Check to see if the library is in your library list or is the current library, by entering the DSPLIBL command. Figure 7.12 shows an example of a library list.

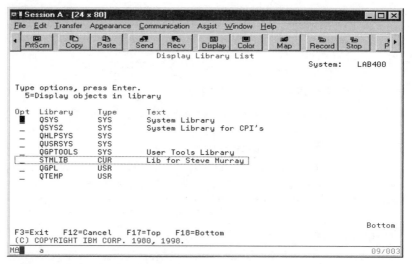

Figure 7.12: An example of a library list.

You cannot delete a library that is on a library list. In the example library list, the library to be deleted is STMLIB, which happens to be the current library for this user. If the library you want to delete does not show up in your library list, you can skip to step 5.

2. If the library is the current (CUR) library, change the current library to remove it from the library list. Enter the command:

> CHGCURLIB *CRTDFT

*CRTDFT means that no library should be in the current (CUR) entry of the library list. If objects are created into the current library, then library QGPL is used as the default.

3. If the library is in the user (USR) portion of the library list, remove it from the library list. Enter the command:

> RMVLIBLE <library name>

4. Optionally display the library list to make sure the library is not on the library list any longer. Enter the command:

> DSPLIBL

5. Delete the library. Enter the command:

> ➤ DLTLIB *<library name>*

6. Optionally try to display the library if you don't believe the library was deleted. Enter the command:

> ➤ DSPLIB *<library name>*

Restore the Library

Once the library and its objects have been deleted off of the system, the only way to recover those objects is to restore, or recreate, them from the backup tape. Even if you didn't (or couldn't) delete the library, you can still restore it to see how the process works.

For the most part, there is a corresponding restore command for each save command. In other words, you can only restore objects in a certain way. How the objects are saved determines how the restore can be executed.

> **Note:** You must have at least *USE authority to the restore commands you need to use. If you don't have this authority, contact the system administrator or security officer.

To restore the library, complete the following steps:

1. Make sure the tape is loaded in the tape drive.

2. Access the Restore Library (RSTLIB) display, by doing one of the following:

   ▪ Enter GO RESTORE, and then choose option 2 (Libraries) on the Restore menu.

   ▪ Type RSTLIB on a command line, and press F4.

3. On the Restore Library (RSTLIB) display, do the following:

   a) Specify the following parameters:

      ▪ LIBRARY = the name of the user library to restore (for example, STMLIB).

      ▪ DEVICE = the name of the tape device (for example, TAP01).

   b) Press Enter.

   c) Keep the default values for the other parameters. Figure 7.13 shows example values for the *Library* and *Device* parameters and the other values you should have.

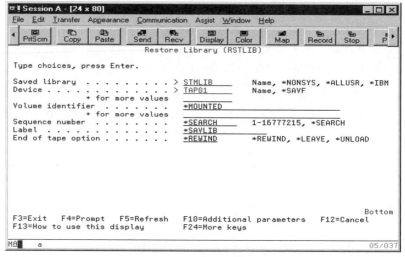

Figure 7.13: Example values for the Library and Device parameters on the Restore Library (RSTLIB) display.

   d) Press Enter. After a few moments, you should receive a message stating how many objects were restored from the tape, similar to the following example:

> 4 objects restored from STMLIB to STMLIB.

This number includes the library object itself, plus the objects in the library.

Display the Library

Are the library and its contents on the system? How can you tell when an object was last saved and restored? After doing a restore of a library, you can answer these questions by displaying the library. To do this, complete the following steps:

1. Enter the command:

    ➢ DSPLIB *<library name>*

2. On the Display Library display:

    a) Examine the list to make sure all of the objects in the library you restored are listed. If the word "More..." appears in the lower-right corner of the display, page down to see more objects. An example of this display is shown in Figure 7.14.

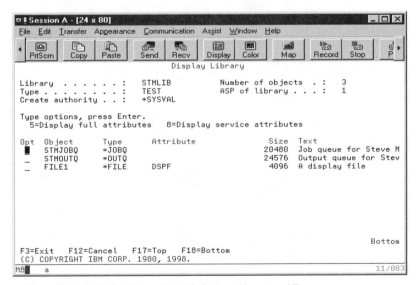

Figure 7.14: A Display Library (DSPLIB) display with restored library.

b) Display an object's attributes to determine when it was last saved and restored. On the option line next to an object:

➢ Select 5 (Display full attributes).

Tip: You can also display an object's attributes by using the command DSPOBJD.

---

c) On the Display Object Description—Full display:

➢ Page down until you see Save/Restore information.

An example of this display is shown in Figure 7.15.

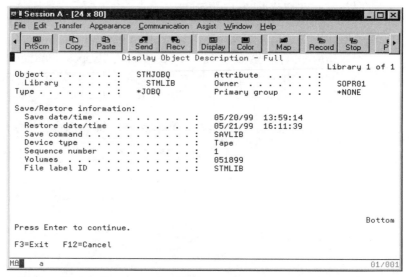

```
☐ ▌Session A - [24 x 80]                                          _ ☐ ✕
 File  Edit  Transfer  Appearance  Communication  Assist  Window  Help
 ◄  ▣      ▣▫     ▣▫     ▣▫    ▣▫     ▣     ▣       ▣      ▣     ▣    ►
    PrtScrn  Copy   Paste   Send   Recv  Display  Color    Map   Record  Stop  P
 ▋                    Display Object Description - Full
                                                      Library 1 of 1
 Object . . . . . . . :    STMJOBQ        Attribute  . . . . . :
   Library  . . . . . :      STMLIB       Owner  . . . . . . . :    SOPR01
 Type . . . . . . . . :    *JOBQ          Primary group  . . . :    *NONE

 Save/Restore information:
   Save date/time . . . . . . . . . . . :    05/20/99   13:59:14
   Restore date/time  . . . . . . . . . :    05/21/99   16:11:39
   Save command . . . . . . . . . . . . :    SAVLIB
   Device type  . . . . . . . . . . . . :    Tape
   Sequence number  . . . . . . . . . . :    1
   Volumes  . . . . . . . . . . . . . . :    051899
   File label ID  . . . . . . . . . . . :    STMLIB



                                                          Bottom
 Press Enter to continue.

 F3=Exit    F12=Cancel

 MA▌    a                                                  01/001
```

Figure 7.15: Save/Restore information on the Display Object Description—Full (DSPOBJD) display.

d) Press Enter to return to the Display Library display.

e) Optionally display the attributes for as many more objects as you wish.

EXERCISE 7:
SAVING A LIBRARY TO AND RESTORING IT FROM A SAVE FILE

Scenario: You need to back up a library and its objects. However, the tape device on your AS/400 is currently in use by another operation. So in the meantime you decide to use a save file. When the tape device is free, you can back up the save file data to tape. (Note: Saving save file data to tape is not discussed here.)

While this exercise is done using a save file, the save and restore commands can also reference tape. In fact, having saved anything to a save file (which is still on-line), it is imperative that the save file contents be saved offline to complete the save process.

Note: You must have at least *USE authority to the RSTLIB (Restore Library) command in order to restore the library. To see if your profile has authority to this command, enter the following command:

DSPOBJAUT OBJ(RSTLIB) OBJTYPE(*CMD)

If you, or a group profile you belong to, don't have at least *USE authority, contact the system administrator or security officer.

Procedures

1. Create a save file in library QGPL.

2. Save a library to this save file.

3. Display the save file to confirm that the save worked.

4. Delete the library.

5. Restore the library from the save file.

6. Display the library to confirm that the restore worked.

7. Check an object's save/restore date and time.

Create a Save File in Library QGPL

1. Sign on with a user ID that has system operator authorities.

2. On the command line:

    ➤ Type CRTSAVF, and press F4.

3. On the Create Save File (CRTSAVF) prompt screen:

    a) In the *Save file* field, type *xxx*SAVF (where *xxx* is your initials).

    b) In the *Library* field, type QGPL.

    > **Note:** You don't want to create the save file in your current library, because that library is the one you created in chapter 2 (*xxx*LIB) and the one you are deleting. When you delete a library, all objects in that library are deleted. You want to use the save file to restore the deleted library.

    c) In the *'Text description'* field, type 'SAVE FILE FOR <*your name*>'.

        Figure 7.16 shows example values for this display.

    d) Press Enter. You will receive a message that the save file was created, similar to the following example:

    ```
    File STMSAVF created in library QGPL.
    ```

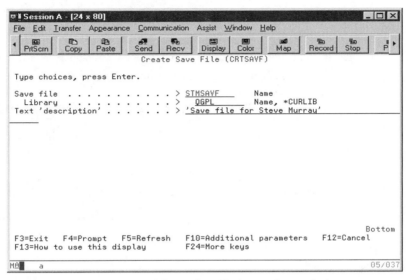

Figure 7.16: An example of the Create Save File (CRTSAVF) entry display.

Save a Library to This Save File

> ***Note:*** Use the library to which you moved and copied objects in chapter 2. This library is *xxx*LIB, where *xxx* is your initials.

1. On the command line:

    ➤ Type SAVLIB and press F4.

2. On the Save Library (SAVLIB) display, do the following:

    a) In the *Library* field, type *xxx*LIB (where *xxx* is your initials).

    > ***Note:*** When saving to a save file, you can only specify one library, but when saving to tape, you can specify up to 300 libraries.

    b) In the *Device* field, type *SAVF.

c) Press Enter to display additional parameters.

d) In the *Save file* field, type *xxx*SAVF (where *xxx* is your initials). Figure 7.17 shows example values for this display.

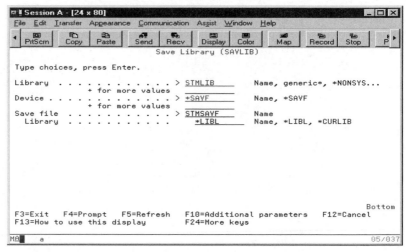

Figure 7.17: An example of the Save Library (SAVLIB) entry display.

e) Press Enter. You will receive a message stating how many objects were saved from the library, similar to the following example:

```
4 objects saved from library STMLIB.
```

Saving a library saves the library object itself and all objects in that library.

Note: If you try to save objects to a save file that already contains data, you receive the following error message:

```
Save file STMSAVF in QGPL already contains data. (C G)
```

Type *C* to cancel the request, or type *G* to replace the existing data with the new information.

Display the Save File to Confirm That the Save Worked

1. On the command line:

    ➤ Enter DSPSAVF *xxx*SAVF (where *xxx* is your initials).

    The Display Saved Objects—Save File display appears. Figure 7.18 is an example of this display, showing that four objects were saved.

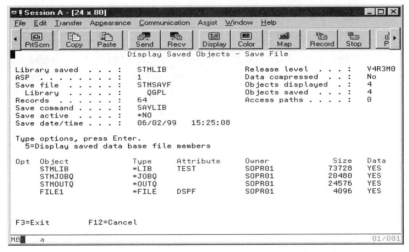

Figure 7.18: An example of the Display Saved Objects—Save File display.

2. On the Display Saved Objects—Save File display:

    a) Notice the similarities between it and the Display Saved Objects—Tape display. (See the "Displaying Tape Contents" topic for an example of that display.)

    b) Examine the list to make sure all of the objects in the library you saved are on the save file. If a plus sign appears in lower-right corner of the display, page down to see more objects.

    c) Look at the other information on the display, and if there is anything you don't understand, read the online help. Just press F1.

d) Press F3 to exit.

To back up save-file contents to tape, use the command SAVSAVFDTA (Save Save File Data). Since a save file still exists on the system, you must use this command to have a copy of the saved objects offline. Once you save the save file to tape, you could delete the save file to free up disk space. Use the command DLTF <*save file name*> to delete a save file.

Delete the Library

Note: Deleting a library also deletes the objects in that library. If you are not the owner of the library, nor the owner of the objects in that library, you must have enough object authority to delete an object. Since the library you saved is one which you created, and since you created the objects in the library, you are the owner and are able to delete the library.

---

1. On the command line:

    ➤ Enter DLTLIB.

    You will receive a message stating that the library was deleted, similar to the following:

    ```
    Library STMLIB deleted.
    ```
    ---

2. If you don't believe the library was deleted, try to display it. On the command line:

    ➤ Enter DSPLIB *xxx*LIB (where *xxx* is your initials).

    You should receive a message saying the library isn't found.

Restore the Library from the Save File

You can easily restore objects that have been deleted. Restoring from a save file simulates restoring from a backup tape.

1. On the command line:

   ➤ Type RSTLIB and press F4.

2. On the Restore Library (RSTLIB) display, do the following:

   a) In the *Library* field, type *xxx*LIB (where *xxx* is your initials).

   b) In the *Device* field, type *SAVF.

   c) Press Enter to display additional parameters.

   d) In the *Save file* field, type *xxx*SAVF (where *xxx* is your initials).

      Figure 7.19 shows example values for this display.

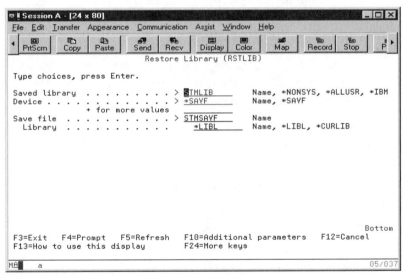

Figure 7.19: An example of the Restore Library (RSTLIB) display.

   e) Press Enter.

      You will receive a message stating how many objects were restored from your library, similar to the following example:

```
4 objects restored from STMLIB to STMLIB.
```

This number includes the library object itself, plus the objects in the library.

Are the library and its contents on the system? How can you tell when an object was last saved and restored? After doing a restore of a library, you can answer these questions by displaying the library and checking an object's description.

Display the Library to Confirm That the Restore Worked

1. On the command line:

    ➤ Enter DSPLIB *xxx*LIB (where *xxx* is your initials).

    The objects in that library should be listed.

2. On the Display Library display:

    ➤ Examine the list to make sure all of the objects in the library you restored are listed. If the word "More..." appears in the lower-right corner of the display, page down to see more objects.

    An example of this display is shown in the "Saving and Restoring a Library Using Tape" topic.

3. Do not exit the Display Library display.

Check an Object's Save/Restore Date and Time

1. On the option line next to an object on the Display Library display:

    ➤ Type 5 and press Enter.

    > **Tip:** You can also display an object's attributes by using the command DSPOBJD.

2. On the Display Object Description—Full display, as shown in Figure 7.20:

a) Page down until you see the Save/Restore information.

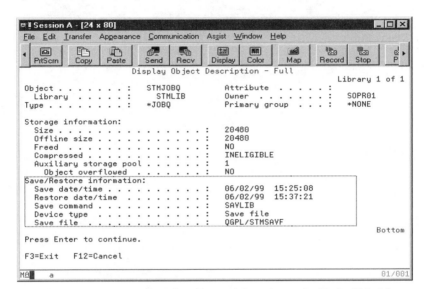

Figure 7.20: An example of the Save/Restore information on the Display Object Description—Full (DSPOBJD) entry display.

b) Press Enter to return to the Display Library display.

c) Optionally, display the attributes for as many more objects as you wish.

RESOURCES

The following AS/400 manuals can be used as references to the material in this book. You can order hardcopy versions of these manuals from IBM, or view most of them online, if the Softcopy Library has been installed. These publications are also available for viewing on the Internet at the following URL:

```
http://publib.boulder.ibm.com/pubs/html/as400/onlinelib.htm
```

See chapter 1 for more information on finding AS/400 manuals on the Internet.

> **Note:** The number preceding the manual title (for example, SC41-3200) indicates the document number used in ordering manuals. The version and release number following the manual title (for example, V4R3) indicates the last version and release of OS/400 for that manual title.

AS/400 Hardware and Software Overview

GA19-5486   *AS/400 Advanced Series Handbook* (an IBM Redbook)

Basic OS/400 Operational Concepts

SC41-3200   *AS/400 System Operation for New Users V3R1*

SC41-4203   *AS/400 System Operation V3R6*

SC41-5161   *Getting Your AS/400 Working for You V4R2*

SC41-5001   *OS/400 InfoSeeker – Getting Started V4R1*

SC41-5002   *OS/400 InfoSeeker Use V4R1*

SC41-5722   *OS/400 CL Reference V4R3*

SC41-5721   *OS/400 CL Programming*

Object Management

SC41-5722   *OS/400 CL Reference V4R3*

SC41-5721   *OS/400 CL Programming*

Job Control and Work Management

SC41-4203   *AS/400 System Operation V3R6*

SC41-5306   *OS/400 Work Management V4R3*

SC41-5206   *AS/400 Basic System Operation, Administration, and Problem Handling V4R3*

Message Handling

SC41-3200   *AS/400 System Operation for New Users V3R1*

SC41-4203   *AS/400 System Operation V3R6*

SC41-5206   *AS/400 Basic System Operation, Administration, and Problem Handling V4R3*

Print Control

SC41-4203   *AS/400 System Operation V3R6*

SC41-5206   *AS/400 Basic System Operation, Administration, and Problem Handling V4R3*

SC41-5713   *OS/400 Printer Device Programming V4R3*

Device Management

SC41-4203   *AS/400 System Operation V3R6*

SC41-5206   *AS/400 Basic System Operation, Administration, and Problem Handling V4R3*

SC41-5406   *OS/400 Communications Management V4R2*

Save and Restore

SC41-4203   *AS/400 System Operation V3R6*

SC41-5206   *AS/400 Basic System Operation, Administration, and Problem Handling V4R3*

SC41-5304   *OS/400 Backup and Recovery V4R3*

In addition, a good source of online education is the "AS/400: Getting to Know Your System" course. This course is shipped free on CD-ROM with all AS/400 systems. Use this course as a refresher study as needed.

INDEX

A

ACTIVE status of devices, 116, 257, 261-263, **262**, **263**, 271-272, 284
ACTIVEWRITER status, 259
Add Entry To Job Queue (ADDJOBQE), 139
Advanced assistance level, 26, 27
Advanced Certification through RCTC, xiv
application messages, 150
AS/400 Associate System Operator, xv
"AS/400 Getting to Know Your System," 40
AS/400 Online Library on the Internet, 29, 38-39
AS/400 University, xiii-xiv
assistance levels, 26-29
    Advanced, 26, 27
    Basic, 26, 27
    Change Profile (CHGPRF) to change, 28
    displaying messages in basic and intermediate, 162-163, **162**
    Intermediate, 26, 27
    print management, 198, **198**
    QASTLVL system value in, 29
Associates Degree through RCTC, xiv
attributes, 3, 64
auditing, object auditing values, 88

authority, authorizing objects, 5, 72-73
autoconfiguration of devices, 256
auxiliary storage pool (ASP), 4, 295-296

B

backups (*See* save and restore)
Barsa, Al, xiv
Basic assistance level, 26, 27
Basic System Operation, Administration, and Problem Handling, 40, 302
batch job processing, 6, 7-8, 98, 104, 105-106, 105
    print management for, 208
    qualified job names in, 108
    Submit Job (SBMJOB) for, 107, **107**
    submitting a job for, 106-108
blank fields in data entry displays, 20
bookshelves in Softcopy Library, 37-38
Bottom to indicate end of items in list displays, 23
break message handling program, 174
*BREAK messages, 174, 179-180
break messages, 157, **157**

Note: Boldface numbers indicate illustrations.

C

call stack for job management, 122

CD-ROM (OPT) devices, 254, 277-278
  save and restore, 299

certification, xiv, xv-xvi

Change Job (CHGJOB), 122-129, **123**, 140

Change Message Queue (CHGMSGQ),
  175-176, **175**, 179-180, **180**

Change Object Description (CHGOBJD), 82

Change Profile (CHGPRF), 19, 28, 219-221,
  220

Change Spooled File Attributes (CHGSPLFA),
  211-214, **211**, 246-247, **247**

CISCO Networking Academy, xiii

CL commands, 40-55
  abbreviations for, 41
  back up to previous (F9), 44
  Command Entry to enter, 42-44, **43**, 76
  command line to enter, 42-44
  default values for parameters of, 50
  entering, 48-55
  F10 display additional parameters for, 51
  F11 toggle between keywords and choices
    for, 51
  F3/F12 exit without running, 50
  F4 display all values of parameter for, 50
  F5 reset all parameters for, 51
  F9 display all parameters for, 51
  format or syntax of, 42
  free-format entry of, 53
  function keys for parameters for, 50-51
  if you forget the name of, 47-48, **48**
  keyword form entry for, 54-54
  keywords for, 51-52, 53-54
  library creation exercise using, 55-62
  list of, 44-48
  Major Command Groups menu for, 44, **44**
  names of, 41
  parameters for, 42, 49-50
  plus sign (+) for more values for, 50
  positional form entry for, 54-55
  print list of, using Print Screen, 235-236
  prompt for (F4), 43
  prompting for, 49-52, **49**
  re-using, 43
  required vs. optional parameters for, 50
  Select Command display for, 47-48, **48**
  spooling of, 45-47, **45-47**
  structure of, 41
  where to enter, 42-44

classes for jobs, 103

Cleanup (CLEANUP) menu, 17

Command Entry, 42-44, **43**, 76

command line, 12, 42-44

command prompting, 49-52, **49**

common elements in, 9

Communication Status (CMNSTS), 272-276

communications jobs, 6

complex work management system, 100

Configuration description for devices, 254,
  268-269

continuously powered main store, 296

controllers, device, 265-267, **266**

copying objects, 72, 89-91, 90, 91

Create Duplicate Object (CRTDUPOBJ), 72,
  90-91, **91**

Create Library (CRTLIB), 56-58, **57**, **58**,
  59-61, **60**, **61**

Create Save File (CRTSAVF), 330-331, **331**

credit certification at RCTC, xiv

Customize Your System, Users Devices
  (SETUP) menu, 18

D

DASD, 4

data, 3

data entry (See entry displays)

database management and DB2/400, 4

default printers, 220

default values for command parameters, 20, 50

Delete Library (DLTLIB), 95, 323-325, 324, **334**

deleting objects, 73, 95

delivery methods for messages, 174

device descriptions for printer writers/devices, 192-193

device management

  5250 twin-ax workstations, 281

  ACTIVE status in, 257, 261-263, **262**, **263**, 271-272, 284

  ACTIVE status prohibits varying off in, 261-263, **262**, **263**

  ACTIVEWRITER status in, 259

  autoconfiguration of devices in, 256

  CD-ROM (OPT) devices and, 254

  Communication Status (CMNSTS) in, 272-276

  Configuration descriptions in, 254, 268-269

  controllers and attached devices in, 265-267, **266**

  display all controllers attached to a line for, 272-276

  display all devices attached to controller for, 287-288

  display all devices on system for, 252-255

  display CD-ROM device for, 277-278

  display devices messages for, 264, **265**

  display lines on system for, 290-291

  display tape devices for, 278-279

  display workstation devices for, 279-280

  Electronic Customer Support (QESLINE) line and, 276

  error messages for, 288-290, **289**

  Ethernet (ELAN) line configuration and, 273-275

  Facsimile (FAX) line configuration and, 273-275

  find controller of workstation devices for, 286

  GO DEVICE command for, 253

  IBMLINK (QTILINE) line for, 276

  interpreting status of devices in, 256

  list controllers and devices for, 267-270, **269**, **270**

  list devices that are varied on for, 284-286

  listing *ALL devices in, 255

  printer (PRT) devices in, 254, 258-259

  QAUTOVRT for virtual devices in, 281

  resource names for tape, diskette, CD-ROM devices in, 265

  sign off workstation, sign on to another for, 281-282

  SIGNON DISPLAY status in, 257, 284

  status of devices for, 252-260

  synchronous data link control (SDLC) line configuration in, 274

  tape (TAP) devices in, 254, 259-260, **260**

  token ring (TRLAN) line configuration and, 274-275

  twin-axial data link control (TDLC) line configuration and, 274-275

  VARIED OFF status in, 257, 259, 260, 270-272

  VARIED ON status in, 260, 270-272, 284

  Vary Configuration (VRYCFG) in, 260, 270-272

  VARY OFF PENDING status in, 263

  vary off workstation devices for, 280-281, 282-283

  VARY ON PENDING status in, 257, 259, 263, 271, 284

  vary on workstations for, 284

  varying controllers on and off for, 270-272, **271**

  varying devices on and off for, 260-264

device management (*continued*)
  virtual devices, QAUTOVRT for virtual devices and, 281
  virtual printer (VRTPRT) devices in, 257
  virtual workstation (VRT) devices in, 257-258, **258**
  why devices are varied off/on in, 261
  Work with Configuration Status (WRKCFGSTS) for, 253-260, **253**, 265-270, **266**, **268**, 272-276, **273**, 278-280
  working with devices, controllers, lines exercise for, 277-291
  workstation (DSP) devices in, 254, 256-258, **258**
Device Operations menu, 14-15, **14**
Device Status (DEVICESTS) menu, 17
disk failures, 295
Disk Space Tasks (DISKTASKS) menu, 17
disk storage, 4
diskette devices for save and restore, 299
display files, creation of, 79-80, **80**
Display Job Description (DSPJOBD), 233-234, **233**
Display Library (DSPLIB), 69, 327-328, **327**, 336
Display Message Description (DSPMSGD), 170
Display Messages (DSPMSG), 144, **144**, 160-166, **160**, 174, 184-186
Display Object Authority (DSPOBJAUT), 73, 83-85, **84**
Display Object Description (DSPOBJD), 52, 86, **87**, 88, 336-337, **337**
Display Tape (DSPTAP), 313, 321-323, **322**
display type, 9-14
  common elements in, 9
  entry displays as, 9, 18-21
  information displays as, 9, 23-24, **23**, **24**
  list displays as, 9, 21-23
  menu displays as, 9, 12-18
  sign-on screen display as, 9-11, **10**
Display Work Station User (DSPWSUSR), 24
Domino, xiv
Duplicate Tape (DUPTAP), 313

E

e-business/e-commerce, 5
ease of using OS/400, 2
economy of OS/400, 2
Edit Object Authority (EDTOBJAUT), 73
Electronic Customer Support (QESLINE) line, 276
ellipsis (...) to indicate more choices in data entry displays, 20
End Job (ENDJOB), 119-120, **119**
END status code, 116
End Writer (ENDWTR), 226, **226**
entering CL commands, 48-55
entry displays, 9, 18-21
  blank fields in, 20
  Change Profile (CHGPRF) display, 19
  changing existing entries in, 20
  default values in, 20
  ellipsis (...) to indicate more choices in, 20
  Help for, 33-34, **34**
  parameters (F10) for, 20
  prompting (F4) for more choices in, 20
  user-assigned values in, 20
error handling
  device management, 188-290, **289**
  error message, **172**
  tape errors, 312-313
Ethernet (ELAN) line configuration, device management, 273-275
Evans, Wayne, xiv
extended help, 35-36
extended lists, 23

Note: Boldface numbers indicate illustrations

F

F1 Help, 23-24, **23**, **24**, 29-30, 36
F3/F12 exit without running CL commands, 50
F3/F12 step back through menus, 15
F4 display all values of parameter for CL commands, 50
F4 prompt for choices in data entry displays, 20
F4 prompt for CL commands, 43
F5 reset all parameters for CL commands, 51
F6 for Viewed Topics in Help, 33
F9 display all parameters for CL commands, 51
F9 to back up to previous CL command, 44
F10 and F11 toggle between columns in list displays, 23
F10 display additional parameters for CL commands, 51
F10 to display parameters in data entry displays, 20
F11 toggle between keywords and choices for CL commands, 51
F23 prompts for more options in list displays, 22
F23 to Set Initial Menu, 16
Facsimile (FAX) line configuration, device management, 273-275
File (FILE) objects, 64
Files (FILE) menu, 17
finding objects, 85-86
first in first out (FIFO) processing order in job queues, 111-112
free-format command entry, 53
function keys, 12
function keys for command parameters, 50-51

G

General Purpose Library (QGPL), 80
General System Tasks (SYSTEM) menu, 13-14, **14**, 18
GO command for menus, 13, 15, 16-18

GO DEVICE command, 253
GO PRINTER command, 222
GO RESTORE menu, 299
Grant Object Authority (GRTOBJAUT), 73
Grenham, Dick, xiv
group ownership of objects, 66-67

H

Help, 29-40
  AS/400 Online Library on the Internet for, 29, 38-39
  assistance levels in, 26-29
  bookshelves in Softcopy Library for, 37-38
  context-sensitive, 30
  entry displays and, 33-34, **34**
  extended, 35-36
  F1 for, 29-30, 36
  F6 for Viewed Topics in, 33
  hypertext links in, 32-33
  Information Assistant for, 29, 36, **37**
  information displays and, 23-24, **23**, **24**, 35
  InfoSeeker for, 29, 37-38
  list displays and, 34, **35**
  menu displays and, 30-33, **30-33**
  message management, 168-171, **169**
  More... to indicate additional help in, 31, 34
  online course in, "AS/400 Getting to Know Your System," 40
  online sources of, 29-30
  other resources/books for, 39-40
  Softcopy Library for, 37-38
*HOLD messages, 174
Hold Job (HLDJOB), 117-118, **118**
Hold Spooled File (HLDSPLF), 210, 243-244
Hold Writer (HLDWTR), 227-228, **227**
human error, save and restore, 297
hypertext links, Help facilities containing, 32-33

Note: Boldface numbers indicate illustrations

I

IBM Certified Specialist, xvi
IBM-supplied subsystems for, 6
IBM-supplied user profiles, 5
IBMLINK (QTILINE) line, 276
Information and Problem Handling
  (USERHELP) menu, 18
Information Assistant, 29, 36, **37**
Information Assistant Options (INFO) menu,
  17
information displays, 9, 23-24, **23**, **24**
  Help for, 35
informational messages, 8, 150-151
InfoSeeker, 29, 37-38
Initialize Tape (INZTAP), 302-307, **303**
initiating a job, 7
inquiry messages, 8, 150-151, 156, **156**,
  183-184
interactive job processing, 6, 7, 98, 104,
  128-133
Intermediate assistance level, 26, 27
IPLs, 296

J

Java, xiv
job attributes, 103
job definitions, 122
job descriptions, 7, 101
job management, 6-7, 8, 97-147
  active job statistics, 133-135
  ACTIVE status code, 116
  Add Entry To Job Queue (ADDJOBQE),
    139
  attributes of jobs, displaying, 121-122, **121**
  batch processing in, 6-8, 98, 104, 105-106,
    105
  businesses and malls analogy for, 100-104
  call stack for, 122
  Change Job (CHGJOB) in, 122-129, 123,
    140

classes for jobs in, 103
communications jobs, 6
complex system in, 100
display job queues in, 138-139
Display Messages (DSPMSG) in, 144, **144**
display particular job in job queue of, 139
displaying signed-on users, 129-131, **130**,
  144-145
End Job (ENDJOB) in, 119-120, **119**
END status code for, 116
ending a job in, 141, **141**
ending jobs in, when not to, 120
find job queues for, 109, 138-139
finding signed-on (and temporarily
  signed-off) users for, 131-132
first in first out (FIFO) processing order in,
  111-112
hold a job for, 117-118, 139, **140**, 142, **142**
Hold Job (HLDJOB), 117-118, **118**
holding a job queue for, 112
how many jobs are active in, 134
IBM-supplied subsystems for, 6, 100
information about signed-on users for, 132
initiating a job, 7
interactive processing in, 6, 7, 98, 104,
  128-133
job attributes for, 103
job column of WRKUSRJOB display in, 116
job definitions in, 122
job descriptions in, 7, 101, 108
job names in, 108
job numbers in, 108
job queues for, 104, 108-112, **108**
JOBQ status code for, 116
jobs in, 6, 7, 101, 104
Manage Your System, Users, Devices
  (MANAGESYS) for, 129, 144-145
maximum CPU time for jobs in, 103
maximum storage space for jobs in, 103

Note: Boldface numbers indicate illustrations

messages to signed-on users in, 132

moving job to different job queue for, 126, 140

MSGW status code in, 116

open file display for, 122

output queues for, 106

output queues for, changing, 125

OUTQ status code in, 116

pools for job storage in, 102

print priorities for, 124

priorities for jobs in, 103, 110, 111-112, 122, 124, 125-126

purging jobs in, 103

QBASE subsystem in, 6, 100

QBATCH subsystem in, 6, 100

QCMN subsystem in, 100

QCTL subsystem in, 100

QINTER subsystem in, 6, 7, 100

QSPL subsystem in, 100

QSWSWRK subsystem in, 100

qualified job names in, 108

releasing a job in, 118, 143-144

releasing a job queue in, 112

routing data for, 102

routing entries for, 102

run time priorities for, 125-126

scheduling batch jobs, 8

selecting which jobs to display in, 114

Send Message (SNDMSG) in, 136

signing users off the system during, 133

simple system in, 99, **99**

sorting user lists in, 131-132

spooled jobs, 6

status attributes for jobs in, 122

status codes for jobs in, 114, 116, **117**

status column of WRKUSRJOB display in, 116

Submit Job (SBMJOB) in, 107, **107**, 136-138

submitting a job for batch processing in, 106-108

submitting and working with jobs exercise for, 135-147

submitting jobs to job queue in, 136-138

subsystem descriptions (SBSD) in, 6, 101

subsystems in, 6, 100, 126-128

system values for subsystems in, 103

time slice for jobs in, 103, 125-126

type and function columns of WRKUSRJOB display in, 117

types of jobs to display in, 114

user column of WRKUSRJOB display in, 116

user IDs in, 108

user jobs in (See also user jobs), 113-126, 142

user profiles and, 103

user whose jobs to display for, 115

work management demystified for, 98-104

Work with Active Job (WRKACTJOB) in, 133-135, **134**

Work with Job Queue (WRKJOBQ) in, 109-110, **109**, 110-112, 138-139

work with signed-on users for, 145-147

Work with Subsystem (WRKSBS) in, 126-128, **127**, **128**, 134, 135, 143

Work with User Jobs (WRKUSRJOB) in, 113-126, **113**, **114**, 135, 142

workflow in, 6

working with signed-on users for, 128-133

job queues, 104

   Add Entry To Job Queue (ADDJOBQE), 139

   Change Job (CHGJOB), 140

   creation of, 78-79, 79, 78

   display particular job in job queue, 139

   display, 138-139, 138

   ending a job, 141, **141**

job queues (*continued*)

find, 138-139, 138

finding, 109

first in first out (FIFO) processing order in, 111-112, 111

hold a job, 139, 140, 139

holding, 112

moving job to different job queue, 140

moving jobs to different job queues, 126

priorities, 124

priorities of jobs in, 110

priorities of jobs in, 111-112, 111

priorities, 125-126, 125

releasing, 112

run time priorities, 125-126, 125

Send Message (SNDMSG), 136

Submit Job (SBMJOB), 136-138, 136

submitting and working with jobs exercise,135-147, 135

submitting jobs to job queue,136-138, 136

time slice, 125-126, 125

Work with Job Queue (WRKJOBQ), 109-110, 109, 109

Work with Job Queue (WRKJOBQ), 110-112, 110

Work with Job Queue (WRKJOBQ), 138-139, 138

working with, 110

job queues, 108-112, **108**

JOBQ status code, 116

jobs, 6, 7, 101, 104

K

keyword form command entry, 54-54

keywords for CL commands, 51-54

L

labels for tapes, 302, 309-311, **309**, **310**

levels of security, 6

libraries, 3, 65

copying objects to/from, 89-91, **90**, **91**

Create Library (CRTLIB) in, 56-58, **57**, **58**, 59-61, **60**, **61**

create objects in, 76-81

creation of, using menu path method, 56-58, **57**, **58**

creation of, using menus and commands, 55-62

Delete Library (DLTLIB) in, 95, 323-325, **324**, 334

deletion of, 61-62, 95

determine if objects have changed in, 88

display file object creation in, 79-80, **80**

Display Library (DSPLIB) in, 69, 94-95, 94, 327-328, **327**, 336

finding objects in, 81-82, **82**

finding, 85-86

General Purpose Library (QGPL) and, 80

job queue object creation in, 78-79, **79**

Library Commands menu for, 70, **70**

library lists and, deleting, 324

listing objects in, 94-95

moving objects between, 91-94, **92**, **93**

output queue libraries and, 208

output queue object created in, 76-77, **78**

place objects in, 75-95

print list of objects using Print Screen, 235

QSYS, 3-4

recreation of, 61-62

renaming, 87

Restore Library (RSTLIB) in, 313, 325-327, **326**, 334-336, **335**

save and restore a library exercise for, 329-337

Save Library (SAVLIB) in, 313, 319-321, **320**, 331-332, **332**

show objects in, 88

Work with Libraries (WRKLIB) in, 69, **81**, 81, 88-89
Libraries (LIB) objects, 64
Libraries (LIBRARY) menu, 17
Library Commands menu, 70, **70**
library lists, deleting, 324
licensed internal code (LIC), Save Storage (SAVSTG), 318
licensed program products (LPP), 299
list displays, 9, 21-23, **22**
    Bottom to indicate end of items in, 23
    commands for options in, 22
    extended lists in, 23
    F10 and F11 toggle between columns in, 23
    F23 prompts for more options in, 22
    Help for, 34, **35**
    More... to indicate more items in, 22-23
    options in, 22
listing objects, 94-95
local printers, 221-231

M

Main Menu, 11, **11**, 13
main storage (See also storage management), 4
Major Command Groups menu, 44, **44**
Manage Your System, Users, Devices (MANAGESYS) menu, 17, 129, 144-145
Marchesani, Skip, xiv
maximum CPU time for jobs, 103
maximum storage space for jobs, 103
members, 67
memory (See also storage management), 4
menu display, 9, 12-18
    blank lines or missing options in, 11, 13
    Cleanup (CLEANUP) menu as, 17
    command line in, 12
    Customize Your System, Users Devices (SETUP) menu as, 18
    Device Operations menu as, 14-15, **14**

Device Status (DEVICESTS) menu as, 17
Disk Space Tasks (DISKTASKS) menu as, 17
F3/F12 step back through, 15
Files (FILE) menu as, 17
function keys in, 12
General System Tasks (SYSTEM) menu as, 13-14, **14**, 18
GO command for, 13, 15, 16-18
help for, 30-33, **30-33**
Information and Problem Handling (USERHELP) menu as, 18
Information Assistant Options (INFO) menu as, 17
Libraries (LIBRARY) menu as, 17
library creation exercise using, 55-62
Main Menu as, 11, **11**, 13
main parts of, 12
Manage Your System, Users, Devices (MANAGESYS) menu as, 17
menu ID of, 12, 15
menu path for, 13-15, **14**
message line in, 12
Operational Assistant (ASSIST) menu as, 16-17
options in, 12
Power On and Off Tasks (POWER) menu as, 17
Printer (PRINTER) menu as, 15, **15**, 17
Problem Handling (PROBLEM) menu as, 18
Restore (RESTORE) menu as, 18
Save (SAVE) menu as, 18
Set Initial Menu (F23) in, 16
Status (STATUS) menu as, 18
Tape (TAPE) menu as, 18
Technical Support Tasks (TECHHELP) menu as, 18
title of, 12
menu ID, 12, 15

menu path for, 13-15, **14**

Message Handler, 8

message identifiers/message IDs, 170

message line, 12

message management (*See* also message
   queues, below), 8, 149-189

   *BREAK messages in, 174, 179-180

   *HOLD messages in, 174

   *NOTIFY messages in, 174, 177, 181

   alternative display for sending messages in,
      158, **158**

   application messages in, 150

   attributes of message queues for, 173-175

   break message handling program for, 174

   break message to workstation message
      queue in, 157, **157**, 181-183, **182**

   categories of system messages in, 170

   Change Message Queue (CHGMSGQ) in,
      175-176, **175**, 179-180, **180**, 181

   characteristics of messages in, 150

   default replies in, 171, **172**

   delivery methods for, 174

   delivery modes for, 178

   device messages in, 264, **265**

   Display Message (DSPMSG) in, 160-166,
      160, 174, 178, 184-186

   Display Message Description (DSPMSGD)
      in, 170

   display messages at basic and intermediate
      assistance level for, 162-163

   display system operator messages and reply
      in, 184-186

   displaying messages, 159-166

   error messages in, 168-173, **172**

   Help for messages, 168-171, **169**, 187

   informational messages in, 8, 150-151

   informational messages to users in, 155

   informational messages to workstations in,
      155, **155**

inquiry message replies in, 162

inquiry messages in, 8, 150-151, 156, **156**,
   183-184

interrupt your current job, start interactive
   session for, 153-154, 159, 187-189

Message Handler and, 8

message identifiers/message IDs for, 170

message queues in, 8, 150, 151, 155, **161**

message-waiting (MW) status indicator for,
   152

printer messages and, 172-173, 222, 225,
   229-231, **230**, 264

program for, 174

QCPFMSG system message file for, 170

QSYSOPR message queue for, 151,
   164-166, **165**, **166**, 167, 183-184,
   187-189, **188**, 264

removed messages cannot be restored in,
   167

removing all messages in queues in, 167-168

removing individual messages in, 167

removing messages not needing replies in,
   168

removing messages in, 152-153, 166-168,
   187

replying to messages in, 162, 184-186, **186**

replying to system and error messages in,
   172

Select Assistance Level window for,
   162-163, **162**

Send a Message display for, 158, **158**

send a message to yourself as practice in,
   178, 180

Send Break Message (SNDBRKMSG) in,
   157, 158, 180, 181-183, **182**

send inquiry to QSYSOPR in, 183-184

Send Message (SNDMSG) in, 8, 154-158,
   154, 178, 180, 183-184, **184**

sending messages in, 153-158

Note: Boldface numbers indicate illustrations

severity codes for, 174-175

severity codes of error messages in, 171

signed-on user messages in, 132

sources of messages for, 150

system messages in, 150, 168-173

system operator messages in, 164-166, **165**, **166**

System Request to interrupt current job for, 154, 159, 187-189, **188**

types of messages in, 150

user message queue for, 151, 155, **161**

user messages in, 150

Work with Message Queue (WRKMSGQ) in, 176, **176**

Work with Messages (WRKMSG) in, 163, 163, 174, 185, **185**

working with user/system messages exercise in, 177-189

workstation message queues in, 151-152, **152**, 155, **161**, 181-183, **182**

message queues (*See* also message management, above), 8, 150, 151, 155, **161**

attributes of, 173-175

Change Message Queue (CHGMSGQ) for, 175-176, **175**, 179-180, **180**

print list of objects in, using Print Screen, 237-238

Work with Message Queue (WRKMSGQ) in, 176, **176**

methods, 3

Microsoft Authorized Technical Education Center, xiii

modifications to OS/400, 2-3

More... to indicate additional help in Help system, 31, 34

More... to indicate more items in list displays, 22-23

Move Object (MOVOBJ), 72, 92-94, **92**, **93**

moving objects, 72, 91-94, **92**, **93**

MSGW status code, 116

N

names for objects, 64-65, 64

non-credit certification at RCTC, xiv

*NOTIFY messages, 174, 177

O

objects, object management, 3, 63-95

attributes in, 3, 64

auditing values for, 88

authorization in, 72-73

Change Object Description (CHGOBJD) in, 82

content of, 67

copying of, 72, 89-91, **90**, **91**

Create Duplicate Object (CRTDUPOBJ) in, 72, 90-91, **91**

creation of, 66-67

data in, 3

deleting, 73, 95

description of, 67

display file object creation in, 79-80, **80**

Display Object Authority (DSPOBJAUT) in, 73, 83-85, **84**

Display Object Description (DSPOBJD) in, 86, **87**, 88

Edit Object Authority (EDTOBJAUT) in, 73

explicit creation of, 66-67

File (FILE) objects in, 64

finding, 67-70, 81-82, **82**, 85-86

Grant Object Authority (GRTOBJAUT) in, 73

group ownership of, 67-68

job queue object creation in, 78-79, **79**

Libraries (LIB) objects in, 64

libraries for, 3, 65,, 69-70

library contents display of, 69

listing, 94-95

objects, object management (*continued*)
members in, 67
methods in, 3
Move Object (MOVOBJ) in, 72, 92-94, **92**, **93**
moving, 72, 91-94, **92**, **93**
names for, 64-65
object creation exercise in, 75-95
output queue object creation in, 76-77, **78**
ownership of, 66-67
Program (PGM) objects in, 64
Q not used as first letter of, 65
QSYS library in, 3-4
qualified names for, 65, 66, 80
reference to, by name not location, 65
Rename Object (RNMOBJ) in, 73-74, **74**, 87
restoring, 75
saving, 75
simple names for, 65
System Request to find, 68, **69**
types of, 64
User profile (USRPRF) objects, 64
Work with Objects (WRKOBJ) in, 67, 71-75, **72**, 82, **82**, 85-86, **85**
Work with Objects Owned (WRKOBJOWN) in, 69
working with, 71-75
online course, "AS/400 Getting to Know Your System," 40
online help, 29-30
Operational Assistant (ASSIST) menu, 16-17, 24-26, **26**
options, 12
options in list displays, 22
OS/400,1-62, 299
assistance levels in, 26-29
CL commands in, 40-55
database management in, 4
device management, 251-291

display types in, 9-24
ease of using, 2
economy of, 2
Help, 29-40
job/work management, 6-7, 97-147
major functions of, 3-8
message management in, 8, 149-189
modifications to, 2-3
object management in, 3-4, 63-95
Operational Assistant in, 24-26, **26**
print management, 8
program temporary fixes (PTF) for, 2-3
purpose and benefits of, 2-3
releases of, 2-3
responsiveness of, 2
security management in, 5-6
single-level storage in, 4
storage management, 4
updates to, 2-3
user management in, 5
versatility of, 2
versions of, 2-3
OS/400 Backup and Recovery, 301, 318
OS/400 InfoSeeker, 38
output queues, 106, 192-194, **193**, 206, 220-221
assigning jobs to different, 125
Change Profile (CHGPRF) and, 220-221, 232-234
changing of, 232-234, 232
clearing of, 249-250
creation of, 76-77, **78**
deleting spooled files from, 249
Display Job Description (DSPJOBD) in, 233-234, **233**
find spooled files in, 246
libraries for, 208
moving jobs between, 212, 244-245
print priorities in, 124

printer writer attached to, 242-243

QDFTJOBD and, 233

Work with Output Queue (WRKOUTQ) in, 201-203, 204, 242-243

Work with Writer (WRKWTR) in, 246

working with all, 201-203

working with one, 203

OUTQ status code, 116

ownership of objects, 66-67

P

parameters (F10) for in data entry displays, 20

parameters for CL commands, 42, 49-50

passwords, 6, 10

plus sign (+) for more command parameter values, 50

pools for job storage, 102

positional form command entry, 54-55

power failures, 296-297

Power On and Off Tasks (POWER) menu, 17

print management, 8, 191-250

ACTIVEWRITER status of writer in, 259

auditing what is printing in, 217-218

basic vs. intermediate assistance level for, 198, **198**

batch jobs in, 208

change attributes of printer output in, 211

change output queues in, 232-234

Change Profile (CHGPRF) in, 219-221, **220**, 232-234

Change Spooled File Attributes (CHGSPLFA) in, 211-214, **211**, 246-247, **247**

changing same attribute on multiple jobs in, 213-214

clearing output queues in, 249-250

common printing problems and solutions in, 218, 219

copies, number of, 212, 246-247, **247**

date/time of job creation in, 205, 207

default printers for, 220

deleting spooled files in, 249

device descriptions for printer writers/devices in, 192-193

Display Job Description (DSPJOBD) in, 233-234, **233**

display messages in, 264

display printer output by printer in, 204, **204**

display printer output for a user in, 195

display spooled files in, 238-241, **239**

Display User Profile (DSPUPRF) to change output in, 194

displaying completed printer output in, 217-218

displaying printer output by job in, 200-201, **200**

duplex (both-side) printing in, 213

end printer writer in, 225-226, **226**

End Writer (ENDWTR) in, 226, **226**

exploring different views of printer output in, 205-208, **205**

find spooled files in, 238-241, **239**, 246

finding printer output in, 194-204

form type or kind of paper to use in, 207, 212

GO PRINTER command for, 222

hold printer output in, 209-210, 243-244

hold printer writer in, 227-229, **227**

Hold Spooled File (HLDSPLF) in, 210, 243-244

Hold Writer (HLDWTR) in, 227-228, **227**

information about printer jobs and, why they don't print, 218

job control (*JOBCTL) authority to, 194

libraries for output queues in, 208

local printers in, 221-231

managing printer output with, 205-214

message/message queue printing in, 172-173

print management (*continued*)
messages for printers and, 222, 225
messages for printers and replying, 229-231, **230**
moving jobs between output queues in, 212, 244-245
number of pages in job in, 205
output queues and, 192-194, **193**, 206, 208, 212, 220-221, 223, 232-234, 244-245
page ranges to print in, 213
preview before printing in, 208-209, **209**
print queues and, 8
Print Screen key and, 234-238, **236**
printer devices in, 192, 206, 212, 220
printer device files in, 194
printer writer attached to output queue in, 242-243
printer writers, 192, 223
priority of jobs in, 124, 205, 207, 213
problems with printing and, 215-221, 241-243
QDFTJOBD in, 233
QSYSOPR messages in, 264
qualified job names in, 207
queues in, 8, 192
release printer output in, 210
release printer writer in, 227-229
Release Spooled File (RLSSPLF) in, 210, 247-248
Release Writer (RLSWTR) in, 228, **228**
remote printers and, 231
save file after printing in, 213, 248
spool control (*SPLCTL) authority in, 194
spooled files in, 192-194, **193**
spooling in, 8
Start Printer Writer (STRPRTWTR) in, 224-225, **224**
status of jobs in, 197-198, 205, 215-217, **216**, **217**, 222, 241-242

terms used in, 192
user data fields in, 206
user ID for jobs in, 199
user profile authorities for, 194
VARIED OFF status of writer in, 259
VARY ON PENDING status of writer in, 259
virtual printer (VRTPRT) devices and, 8, 257
where output prints and, 219-221
Work with All Printers display for, 204, **204**, 221-231, **222**
Work with All Spooled Files display for, 210
Work with Output Queue (WRKOUTQ) in, 201-203, 204, 242-243
Work with Printer Output display for, 199, **199**, 218
Work with Spooled Files (WRKSPLF) in, 195-199, **196**, **197**, 201, 204, 215, 238-241, **239**
Work with User Jobs (WRKUSRJOB) in, 200-201, **200**
Work with Writer (WRKWTR) in, 204, 246
working with all output queues in, 201-203
working with one output queue in, 203
working with spooled files exercises for, 231-250
print priorities, 124, 205, 207, 213
print queues, 8, 192
Print Screen key, 234-238, **236**
Printer (PRINTER) menu, 17
printer (PRT) devices, 254, 258-259
printer devices, 192, 206, 212, 220
Printer menu, 15, **15**
printer writers, 192, 223
priorities of jobs, 103, 110, 111-112, 122, 124
print management,, 124, 205, 207, 213
Problem Handling (PROBLEM) menu, 18

Note: Boldface numbers indicate illustrations

Program (PGM) objects, 64
program failure, save and restore, 297
program temporary fixes (PTF) for OS/400,
  2-3, 276
prompting (F4) for more choices in data entry
  displays, 20
prompting for commands, 49-52, **49**
purging jobs, 103
purpose and benefits of OS/400, 2-3

Q

QASTLVL system value, assistance level, 29
QBASE subsystem, 6, 100
QBATCH subsystem, 6, 100
QCMN subsystem, 100
QCPFMSG system message file, 170
QCTL subsystem, 100
QDFTJOBD, 233
QGPL, 80
QINTER subsystem, 6, 7, 100
QSECOR (Security Officer) profile, 5
QSECURITY values in, 6
QSPL subsystem, 100
QSWSWRK subsystem, 100
QSYS library, 3-4
QSYSOPR (System Operator) profile, 5
QSYSOPR message queue, 151, 164-166, **165**,
  166, 167, 183-184, 264
  Help for, 187-189, **188**
qualified names, 65, 66, 80, 108, 207
queues (*See also* message management; printer
  management), 192
QUSER (End User) profile, 5

R

recovery (See save and restore)
referencing objects, 65
Release Spooled File (RLSSPLF), 210,
  247-248

Release Writer (RLSWTR), 228, **228**
releases of OS/400, 2-3
remote printers, 231
Rename Object (RNMOBJ), 73-74, **74**
renaming objects, 73-74, **74**, 87
Restore (RESTORE) menu, 18
resource names for tape, diskette, CD-ROM
  devices, 265
responsiveness of OS/400, 2
Restore Library (RSTLIB), 313, 325-327, **326**,
  334-336, **335**
restoring objects, 75
Rochester Community and Technical College
  (RCTC), xiii-xiv, xv
routing data, 102
routing entries, 102
RPG, xiv
run time priorities, 125-126

S

Save (SAVE) menu, 18
save and restore, 75, 293-337
  *LABELS format in, 309-311, **309**, **310**
  *SAVRST format in, 311-312, **311**
  *USE authority in, 329
  abnormal ends and, 296
  automatic unloading of tapes for, 307
  auxiliary storage pool (ASP) for, 295-296
  backup and recovery plans for, 294
  CD-ROM for, 299
  cleaning tape units for, 301-302
  clearing a tape for, 307
  complete system loss and, 297
  continuously powered main store for, 296
  Create Save File (CRTSAVF) in, 330-331,
    331
  date/time of object save/restore in, 336-337
  Delete Library (DLTLIB) in, 323-325, **324**,
    334

save and restore (*continued*)

density of tapes for, 306-307

disk failures and, 295-296

diskette devices for, 299

Display Library (DSPLIB) in, 327-328, **327**, 336

Display Object Description (DSPOBJD) in, 336-337, **337**

display save files for, 333-334

Display Saved Objects for, 333-334

Display Tape (DSPTAP) in, 313, 321-323, **322**

display tape contents for, 307-309, **308**, 321-323, **322**

Duplicate Tape (DUPTAP) for, 313

errors on tapes and, 312-313

failures that can occur and, 295

GO RESTORE menu for, 299

human error and, 297

initializing a tape (INZTAP) for, 302-307, **303**

IPLs and, 296

labels for tapes in, 302, 309-311, **309**, **310**

media for storage in, 298-299

non-labeled tapes for, 304

power failures and, 296-297

preparing tapes for, 300-313

program failure and, 297

recoverable vs. unrecoverable errors in, 312-313

recovering saved data for, 299

Restore Library (RSTLIB) in, 313, 325-327, **326**, 334-336, **335**

restricting access to, 318-319

rotating backup tapes in, 300-301

running simple backups in, 313-328

save and restore a library exercise for, 329-337

Save Changed Object (SAVCHGOBJ) in, 317-318

save commands for, 316-318

Save Configuration (SAVCFG) in, 318

Save Directory (SAV) in, 317

Save Documents, Folders, Objects (SAVDLO) in, 317

save files in, 318, 330-331

Save Library (SAVLIB) in, 313, 317, 319-321, **320**, 331-332, **332**

save menu for, 314-316, **314-315**

Save Object (SAVOBJ) in, 317

Save Save-File Data (SAVSAVFDTA) in, 318

Save Storage (SAVSTG) in, 318

Save System (SAVSYS) in, 316

saving individual objects in, 294

standard labels for tapes in, 304

system failure and, 296

system power control network and, 296

tape devices for, 299

tape formats supported by AS/400 for, 300

volume labels for tapes in, 305, 309-311, **309**, **310**

what can be saved by, 297-298

what can't be saved by, 298

why save AS/400 data and, 295

Save Changed Object (SAVCHGOBJ),317-318

save commands, 316-318

Save Configuration (SAVCFG), 318

Save Directory (SAV), 317

Save Documents, Folders, Objects (SAVDLO), 317

save files, 318, 330-331

Save Library (SAVLIB), 313, 317, 319-321, **320**, 331-332, **332**

save menu, 314-316, **314-315**

Save Object (SAVOBJ), 317

Save Save-File Data (SAVSAVFDTA), 318

Note: Boldface numbers indicate illustrations

Save Storage (SAVSTG), 318
Save System (SAVSYS), 316
security management, 5-6
   levels of security in, 6
   passwords in, 6
   QSECURITY values in, 6
   user IDs in, 6
   viruses and, 5
Select Command display, 47-48, **48**
Send Break Message (SNDBRKMSG), 157,
   158, 180-183, **182**
Send Message (SNDMSG), 8, 136, 154-158,
   154, 178, 180, 183-184, **184**
Set Initial Menu (F23), 16
severity codes for messages, 171, 174-175
sign-on screen display, 9-11, 10
   password field in, 10
   user ID field in, 10
SIGNON DISPLAY, 257, 284
simple names for objects, 65
simple work management system in, 99, **99**
single-level storage, 4
   auxiliary storage pool (ASP), 4, 295-296
Softcopy Library, 37-38
spooled files, 192-194, **193**
spooled jobs, 6
spooling, 8
spooling CL commands, 45-47, **45-47**
Start Printer Writer (STRPRTWTR), 224-225,
   224
Status (STATUS) menu, 18
status attributes for jobs, 122
status of jobs in print management, 215-217,
   216, **217**, 222, 241-242
storage, 4
   auxiliary storage pool (ASP) in, 4, 295-296
   DASD and, 4
   disk, 4
   main (memory), 4

Save Storage (SAVSTG) in, 318
   single-level storage in, 4
Submit Job (SBMJOB), 107, **107**, 136-138
subsystem descriptions (SBSD), 6, 101
subsystems, 6, 100, 126-128
Sylvan Prometric testing facilities, xiii-xiv
synchronous data link control (SDLC) line configuration, device management, 274
syntax of CL commands, 42
system failures, 296
system messages, 150
System Operation for New Users, 39-40
System Operation SC41-4203, 40
system operator messages, 164-166, **165**, **166**
system power control network, 296
System Request to find objects, 68, **69**
system values for subsystems, 103

T

tape (TAP) devices, 254, 259-260, **260**
Tape (TAPE) menu, 18
tape devices for save and restore, 278-279, 299
Technical Support Tasks (TECHHELP) menu,
   18
time slice for jobs, 103, 125-126
title of menu, 12
token ring (TRLAN) line configuration, device
   management, 274-275
twin-axial data link control (TDLC) line configuration, device management, 274-275

U

updates to OS/400, 2-3
user authorities in, 5
user ID, 6, 10, 199
user jobs, 113-126, 142
   ACTIVE status code of, 116
   attributes of, displaying, 121-122, **121**
   call stack for, 122

user jobs (*continued*)

Change Job (CHGJOB) in, 122-129, **123**

End Job (ENDJOB) in, 119-120, **119**

END status code for, 116

ending, when not to, 120

Hold Job (HLDJOB) in, 117-118, **118**, 142, **142**

job column of WRKUSRJOB display for, 116

job definitions in, 122

JOBQ status code in, 116

moving jobs to different job queues in, 126

MSGW status code in, 116

open file display for, 122

output queues for, changing, 125

OUTQ status code in, 116

print priorities and, 124

priorities for, 122, 124, 125-126, 125

releasing, 118, 143-144

run time priorities in, 125-126

selecting jobs to display for, 114

status attributes for, 122

status codes for, 116, **117**

status column of WRKUSRJOB display for, 116

status of, 114

time slice in, 125-126

type and function columns of WRKUSRJOB display for, 117

types of jobs to display for, 114-115

user column of WRKUSRJOB display for, 116

user whose jobs to display in, 115

Work with User Jobs (WRKUSRJOB) in, 113-126, **113**, **114**, 142

user management, 5

authorities in, 5

IBM-supplied user profiles in, 5

QSECOR (Security Officer) profile in, 5

QSYSOPR (System Operator) profile in, 5

QUSER (End User) profile in, 5

user authorities in, 5

user profiles in, 5

user message queues, 151, 155, **161**

user messages, 150

User profile (USRPRF) objects, 64

user profiles, 5

Display User Profile (DSPURPRF) in, 194

job management and, 103

print management authorities in, 194

user-assigned values in data entry displays, 20

V

VARIED OFF status, 257, 259, 260, 270-272

VARIED ON status, 260, 270-272, 284

Vary Configuration (VRYCFG), 260, 270-272

VARY OFF PENDING status, 263

VARY ON PENDING status, 257, 259, 263, 271, 284

varying devices on and off, 260-264

versatility of OS/400, 2

versions of OS/400, 2-3

virtual devices

QAUTOVRT for virtual devices, 281

virtual printer (VRTPRT) devices, 8, 257

virtual workstation (VRT) devices, 257-258, **258**

viruses, 5

volume labels for tapes, 305, 309-311, **309**, **310**

W

Web servers, xiv

work management (*See* job management)

Work with Active Job (WRKACTJOB), 133-135, **134**

Work with All Spooled Files display, 21-22, **22**, 210

Note: Boldface numbers indicate illustrations

Work with Configuration Status
(WRKCFGSTS), 34, 253-260, **253**, 265-267,
266, 267-270, **268**, 272-276, 273, **273**, **274**,
278-280
Work with Job Queue (WRKJOBQ), 109-110,
109, 110-112, 138-139
Work with Libraries (WRKLIB), 69, 81, **81**
Work with Message Queue (WRKMSGQ),
176, **176**
Work with Messages (WRKMSG), 163, **163**,
174, 185, **185**
Work with Objects (WRKOBJ), 67, 71-75, **72**,
82, **82**
Work with Objects Owned (WRKOBJOWN),
69
Work with Output Queue (WRKOUTQ),
201-203, 204, 242-243
Work with Printer Output, 199, **199**
Work with Spooled Files (WRKSPLF), 41, **47**,
48, 195-199, **196**, **197**, 201, 204, 215,
238-241, **239**

Work with Subsystem (WRKSBS), 126-128,
127, **128**, 134, 135, 143
Work with User Jobs (WRKUSRJOB),
113-126, **113**, **114**, 135, 142, 200-201, **200**
Work with Writer (WRKWTR), 204, 246
workflow in, 6
workstation (DSP) devices, 254, 256-258, **258**,
279-280
  5250 twin-ax workstations, 281
  display workstation devices, 279-280
  find controller of workstation devices, 286
  QAUTOVRT for virtual devices, 281
  sign off workstation, sign on to another,
  281-282
  vary off workstation devices, 280-281,
  282-283
  vary on workstations, 284
workstation message queue, 151-152, **152**, 155,
161
  Send Break Message (SNDBRKMSG),
  181-183, **181**, **182**